EXPOSÉ

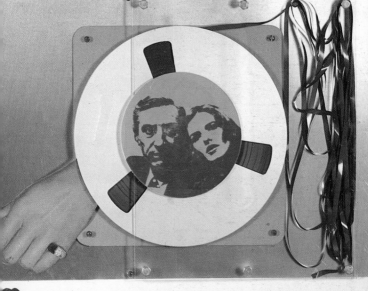

Potentially More Explosive than Watergate!

THE WASHINGTON CONNECTION exposes the facts behind these headline-making Congressional scandals . . .

—The Korean Scandal, and in particular, Tongsun Park, the Korean businessman who had been giving bribes for years to Congressmen, Senators and Governors in return for favored treatment of bills involving South Korea.

—What it means to be a woman (or male) employee in certain Congressional offices. The Colleen Gardner–Congressman John Young story *in detail*!

—The truth behind the energy fiasco.

Robin Moore created three separate teams of investigative reporters to bring you the facts about corruption and abuse of power in Washington, D.C. THE WASHINGTON CONNECTION is their story too of long days and months of intensive painstaking research.

THE
WASHINGTON
CONNECTION

ROBIN MOORE
LEW PERDUE
WITH NICK ROWE

CONDOR

NEW YORK

THE WASHINGTON CONNECTION

CONDOR

PRINTING HISTORY
CONDOR edition published August 1977

ISBN 0-89516-004-8
Library of Congress Catalog Card Number: 77-76522

Printed in the United States of America

CONDOR PUBLISHING COMPANY, INC.
521 Fifth Avenue,
New York, N.Y. 10017

Contents

Introduction

The Washington Connection started, as did so many other investigations in Washington, with the advent of one Liz Ray. It was back in 1974 that I got the phone call from Ms. Ray telling me that she had a story for me that would make *The Happy Hooker* read like *Mother Goose*. She gave me some hint of what the book was about and a phone number for me to call. Unfortunately I was finishing up a project at the time and when I finally phoned back to Liz Ray she had already taken off for a career in Hollywood.

Imagine my surprise when two years later Liz Ray burst upon the scene with her stories of mistressing for such worthies in the United States Congress as Wayne Hays, Ken Gray, Senator Mike Gravel and others.

So I got on the telephone and called my old friend in Washington, D.C., Clancy Isaac, who would become my chief of staff on this project.

Here's how Clancy remembered this incident.

"It was April 12, 1976. The voice was familiar—it was that of Robin Moore—a friend of over twenty five years.

"I thought the call was social. It wasn't. Robin expressed interest in writing and producing a book on the Washington scene. My immediate response was, naturally, 'Yet another book on Washington?' it seemed as though everyone was in on that act. But everyone was *not* Robin Moore.

"His objective was to go to the guts of abuse of power, arrogance in power, misuse of trust in our nation's Capitol and in our government. He wasn't interested in merely a frothy sex exposé although he admitted his appetite had been whetted by Elizabeth Ray's revelations.

"Was the Wayne Hays-Elizabeth Ray saga a tip of an iceberg? How far-reaching did contempt for the taxpayer's money go? How many of those elected to public office and those appointed to positions of responsibility had forgotten that they were servants of the people, not their masters? How many fail to realize that the green check they receive every two weeks from the Treasury is, in reality, signed and endorsed by the people of the United States to be used for their welfare and not to be abused in adding to the payee's comfort, wealth and power. Temptations of sex, money and power for the Senator, Congressman, Secretary, Under Secretary, Assistant Secretary and a GS-16 (senior management in the Civil Service System) are enormous. The weak will submit—but, we would expect that those in whom constituents have put their faith and those who hold high positions in the Executive Branch, in the Judicial Branch and in the Civil Service would have the strength to resist such temptation. Robin Moore wanted to find out.

"As a consultant in an Executive Department of the government, I was hired to develop a communications program to increase the public's belief in the credibility of the government's position on one of our most perplexing national problems—energy. I was paid a relatively high daily fee for nine months and it had been the most frustrating experience of my life. I was simply unable to overcome a cumbersome bureaucracy and accomplish any of my objectives."

A few days after my call to Clancy, Colleen Gardner burst upon the scene confirming much of what Liz Ray had described and adding her own tale of sexual activity. Naturally I asked Clancy if he knew how we could talk to Colleen Gardner and incorporate her into the book that was just beginning to form in my mind.

Clancy got in touch with Colleen's lawyer, who indicated that Colleen's story was indeed for sale. But after several days of being badgered by the press, Colleen clammed up and said she did not want to write a book or in any way contribute to a literary exploration of sex life on Capitol Hill. This was never my intention. Rather I was interested in *abuse of power and the abuse of people*.

The question weighing heavily on my mind was, can a writer from Connecticut sally forth into the Washington scene and find explosive information where the professionals who live in Washington and know their own backyard, have not succeeded.

Clancy strongly encouraged me to come down to Washington and look around. So to Washington I hied myself for the first of many visits. It was a hot June in 1976 when Clancy introduced me to a hostess who was reputed to know everything about the seamier side of Washington, D.C. Our hostess in turn introduced me to a former Administrative Assistant on Capitol Hill and this was where the chain started.

A list of Congressmen and a litany of their misdeeds was presented to me. It was interesting as the months rolled on to see how many of the names on that list were suddenly exposed by the local newspaper or congressional investigators. There was of course the problem of Clancy and myself trying to track down these legislators and find instances of abuse of power or people in their activities. I couldn't help feeling that perhaps Colleen Gardner might be a key to this situation and even though she had announced she did not want to say any more about sex on Capitol Hill, I decided to try and meet her.

Colleen Gardner's mother, Dr. Isabela Chaly Conserta, is a woman lawyer licensed to practice in Venezuela. She is interested in women's rights and had complained bitterly about the alleged humiliations her daughter had been subjected to by the Congressman who employed her. I called Chaly on the telephone and made a date to meet her in the cocktail lounge in the Mayflower Hotel.

We discussed at some length her feelings about women's rights and what went on in the offices of the Congressmen on Capitol Hill. I told her about the book I wanted to write and suggested that maybe she and I could work together to bring out the problems that women (and men) face on Capitol Hill. They are virtual chattels of their employers. There is no redress from a Congressman's decision regarding his employees. Furthermore if an employee is fired, or for that matter quits without adequate reason, a Congressman can destroy any chances of the employee getting another job on Capitol Hill.

After Chaly and I had talked for a couple of hours she said that she would like to have me meet her daughter, Colleen. This of course was what I was hoping would happen. Two days later, Colleen, her mother and I met again at the Mayflower and discussed the possibilities of Colleen and her mother working with me on the book. We still had no title or overall theme. Indeed I was wondering whether or not I would ever do the book. I felt very much the outsider in Washington. In fact as news of my efforts surfaced I was called, with some justification, a carpetbagger. My bag, it was intimated, was corruption, cops, wars and whores. "But isn't that precisely the Capitol Hill scene?" I retorted.

With Clancy's help I continued to bore into the Washington arena of action and finally I discovered a girl who might be another key to the theme of the book.

Betty Jane Ackerman was from my part of the world, Hartford, Connecticut. Betty and I discussed using the tapes of her conversations with Congressman Don Reigle in the book which by now had been named *The Washington Connection*. Congressman Reigle had announced that he was going to run for the Senate office from Michigan.

Betty told me the rather astounding news that she had many hours of taped conversation with Reigle which she had given to a former boyfriend. I asked if we could get them back and she said she didn't think so. Her current companion, David Taylor, who was also her lawyer, brought up a name which although it meant nothing to me at the time would play a large role in subsequent investigations on behalf of *The Washington Connection*. What I thought David Taylor told me and Betty Ackerman confirmed was that the former boyfriend's name was "Thompson Park." I suggested that maybe Mr. Park would like to sell back the recordings. Betty laughed and said no she was sure he would not be interested in doing that. I asked her why she had given this "Thompson Park" these very sensitive tapes, and Betty said that at the time he was very close to her and it was a catharsis on her part to forget her past with Reigle and intensify her relationship with Park by having him hear her most intimate conversations with a previous lover.

Now I felt we were really getting somewhere on *The Washington Connection*. We had Colleen Gardner and her story and we had Betty Ackerman and her story.

In September 1976 Clancy and I learned that "Thompson Park" was actually Tongsun Park, the Korean businessman who had been giving bribes for years to Congressmen, Senators and even Governors in return for favored treatment of bills involving South Korea.

The original purpose of the book had been to get it out in paperback just before the elections. However, in September I cancelled this goal. I realized that we could probably affect a number of Congressional elections in the House of Representatives and the Senate, and even provide voters with second thoughts on some of President Ford's stalwarts. However, it is only fair to point out that, although the Detroit *News* devoted its front page to the Reigle tapes on Sunday, October 17, 1976, Reigle was elected Senator from Michigan. But it must be remembered that when a United States Senator or Representative allows himself to be compromised as did Reigle, he opens himself up to blackmail by the likes of Tongsun Park, and this has to be detrimental to the interests of the American people. Congressman Young, whose sexual behavior with the female members of his staff was well aired by the *New York Times*, the *Washington Post*, and of course the newspaper in his hometown of Corpus Christi, Texas, has been reelected by his constituents. Perhaps if they had actually heard Colleen's tapes, Young would have been defeated. Now we will not know.

Publicity regarding the Ackerman-Reigle tapes upset Betty to such an extent that she decided to resign from the *The Washington Connection*.

With the elections safely over I began to investigate Tongsun Park with some fervor. He is a fascinating denizen of the Washington netherworld. A source who is an old friend of mine as well as a friend and former business associate of Tongsun Park filled me in on the man. Even to his friends he is something of an enigma.

My source told me that basically T.S.P. is one of the most inept businessmen he has ever come across. Nevertheless, with the backing of the South Korean government he made a small fortune in importing American rice into South Korea with the proviso that he would spend a great deal of the money he made taking care of Congressmen and Senators on Capitol Hill.

As my source put it, Park felt that if he was traveling he was working. If you wanted to sell Park the building across the street in Washington, D.C. you had to convince him that it was necessary to go to Hong Kong to make the deal.

I resolved that it would be worthwhile to discover as many hard facts on the elusive Mr. Park as possible and much of this book recounts how my investigative team unearthed information, which as this book goes to press is being used by the House Ethics Committee in its probe into Congressional figures who took favors and money from the South Korean to bring about favorable legislation.

So, month by month, I found myself drawn into the vortex of this increasingly less alien world of Washington intrigue. Over and over again I made up my mind to give up on the book. But Clancy and other writers kept me going. My old Green Beret friend, Nick Rowe, who wrote a remarkable book about his experiences as a prisoner of the Viet Cong for five years, came aboard along with his wife, Jane. They took over the Colleen Gardner project.

And then Tongsun Park became hot. The Justice Department announced they were going to subpoena Park's records. And a little while later, it is believed that Park employees in his Washington office put all of his records, correspondence and other documents through the shredder.

INTRODUCTION

Lewis Perdue, a brilliant young investigative reporter who joined us, anticipated this move and in an old investigative reporter's trick, he and Ken Cummins, with the aide of an employee of the Park organization, began picking up the garbage behind Tongsun Park's office-residence. In an operation that would put the Justice Department or the C.I.A. to shame, Lew and his staff, now increased to six worked 18 and 20 hours a day sorting out the shreds and pasting them back together. He even found carbon paper typewriter ribbons in the garbage which could be deciphered, and all the letters written on the ribbons were recast.

At this point, having created three separate investigative teams together to investigate Park and associates, the abuse of power in the Congress, and the truth behind the energy fiasco, I realized that *The Washington Connection* was much bigger, and potentially much more explosive than Watergate. The reporters had dug up information which showed that the "bad apples" in high places were *not* the exception to the rule as we would like to believe, but that business as usual on Capitol Hill involved the taking of bribes, the shocking exploitation of female (and male) staff members; and that in the realm of energy, the cross-fertilization of staff between government and the oil companies where people work for a government agency for a couple of years and then take their knowledge of the workings of the agency, and use it to the advantage of the oil company, were common day-to-day events.

To a naive voter, and most of us, alas *are* naive about the inner workings of our government, it is shocking to realize that our hard earned tax dollars are being used to keep Members of Congress in life styles we cannot ourselves afford. Worse, that people on their staffs are not protected by the same laws which protect employees in business organizations, where labor protection laws are created by Congress. These Congressional employees find themselves at the mercy of the Congressmen, who enjoy despotic powers over their lives and fortunes.

The Washington Connection was now moving ahead at full speed. In the same way that dark-horse presidential candidate Jimmy Carter picked up support as he won primaries, so too did *The Washington Connection.* Anonymous phone tips came in by the score, and one lead led to another. Even Suzi Park Thompson, former aide to former Speaker of House Carl Albert, gave us help and information.

The Washington Connection contains three separate but related stories . . . stories without endings.

The Tongsun Park Korean scandal investigation began hearings in June 1977. The House International Relations subcommittee is expected to hear that Tongsun Park, the mysterious Korean millionaire was in fact associated with the South Korean government of President Park Chung Hee. Further along in the summer of 1977 the House Ethics Committee will hold hearings to determine which Congressmen, if any, accepted gifts or cash from T.S.P. to keep aid and money flowing to South Korea. These hearings will without question highlight the biggest Congressional scandal ever. But can Congress police their own house? As we go to press, former Watergate prosecutor Leon Jaworski has been appointed special prosecutor.

Can anyone truly stop the abuse of power and of people in the Congressional offices of the Capitol? We believe the people of the United States can and will by the application of pressure in their home districts.

The "energy fiasco" is still with us. Can we take steps to create a sound and beneficial energy plan?

As *The Washington Connection* is being rushed to press we look to the American people to review this information that reflects the corruption in our government. We feel that the shocking facts of "business as usual" *must* be exposed.

The assistance and the "shredded documents" and bags of shreddings we furnished to the House Ethics Committee reveals the facts, but not the story behind the facts . . . they are presented here in *The Washington Connection*.

By the middle of the summer of 1977 we had built such a powerful prototype book in *The Washington Connection* that rather than let the staff drift away with the completion of this book, we are reorganizing the staff to bring you a new *Washington Connection* book whenever one is necessary to investigate and expose corruption. Corruption seems to be the one truly incurable disease throughout the world.

About the Author

ROBIN MOORE was born in Boston, Mass, and he has been writing all his life. After flying combat missions during World War II, he entered Harvard University and graduated in 1949. After a stint as correspondent for the *Boston Globe*, he worked in the television industry, and as a public relations executive for the Sheraton Hotel chain. He quit the hotel business to write full time. Among the best selling novels he authored are *The French Connection*, *The Green Berets*, *The Fifth Estate*, *Dubai*, several of which became award-winning motion pictures. His current bestseller is *The Mafia Wife*.

1. The Korean Connection

by Lew Perdue and Ken Cummins

A blind alley at dead of night

Lew Perdue and Ken Cummins had both gone to Washington with high ideals, determined to find investigative reporting assignments. Although still only in their mid-twenties, between them they had years of experience on Kansas and New York state papers. Both had always known exactly what they wanted to do with their lives: *be reporters*. Both had a burning zeal to unmask wrongdoers, and a strong conviction that reporters were the best people to show society its ugly underside. So when Clancy Isaac Jr. came to them with the news that Robin Moore was putting together teams of reporters to investigate an idea which was consuming him with its enormity—abuse of power—they knew they had met a kindred spirit. When Clancy told them that their assignment would be to explore the labyrinth which lay around Tongsun Park, the mysterious Korean millionaire socialite, they leaped at the chance and went straight to work.

They found that, as always, investigative journalism is made up of long days, long months and legwork, of poring through dusty files. It seems as though ninety per cent of the leads lead nowhere. Breaks rarely *happen* to reporters—despite the way it always appears in

3

movies about reporters at work—breaks are the end result of intensive, painstaking research. Rumors about Park abounded in Washington, but solid facts were hard to come by. For someone who "knew everybody," Park seemed to be a very private person indeed.

Then one miserable March day, which they had spent chasing futile leads, Lew Perdue had an idea. Digging in garbage cans is the last resort of the reporter who has come up against one stonewall too many. Garbage cans generally contain only garbage, stuff that *nobody* in the world could possibly need. It was late at night, it was bitterly cold, one of those nights when the city suddenly becomes frighteningly silent, unnaturally empty, yet uncannily watchful as though behind the darkened windows of the buildings eyes are watching, thousands of hostile eyes looking down on two figures alone in the night. It was in this atmosphere of chill and depression that Perdue decided to finish up the long day's work which had begun at six o'clock the previous morning, by seeing what might be found in the garbage cans of Pacific Development, Inc. at 1604 K Street. Pacific Development was Tongsun Park's flagship company, and he lived "over the shop" in a luxuriously appointed suite furnished with antiques, and a unique collection of jade and South Korean chests.

It is in the four-foot wide alley which lay behind 1604 that our story begins. It was a blind alley with a difference, for it was to lead the two young men into the heart of corruption in Washington, D.C.

Number 1604 is a dark-brown townhouse, sandwiched between a "fifties" building occupied by Pan Am, and another brick townhouse occupied by Burger King. As they parked their car and walked furtively towards the alley, they were both very jumpy. Earlier in the day Perdue had driven past 1604, and had noticed the very hefty muscular guard on duty. The back door to Pacific Development was located between the large 55-gallon oil drums that contained the garbage, and the opening to the alley. As they approached the alley they both thought unhappily about the burly guard, for although the exhaust fan from the Burger King covered any sounds that they might make, it also had the disadvantage of cloaking the sounds made by other people. As they stared into the dark little alley, it looked like the perfect place for an ambush.

But once they reached the garbage cans, they knew that they had found something very important. They had noticed a light burning in the otherwise darkened building. Could it be that unknown to them an anonymous friend was looking down on them from inside the P.D.I. office? As they stared into the garbage in the dim light, they knew that inside P.D.I. someone had been working overtime with a shredder destroying documents.

The person operating the shredder had made two extraordinary mistakes, first in only shredding the material once, and then in not burning the shredded documents but simply dumping them in the garbage. The shredder's error was to prove invaluable for Perdue and Cummins. They knew as they lugged the bags of paper spaghetti back to the car that they had at least a sporting chance of finding out something about the mysterious Korean and his network of companies and connections which stretched all the way to Capitol Hill, and on to Seoul, South Korea. Connections which it appeared, reached into every level of American society.

We see society as neatly broken up into compartments—perhaps because it's easier for us to deal with it like that. Good guys, respectable guys, lawyers, Congressmen and the like inhabit one compartment. Bad guys on the wrong side of the law inhabit another compartment. But the truth of the matter is that society is *not* fragmented, and people holding the highest offices in the country, our appointed representatives, whom we naively believe will somehow be "better" than we are, *do* rub shoulders with the more disreputable members of society. Not only that, they also do business with them. Tongsun Park is interesting because he operated a kind of spider's web of influence in which the respectable were joined with the disreputable. In fact one of his chief executives Robert J. Conkling, a former lobbyist, former Nixon campaign worker, was *also* a convicted rapist and arsonist. But those facts did not prevent Conkling from being accepted in the two-faced world of Washington society, where power, and proximity to power is what really counts.

It was 12:30 A.M. on the morning of March 15, 1977 by the time Perdue dragged the green plastic bag they had taken from the alley, into the foyer of his development townhouse. Although he had been working since six o'clock the previous morning, the sheer excitement of the discovery gave him a new lease of energy. It was clear almost at once that what he and Cummins had stumbled upon was a treasure trove of information—names, dates and places, in short the all-important leads for stories that they had been so hungry for. Sometimes there were five or six strips of paper sticking together which showed intriguing names. Who was Bong Y. Lee, for example? Who was Spencer Robbins?

In the early hours of the morning, Perdue didn't come across much on Park, but he knew that now he and Cummins had a chance of finding out more about the man and P.D.I.

The reporters had rented an office in a downtown Washington D.C. office building, and furnished it with ancient battered desks and files which looked as though they were ready for the junk yard. Soon, they were joined by Wendy Kramer, Rich Sokolow, Jim Mintz and Don Zullo, all of whom had worked as interns for syndicated columnist Jack Anderson. The newcomers interviewed people, and spent upwards of 18 hours a day piecing together the shreddings. It was an insane kind of jigsaw puzzle. Up close, each strip of shredded paper was unique. The first step was to group paper of one color together, then rearrange the groups in appropriate lengths and then according to matching typefaces, color of type, etc. Once relative order had been imposed upon the lookalikes, each strip was pinned onto cardboard. Strips were lined up, and slowly, strip would meet strip to form part of a word, part of a page and finally a whole page. The word "Agnew" first appeared on a strip similar to one with "Tongsun," and when the strips were put together they read "Flight to New York—Mr. Tongsun Park, Mr. S. Agnew."

Tongsun Park's employees, seemed to be trying to get rid of everything which might be incriminating in case questions were to be asked. It was also clear as more documents were pieced together that Park was fending off the I.R.S., and having difficulties with American Express, who eventually withdrew his card and charge privileges.

After they had been working on the shreddings for a few days, picking up the garbage bags nightly, they realized that they did indeed have a friend inside P.D.I., a friend fearful of retribution should he or she be discovered. The shreddings became easier to reconstruct as time went on because the operator of the shredding machine was making sure that shredded documents placed in the garbage were arranged carefully so that all the pieces lay close together. Without this help, their work on the shreddings would have been made still more laborious than it already was.

Why the Koreans were lobbying in Washington

The main reason the South Koreans concentrated their persuasive powers on Congress was a clause in the fine print of their defense treaties with the United States. If a N.A.T.O. ally is attacked, the U.S. is automatically committed to come to the aid of that ally. But the agreement with South Korea is different. Any request for aid to South Korea *must* be approved by the Congress. So the South Koreans, logically enough, sought methods that would help create a "favorable legislative environment."

In 1968, fate and the North Koreans made Tongsun Park's usefulness to the South Korean government suddenly much greater than it had been previously. In January of that year more than 30 North Korean commandoes, with orders to behead Korean President Park Chung Hee broke into the presidential compound and almost succeeded in reaching their target. In February of that year the Viet Cong bashed the American forces in Vietnam during the Tet offensive, proving that the Americans had bitten off more than they could comfortably chew in Asia. Every country in the area which had aligned itself with the United States, Japan, the Philippines, and, of course, South Korea became anxious about what the future held for them.

At the time, the invasion of his palace probably shook President Park more than the Vietnam offensives, but all the same the American experience in Vietnam was to dominate U.S.-South Korean relations for years. The South Korean government which had about 5,000 troops in Vietnam, watched as anti-war pressure mounted in the U.S. At first a trickle, then a great rush of Congressmen came out against the war. The consequences of a faltering American commitment in Vietnam were soon felt by South Korea. The Nixon administration, normally a good friend of South Korea, reduced the U.S. troop strength in South Korea from 62,000 to about 42,000. To President Park it seemed that the American reservoir of goodwill, that had existed since the Korean War, was drying up. The South Korean government became desperate to insure that a similar situation to that in Vietnam did not occur in their country. It just so happened that Tongsun Park had been busy for years laying the groundwork for just such an eventuality. In 1965 Tongsun Park is said to have convinced intelligence officials in the South Korean government of the idea that he could use his influence with his powerful friends in Congress to lobby for increased military and economic aid to South Korea. Two Congressman, said by some sources to be Cornelius Gallagher, formerly Democratic Congressman from New Jersey, and Richard Hanna, formerly Democratic Congressman from California had helped persuade the South Korean government to name Tongsun Park the sole broker for handling sales of American rice to South Korea. In return for this favor they promised to help obtain U.S. armaments for South Korea. The commissions on these sales would amount to millions of dollars over the years.

Tongsun Park: the man everybody knew, and nobody knew well

In Korea, where the family name comes first, his name is Park Tong Sun. He is said to have been born in the late thirties, and it is known that he came to the United States as a teenager in the early fifties. This was the period of the Korean War, and few Korean families could afford to send their children to America to be educated.

According to several sources, Park's family had originally come from North Korea, where the family fortune had been made in the oil business. An American woman friend of Park's told reporter Mintz that Park once told her that his father had been smart enough to get his money out of North Korea and into West Germany and the United States, and that his family had fled to the South before the North went communist.

Not much is known about the first few years of his life in America, but in 1956 Park enrolled in Georgetown University's Foreign Service School, where his classmates remember him as an accomplished speaker. According to one of his closest friends and a former classmate, he became an "instant personality" on campus. "He looked substantial. He always dressed in suits. I can't remember ever seeing Tongsun without a suit." And it was Park's outward appearance—the parties, the priceless antiques—which people would remember. As a person he was thought of as rather cold, someone not easy to get close to.

Park graduated from Georgetown in 1963, several years behind his classmates, because he took time off after finishing his sophomore year. It is said that those years were not spent with his family in Korea, as has been suggested, but were spent instead in the service of the South Korean Government.

On June 5, 1977 there came a bombshell. Kim Hyung Wook, former Director of the K.C.I.A. identified Tongsun Park as a K.C.I.A. agent who spent millions of dollars to buy support for South Korea amongst U.S. policymakers in the Congress. The *New York Times*, which broke the story, quotes Mr. Kim as saying: "When I was Director of the K.C.I.A., he was my agent. I controlled Park at that time." Mr. Kim also listed the Reverend Sun Myung Moon, leader of the Unification Church, as being aware of K.C.I.A. activities in the U.S.A. although not himself an agent. The Unification Church and the Korean Cultural and Freedom Foundation were said to have been set up both to provide money and cover for the K.C.I.A. agents, and as a propaganda forum both here and abroad. Moon's chief lieutenant, Pak Bo Hi, *is* an agent according to Kim, as is President Park's son-in-law, Han Byung Ki, who was until recently the deputy ambassador to the South Korean observer mission at the U.N. In addition Mr. Kim listed less important agents, Sue Park Thomson, former aide to former House Speaker, Carl Albert; Alexander Kim, a lawyer; his brother Charles Kim, former chairman of the Diplomat National Bank in Washington, D.C.; Jhoon Rhee, head of a chain of karate gyms in Washington. A week or so later in testimony before the House Subcommittee on International Organizations, Kim Hyung stated that Ms. Thomson, the two Mr. Kims and Jhoon Rhee had *not* been agents of the K.C.I.A. And that although Tongsun Park had been in contact with the agency he had not actually been an agent as such, but rather someone of whom the K.C.I.A. had made use when necessary. So the situation on who is or is not an agent, or past agent of the K.C.I.A. remains unclear.

Kim Hyung Wook said that the American C.I.A. had known about Korean bribery plans almost from the beginning in 1970, and this was confirmed by a former head of the Korean desk at the State Department, who had seen C.I.A. cables on the subject. Not only was the C.I.A. aware of the activity, but so too, it is said, were senior Nixon and Ford administration officials. Two reasons are given as to why the bribery information did not come to light at once:

a) the C.I.A. was anxious to protect its highly sensitive sources in South Korea, and

b) the information about K.C.I.A. activities was not gathered together in any one place. The I.R.S., the Department of Agriculture, the F.B.I., the Defense Department and the U.S. Embassy in Seoul all knew what was going on, but, in effect the information got lost in the red tape and bureaucracy of the different government departments.

While a student at Georgetown, Park met many people who are now in public life, and in 1962 he shared a house with two men who are now Congressmen—Representative Lud Ashley of Ohio and John Brademas of Indiana. Fifteen years later, Brademas would be the Majority Whip of the House of Representatives—the third highest position of power in that body—and would publicly admit to receiving nearly $4,700 in campaign contributions from Park for the 1972 and 1974 elections. But Brademas was only one of an unknown number of Congressmen who received contributions from Park. On November 4, 1976, Congressman John McFall, who was then Majority Whip, and a contender for the position of Majority Leader, admitted taking $3,000 in $100 bills from Park to put into his private office account. Five days later on November 9, 1976, former Congressman Richard Hanna of California revealed that he had been Park's silent partner in an import-export business when he was still a member of Congress. He said that the business had earned him nearly $70,000 over a three-year period.

In addition Kim Hyung Wook also told U.S. investigators that President Park is rumored to divert approximately 5 per cent of all foreign investments in his country to Swiss bank accounts. Kim Hyung Wook told how money was channeled to Congressional and Presidential candidates here during the sixties, and how cash-filled envelopes were handed to U.S. Congressmen visiting South Korea. He told of the women, the medals, the honorary degrees, the lavish parties, which awaited the visitors. And he named more past and present Congressmen as recipients of South Korean money, favors or gifts from Tongsun Park: William Broomfield, (R-Mich.), Cornelius Gallagher (former D-N.J.), John M. Murphy (D-N.Y.), Otto E. Passman (D-La.). Other sources named Tennyson Guyer (R-Ohio).

THE KOREAN CONNECTION

Interestingly enough there were those who proved that honesty is a comparatively simple matter, involving no back-breaking physical work. *They* rejected the Korean bribes by the old-fashioned method of returning the cash-filled envelopes. Representative Larry Winn, Jr. (R-Kan.), a member of the House International Relations Committee, sent his secretary to track down the Korean who left an envelope full of $100 bills in his office. The secretary found the Korean a few minutes later—in another Congressman's office. Representative Charles Wiggins (R-Cal.) turned down a Korean offer of "campaign contributions." On a trip to South Korea in 1974, John E. Nidecker, a former White House aide, returned an envelope containing $10,000 in cash. As a result of the revelations about wholesale bribery, all 434 members of the House are being asked to declare whether they received cash or gifts from the Koreans in excess of $100—the legal limit.

Edwin Edwards, Governor of Louisiana, said that his wife got a 'gift' from Park while he was still a U.S. Congressman, ostensibly because Park wanted to help her and the children. (Confirmation of this transaction turned up later in the reconstructed documents). A note in Park's handwriting said, "This will confirm that sometime in the fall of 1971, I handed Mrs. E.E. an envelope containing $10,000 cash. I told her I had not been able to make a political contribution to her husband's campaign but that I wanted to do something for her and the children. It was a gift with no string attached and I asked her not to tell her husband or anyone else about it. The transaction took place over coffee in the coffee shop of the Monteleone Hotel in New Orleans." It ended with Governor Edwards' address. On June 17, 1977, Governor Edwards told newsmen that he did not believe the gift was improper. He went on to defend Tongsun Park, pointing out that Mr. Park had helped him to "sell rice from people in Lousiana to the Koreans." Although the logic is hard to follow, it apparently satisfied the Governor.

According to the *Washington Post*, the F.B.I. is investigating allegations that two additional members of the House of Representatives took bribes from Park totaling "less than $10,000."

Even before the Kim Hyung Wook revelations, U.S. government investigators had reason to believe that Park was not so much a private businessman distributing money in return for favors, as the agent of a foreign government buying support. And it should be noted, even campaign contributions received in good faith from such a source, would in fact be illegal.

How Park made the Korean Connection: the George Town Club

In 1966 Tongsun Park introduced himself to Washington's social and political elite with a bang, when he opened the George Town Club. Kim Hyung Wook has explained how the K.C.I.A. financed the club. Mr. Kim said that he arranged for a $3 million loan from the South Korean government as collateral for Tongsun Park. Park went on a worldwide shopping spree to furnish the club, importing antique chests and other art objects from South Korea, irreplaceable national treasures, which, so it is said, could not have been exported without K.C.I.A. assistance. A brief listing of one very small part of his possessions which was transcribed from a carbon paper typewriter ribbon found in the P.D.I. garbage gives an idea of the scale of Tongsun Park's possessions:

"Description: 7 stamp boxes in hard stone, contents of Box A1 $6,275.00 Contents of Box A2 Contents of Box A3 Contents of Box A4 Contents of Box A5 Contents of Box A6 $633,300.00, $10,650.00, $8,950, $15,300.00" In addition the typewriter ribbon revealed a "king's ransom" in personal jewelry, watches, old jade, ivory.

The George Town Club was a sound investment, both for Park and for the government of South Korea. For although Tongsun Park had excellent connections in the Blue House in Seoul, and in top government circles in South Korea, in 1966 Park was quite without power in Washington D.C. To get power he had to have a direct conduit to those who were already powerful. In 1966, no one was going to come to a party to visit Tongsun Park, but he knew that the powerful would come to a party to meet and talk with others of their kind. All it took was a couple of "seed powers" to attract the bigger fish. Park played on his college friendships with Congressmen and others, and used them as bait to attract the really big power pushers, the wholesalers of the commodity. The George Town Club represented the South Korean Government and Tongsun Park's ploy to bring together influential politicians, rich businessmen and beautiful socialites. The other investors in the club "wanted as many members from the Green Book as possible," said one charter club member, referring to the Green Book, which is the Social Register of Washington. "They admitted a few Blacks and a good many Jews who are barred from most of the high-society clubs in Washington. The club was not ultra-exclusive, but the old guard was definitely represented."

One early club member, a middle-aged lobbyist, described to reporter Mintz the atmosphere at the George Town Club.

"Once it got around that Tongsun's were the parties to attend," the lobbyist said, "he had no trouble. In this town everybody wants to run with the pack. The chauffeur-driven limousines would pull up outside and the 'professional partygoers' came in. The parties were uniquely Washington in that you might know the people ever so slightly, but you probably had no real friends there. He would throw a party at the drop of a hat.

"At the parties were always an interesting cast of characters," the lobbyist continued. "The people were like the cast in a movie about Washington—like old-fashioned embassy parties, or robber baron parties.

"Cocktails at 7:30—the drawing room downstairs

was always jammed. Dinner at 8:30. Often Tongsun would arrive just as the food was hitting the table. There was always entertainment—maybe a guitarist—at dinner. The food was high French. The glasses were always full.

"Afterwards there were speeches. Tongsun would always say 'Koreans are the Irish of the Orient.' Always lots of toasts. At the end you really felt like you'd been to something.

"Sometimes Tongsun would play the violin and it really was like tying two cats together by the tail and throwing them over a fence. I had been told, 'if he ever takes out the violin, run for the door.' Of course we'd all applaud afterwards, and then he'd play for another half hour."

Describing the typical Park party got the lobbyist to thinking about his 10-year relationship with Park.

"It's funny," he began after a pause, "I just realized that though I call Tongsun my friend, I never repaid him for all of the times he invited me to his house or to the club. It's a social law here in Washington that one must return such an invitation within a year. Come to think of it, we never even had a long conversation."

The realization that he was not as close to Park as he had thought is echoed by others who got to know Park at parties. One Congressman, for example, saw Park socially over a 15-year period, and was on first-name terms with him, yet he considers Park "deliberate, calculating, enigmatic."

Many people began to realize that for all of Park's hospitality and his affable manner towards his guests, his friendships were carefully calculated according to who could do him most good, according to who could help him in his power connection. Congressman Hanna who had helped Park in business, had reason to feel bitter towards Park.

"I guess I was his original friend on the Hill," Richard Hanna told the *New York Times*. "He often told me I was his oldest, dearest, closest most valuable friend. Then he turned around and kicked me."

Hanna introduced Park to influential people, but in the later years of their friendship, Hanna says he became convinced that he was being "abused." Hanna claimed that the business association with Park began in 1971.

"This guy was really broke when he came to me," Hanna said. "This was a guy whose credit was no good." Hanna volunteered to use some $90,000 worth of stock that he owned as collateral, so Park could obtain a line of credit with the Equitable Trust Company in Baltimore, Md.

Hanna claims that there were no partnership or corporation documents and that Park told him he would be taken care of "as a member of the family."

However, Hanna's assertions are contradicted by corporation records on file with the office of the Recorder of Deeds of the District of Columbia. According to their records, Hanna was one of the original members of the Board of Directors of Pacific Development, Inc., Park's flagship company. In addition, since his name as a board member appears on the original incorporation dated April 1, 1968, his involvement with

Park's company seems to start at a much earlier date than Hanna asserts.

Hanna said he thought Park sought influence to further his own business interests, and not the legislative needs of South Korea. As for his role in helping Park to his position of considerable influence, Hanna termed it a "sad, tragic . . . mistake." The two men had a falling out in 1975, allegedly over the sale of Hanna's home.

But if some people found Park difficult to deal with, some of his women friends seemed to have a different point of view, remembering him as a kindly and affable host.

One such friend says, "He told us his family had built the biggest oil tanker in the world. We called him, 'the Onassis of the East' which he thoroughly enjoyed. Years ago I was in Korea with (a friend) and we spent some time with Tongsun's mother, who is a real matriarch . . . Tongsun wired us at our hotel, 'hope my family is taking care of you.' Of course they were. (We) were treated royally in Korea—a limousine at the airport with the presidential flag, motorcycle escorts everywhere. But I think that was only partly because of Park's family. I also think the Prime Minister was enamored of (my friend).

"I stayed at Tongsun's house in Georgetown one time, and he kidded me about my bed. 'Frank Sinatra once slept here,' he told me. Tongsun walked us out of his house one day, and there on the steps, waiting for us to leave, was a girl in a mink. We kidded him about all of the girls—about giving them all minks."

Park's social events and the power connections he

21

made through the George Town Club became his launching pad, and Park ascended with dizzying speed between 1968 and 1975 when the George Town Club had at last stopped losing money. President and Mrs. Ford were its most prominent members, and virtually all of Washington society, led by foremost socialite Mrs. Morris Cafritz flocked there. Senator Barry Goldwater, several ambassadors, former Defense Secretary Melvin Laird, former Democratic National Committee Head and Carter appointee Robert Strauss, Supreme Court Justices Stewart, Powell, White and Brennan and their wives could be found at one time or another under Tongsun's roof.

One source, a former Park associate, told the reporters that Park would "make careful lists of everybody that came to his parties, and had lots of pictures and then he'd go back to Korea and tell the government people, "Look at all the top American political powers I know well. You should work through me to get your lobbying done right!"

The source said that President Park was wary of Tongsun Park, but because of the prominence of Park's family, he went along with his schemes. At one point, Tongsun Park was ordered to stop claiming he was a relative of the President. Park apparently stopped doing this actively, but he never denied the rumors.

"He used his parties well," the former Park associate continued. "He'd throw around names like 'Tip' O'Neill and Carl Albert (the former Speaker), and when South Korean officials would come to visit, Park would throw one of his fabled parties and line up all of his highly visible Congressional people for the Koreans to gawk at. When they returned to South Korea, these people would report back that Park was really connected in Washington society. At the same time, the Congressman would be impressed by the Korean visitors, and would get the impression that Park could be useful in dealing with the South Korean government."

"There's no doubt that Park had only one reason for his social life," said one Congressman, who agreed to talk only off the record. "And that reason was to further his economic and political self-interests. Park was not particularly warm. I can't give you one specific example, it was just his entire manner. You ought to talk to some of Park's gals he brought over here from Korea. The chauvinistic attitudes they have over there, that women were only meant to please men. I talked to one of his gals years ago who wanted to get away from Park. You ought to talk to her. This was years ago and I was needling her about Park's attitude toward women . . ."

As an amusing footnote, Suzy Park Thomson when denying that she was a K.C.I.A. agent pointed out that the South Koreans were male chauvinists who would never give such responsibility to a woman.

Tongsun Park's lists

In late 1970 or possibly early 1971, according to several sources, Park met with President Park and South Korean intelligence officials in the Blue House, the South Korean presidential palace. The men discussed strategy in regard to lobbying the U.S. Congress. By that time, the K.C.I.A. had reportedly compiled a list of about one hundred key, or "target" Congressmen. Park reportedly received the list so that he could begin working on the members named.

That list or a copy of it was discovered by a U.S. customs inspector in Anchorage, Alaska when Park came through the airport there on December 8, 1973. Park was returning from Korea. The customs official, D.R. Hazelton, said that he was inspecting Park's luggage since he "seemed to be carrying undeclared gifts." He found the Congressional list in Park's briefcase, and immediately the two men scuffled to obtain possession of the papers.

"He used both hands to grab my arm and hand in an attempt to stop me from opening the folder," Hazelton said in a memo to his superiors. "It was not a paltry or half-hearted attempt; it was forceful and lingered with force until I advised him of my right to search."

Hazelton said he looked at the list, but did not copy it for fear it would provoke violence. He noticed that the names had dollar amounts written beside each one.

One of the first documents that Perdue put together in the two or three nights following the initial garbage pickups in March was a memo from Bong Y. Lee to retired U.S. Navy Captain Spencer Robbins, who was executive vice president of Pacific Development. With it there was a three-page list containing the names of 39 Senators and 74 Representatives—a total of 113 names. Perdue knew that the memo and the list had been shredded at the same time because the shreds of both memo and list were bonded together. It was clear that the P.D.I. source had deliberately shredded this material in such a way as to make sure the papers remained attached.

The memo read in part: "Attached is a U.S. Congressional list with whom TSP has been associating." Since the list contained Democrats and Republicans, the powerful and the powerless, it must be pointed out in all fairness that the list may have been made for perfectly innocent purposes.

Perdue also put together another memo from Bong Y. Lee that was concerned with recent publicity over Park's relationships with Congressmen. The memo was labelled, "Report II" and was dated April 24, 1975.

"I met with Mrs. Sew (sic) Thompson (sic) who is working with House Speaker Carl Albert's office as assistant to the Speaker," the memo began.

"She asked me to extend her sincere personal sympathy with TSP for the articles, news in recent days.

"Also, she is sure that TSP's Congressional friends are reaffirming to maintain good friendship regardless what articles in the newspapers, news (unintelligible) reported throughout nation.

"For your information, Mrs. Thompson is close information source to:

Cong. Wolff (D-N.Y.)

Cong. Brademas (D-Ind.)

Cong. Albert Johnson (R-Pa.)

Cong. Sony Montgomery (D-Miss)

Cong. Matsunaga (D-Hawaii)"

The reporters called all of the offices. Those of Congressmen Wolff, Matsunaga and Brademas did not return any of the telephone calls.

Congressman Montgomery's office returned the call to reporter Jim Mintz on May 3, 1977. An aide told Mintz:

The Congressman might say, 'Well, it's under investigation so I have no comment.' "

"Oh, is the Congressman under investigation?" Mintz asked.

"No, but he might say that," the aide responded. The conversation ended.

Albert Johnson, who had been defeated in the 1976 election told Mintz that he had gone to two parties that Park gave for House Speaker "Tip" O'Neill.

"I was just a run-of-the-mill Congressman who went to some parties," Johnson told the reporter. "I had a nodding acquaintance with Suzi Thomson. I would see her in the hall. I didn't know her." Tongsun Park has described this memo as a forgery.

Park's Political Sympathies: How sincere were they, and where did they lie?

In the sixties Park's political leanings were towards the ultra-conservatives who founded the Young Americans for Freedom, and who worked for and elected conservative New York Senator James Buckley. Park, according to one of his associates of that era, was on the floor of the Republican convention in 1964 when Goldwater was nominated.

But a college classmate who "showed Park around the conservative movement," recalled a breakfast he had with Park and a Congressman in 1974. "Speaking to the Congressman, Park turned and pointed to me and said, 'This fellow introduced me to the conservative movement. For a while I thought that was all there was.' It was the Democrats, the liberals who opened up the real power of America for Tongsun." Remembering the breakfast, he said with a trace of resentment, "Tongsun looked like he was sitting on top of the world." It seemed as though, like his neckties, Park's political beliefs were to be changed when convenient.

The reconstructed shreddings, some interesting links are disclosed

Amongst the shredded documents Perdue and Cummins pieced together was a handwritten memo on a legal pad from Spencer Robbins, which dealt with the Military Assistance program, a matter seemingly far removed from the interests of a rice broker such as Park. The undated memo is a draft, not addressed to anyone, and it reads in part: "Subj: MAP (Military Assistance Program) Discussion with our consultant this date revealed that decision on country (word unclear) figures had been postponed until SEPT but continued consideration was given. Further that the two option figures named would be the figures debated (in Congress) unless a case was made for an increased amount."

It seemed to the reporters that the unnamed "consultant" mentioned in the memo had obviously made close contact with a Congressman involved in the Military Assistance Program appropriations and that this Congressman had outlined his opinion of the upcoming debate on it. At the time of going to press, the question of the identities of the lobbyist and the Congressman has not been resolved.

In the last paragraph, the memo cryptically put the consultant down. "Since our consultant cannot (unclear words) be of assistance, you may wish to reconsider the matter. However (unclear) 'real' material will be required in justifying a higher figure." The memo was signed "SER" as were most of Spencer E. Robbins' memos.

In addition, several other papers pertaining to economic aid to South Korea were pieced together, most of them dating from 1975. Since the Robbins' memo was found tangled with these pieces, the reporters assumed that it, too, dated from 1975.

In addition, Park's association with the South Korean government was cemented further by memos and directives from Bong Y. Lee. (In the *New York Times* of June 30, 1977 Mr. Lee is reported to have told Justice Department and Ethics Committee investigators "how he distributed money and other gifts from Mr. Park to members of Congress." Mr. Lee was also said to have reported to the South Korean embassy in Washington, D.C. information which he gathered on Capitol Hill.)

In the garbage the reporters also found pieces of automobile registration belonging to Jae Bum Park, second secretary at the South Korean embassy. The registration was found among papers belonging to Bong Y. Lee. The Virginia registration renewal was for a 1974 Volkswagen with diplomatic license plate DPL 637. The address on the registration, 6548 Orland Street, Falls Church, Va., was the same as Bong Y. Lee's. The registration papers were found in a pile of what was obviously the result of a cleaning out of Bong Lee's desk. They also found, intact and unshredded,

Lee's daily calendar complete with names and telephone numbers of people he dealt with.

According to the South Korean embassy, J.B. Park has been recalled to South Korea. The reporters lost track of Bong Y. Lee. They called a grocery store in Hyattsville, Md. using information they had gleaned from the calendar and other documents because Lee it seemed had been planning to buy the market. A man with a Korean accent answered the telephone and when he was asked about Bong Y. Lee became agitated, said he could not be found talking to them and hung up.

Several memos from Bong Y. Lee to Spencer Robbins were pieced together by the reporters, and many of them relayed information from the South Korean embassy.

"Korean diplomats are now trying to (unclear) size up the sound of what the State Department has on an official opinion in the matter (TSP). Also specifically Korean Consul is very much concerned about this matter because he is very responsible to protect S.K. nationals residing in this country. They have not received specific information from State Dept. at this moment. I will keep in touch with those who are collecting such info. at S.K. embassy. If any I will let you know immediately." This Bong Y. Lee memo—to either T.S. Park or Robbins—was not dated, but by reason of the other papers it was found with appeared to date from 1975.

The South Korean embassy has repeatedly denied having any such close contact with Tongsun Park or any of his employees.

But leaving aside the tangled question of whom Park represented, it is clear that between 1968 and 1971, Park proved that he could work the halls of Congress as skillfully as he could enliven a dinner party. His skill, however, suffered from the same violin playing that his parties did, and this overestimation of his own abilities would cause him to make mistakes that would eventually force him to flee the country.

Park's blunders on Capitol Hill

An aide to a Congressman from the Southwest spoke to Mintz about Park.

"Tongsun Park and his runner barged into the office on one or two occasions. I assume they came to pay a courtesy call on the Congressman." (He was on the South Korean list which Perdue and Cummins had reconstructed.) She said their courtesy call was not very courteous. "You know, 99 out of 100 visitors that call on a Congressman have an element of courtesy about them; an air of courtliness. Not these two," she remembered. "The runner walked in front of Park and in a heavy accent demanded, authoritatively, demanded to see the Congressman that instant. You understand, they had no appointment." But the Congressman received them anyway.

"Park was in with the Congressman for no more than 3½ minutes," the aide said. "After a thousand years on the Hill, I can spot a spook (undercover agent). The Congressman knew better than to get involved with Park. He can spot a bad guy too."

Another Congressman on the list described Park as "a bullshitter" to reporter Mintz. "He liked to talk about himself and how rich his family was back in Korea . . . Park liked to play the little Korean boy innocent in the ways of Washington, but I knew this was B.S. because Park has attended Georgetown (University)." The Congressman had attended many of Park's parties. But on the only occasion that Park visited his office, he had no appointment.

"He just dropped in, to talk very generally about how our two countries must cooperate and do what's right against the evil spirit of Communism. Park would never ask outright, 'would you do this or that'. He is typical of a type here on the Hill who likes to be in the company of influential people, but Park had more class than most. He always properly knotted his tie."

Reporter Mintz had finished the interview and was heading for the door when the Congressman added a postscript.

"Yeah, he was quite a character. If he ever does come back to this country, I wouldn't want to be on the plane with him."

The reference was to the physical harm that would come to Park if he did come back to the United States. For weeks, the reporters had been receiving reports that the K.C.I.A. would assassinate Park if he ever tried to come back to the U.S. It is said that the South Koreans do not want Park back in the country for fear of what he might reveal about K.C.I.A. operations.

The report was also confirmed by several other Korean sources and a former Tongsun Park business associate.

Park's business interests and business associates

Pacific Development, Inc. was the base for Park's lobbying operation in the United States. The townhouse at 1604 K Street was remodeled to his specifications in 1975. The offices housed a variety of direct employees of P.D.I. as well as consultants.

One totally legitimate businessman who had an office at P.D.I. was C. Wyatt Dickerson. Dickerson served as a consultant to Park in several international export-import deals, but his primary interest was in the oil industry. According to documents he worked on several deals involving Indonesian oil purchases, and on a settlement between Burma Oil Company and a large shipping firm, Japan Line. Dickerson represented Burma Oil and Park represented Japan Line. Park reportedly earned $3 million from the settlement of the dispute over the price of crude oil.

Former Attorney General Richard Kleindienst, had an office at P.D.I. for several months, and received a retainer from Park. In late 1974 and early 1975 Park was trying to set up a "super" business firm, and was courting many former White House officials in hopes of convincing them to join his firm. Kleindienst was retained as Park's corporate counsel in January of 1975 and moved into the P.D.I. office at that time. Kleindienst suddenly ended that relationship three months later, but he said his reason for leaving was the result of a "privileged conversation" he had with Park in March. Sources say Kleindienst left because Park, who was out of the country most of January and February of that year, did not ask him to get involved in any of the business dealings, "and Kleindienst just got bored." Others contend the former Attorney General became suspicious of what he saw going on around him. Park and Kleindienst had known each other socially through the George Town Club since 1969, and Park gave a dinner for Kleindienst at the club in late 1972 after Kleindienst became Attorney General.

William Timmons, former Congressional liaison for the Nixon and now a top Washington lobbyist, was retained by Park during 1975, just after Timmons left the White House, and paid $60,000 for his services that year. Timmons has refused to comment on his business associations with Park.

In 1975, Park was also trying to convince Gerald Warren, the former top White House press aide, to join the business and handle Park's public relations. Warren eventually declined the offer after giving it serious consideration, but Park managed to get Omar Dajany from the World Bank that year. Dajany, a top official at the bank, supplied Park with many valuable contacts with foreign governments that Park was hoping to use to obtain business for American companies.

Also during 1975, Park became friendly with William Henry, a former executive vice president of Gulf Oil, who was also considering joining Park's firm. Park and Gulf were planning to build the world's largest oil tanker, "Korean Universe," at that time.

J.S. Kim, who later set up the A.M.E.P.A. Trading Company was a vice president of P.D.I. and handled the chores of procuring materials and services for the Korean Government.

B.Y. Lee was an employee of P.D.I. who was also working with the retail grocery company that Park owned.

Spencer Robbins, a former U.S. Navy Captain, was executive vice president of the firm and was supposed to oversee the entire operation. The reconstructed documents showed that he worked for most of 1975 on trying to complete several deals for oil pipelines and other construction projects for the Nigerian government—deals that eventually fell through, according to a former Park business associate.

Wishing to confirm his role in Park's business, Perdue and Cummins called Spencer Robbins for days. When he did not return their calls they decided to pay him a visit at his home in Great Falls, Virginia. They found a courteous stonewaller, who described every person they asked about in glowing terms. The exception to this stream of pleasantries was Robert J. Conkling.

"I don't know the man. I don't know what he is doing for Mr. Park, I don't know of his connections to Mr. Park or any of Mr. Park's companies," said Spencer Robbins.

The two journalists would later learn this was a falsehood since Robbins and Conkling worked together on the Harper's Ferry Arms Company arrangement. It would later be obvious from documents obtained from a Park associate, that Robbins and Conkling not only knew one another, but did not relish the association.

"What about the documents, the shredded documents?" Cummins asked unexpectedly in the middle of a very light moment. Robbins was not taken aback.

"What documents?" he asked calmly.

"The ones you are shredding," Cummins said.

"We are not shredding any documents," Robbins said.

"Where did you get an idea like that?"

"Well, we have a source who has told us that you are shredding documents that the Justice Department and the House Ethics Committee investigators have requested," Cummins said. Neither he nor Perdue mentioned the shreds they had been collecting and reconstructing.

"I can only say that your source is wrong," Robbins told them. "However, I will say that we do have a shredder, but we haven't been shredding documents. What shredding that is going on is the normal phasing down of a business," Robbins said, apparently contradicting himself.

"You mean P.D.I. is going out of business?" Cummins asked.

"No, only phasing down. Now, we have a shredder and are disposing of duplicates that we no longer need. I mean, there are so many copies that have to go to this person and that in a corporation that are needed when that corporation is going strong, but these are no longer needed by us now."

Cummins was incredulous remembering the many telexes, the Edwin Edwards gift memo in Tongsun Park's hand and so many other originals they had reconstructed.

"So you're saying that you have not shredded any originals?" Cummins asked.

"That's right," Robbins said. At that point they left, knowing they would get nothing out of him.

One company affiliated with P.D.I. and with one of Park's Korean companies, the Hannam Supermarket Corporation, was Pacific Enterprises Inc. located in Los Angeles. The company, according to its manager, is in the grocery import-export business. The manager, who was located at P.D.I. in Washington for a short period, said that the Hannam Supermarket corporation owned a chain of more than 100 grocery stores in South Korea.

The Hannam company is only one of seven companies that are members of the Miryung Group which is owned by Park and headquartered in Seoul, Korea. Henry Chang is the executive vice president of the group and serves as its chief operating officer. The group consists of the Miryung Moolsan Co., Miryung Tongsang Co., Miryung Navigation Co., Miryung Electronics Co., the Soong Eui Educational Foundation and the Hannam Supermarket Corporation.

THE WASHINGTON CONNECTION

Miryung Moolsan handled Park's rice export-import business. On March 21, 1972, OSROK, the South Korean agency responsible for overseas purchasing for their country wrote to all of the major rice exporting firms in the United States:

"In order to insure more satisfactory transactions for our rice trade, we are pleased to inform you that Mr. Tongsun Park, President and chief executive officer of the Miryung Moolsan Company of Seoul, Korea, has once again, as in the past, agreed to serve as an intermediary. In fact, his service will be required for all our rice trade with the United States in the future."

But most of the rice sold to South Korea was done so under the Federally subsidized "Food for Peace" program, and because of this, the $1 per ton commission that Park was getting had to be hidden from the attention of the Department of Agriculture which managed the program. Much of the commission money was funneled through dummy bank accounts to launder it before it was paid to Park. From 1971-1974, more than 60 per cent of all rice sales to South Korea under the "Food for Peace" program were made through the Connell Rice and Sugar Company of New Jersey.

"It's the most amazing thing I've ever seen," commented a Department of Agriculture investigator. "And I don't think we've tracked it all down, yet. This guy seemed to know everybody and have his finger in everything." The investigator began looking at Park in early 1976 in connection with the subsidized PL-480 rice shipments program, but the investigation quickly widened into other areas, and is continuing today.

According to the I.R.S. documents, many of the commission payments were paid through accounts opened in the names of the Bowsprit Co. and Three Star Navigation, two more Park firms. In August 1974, according to the I.R.S. records, Park received $110,-000 through his Bowsprit account at the Bank of Bermuda. A $1.4 million payment was made in September 1974 and another for $1.3 million was made in October 1974. The payments were wired to the Three Star Navigation accounts at the same bank.

Three Star Navigation, Bright Star Navigation and Fire Star Navigation were companies that Park set up with the aid of another business associate, Milton Nottingham, and were Liberian chartered corporations set up to register tankers and bulk cargo ships.

Before becoming involved with Park, Nottingham operated a small but financially successful shipping operation. When he went into business with Park, all of his former clients were absorbed into the Pan Mediterranean Shipping Corporation, which was owned jointly by Nottingham, Park and Grover Connell who owned the Connell Rice and Sugar Company.

It is alleged that Connell and Park tried to keep their involvement with the company a secret, but when the U.S. Department of Agriculture pressed for full disclosure of the corporation's backers, their roles became clear, and Pan Mediterranean folded. Park then turned all of his shipping affairs over to Bong Y. Lee, and started another shipping company, Pacific Cargo, Inc.

The other companies in the Miryung Group that the reporters were able to find information on, included

Miryung Tongsang, which owns stone quarries and exports stone products; the Miryung Navigation Co. which owns and charters oil tankers and bulk cargo carriers, and the Soong Eui Education Foundation which runs a girls' school in Seoul.

To keep his profits from being fully taxed by the United States government, Park set up an investment firm in Bermuda called Fontas Ltd. This investment firm then parceled out funds as they were needed for Park's ventures. We must point out that at the time of going to press Park's status as a non-resident alien is not clear. Several years ago the I.R.S. is said to have accepted his status as a non-resident alien, but then they later reversed themselves. To maintain non-resident status an individual cannot spend more than a certain number of days each year in the United States. If Tongsun Park was indeed a non-resident alien, then he would *not* be obliged to pay U.S. taxes on his income. It was the change in the I.R.S. thinking regarding Park's non-resident alien status that led to the $4.5 million lien on his assets, while the I.R.S. considered whether or not he owed them back taxes.

Park's business interests also extended to Abu Dhabi Hong Kong and Indonesia, and he had offices in Morocco and Egypt.

Some of the names which turned up in the shreddings were those of Robert J. Conkling, the former Washington lobbyist, who was hired by Tongsun Park to straighten out the affairs of the Harper's Ferry Arms Company, when he came out of prison. Francis Rosenbaum who had been found guilty of swindling the U.S. Navy and the Penn Central Railroad of millions of dollars. Cornelius Gallagher, a former Congressman who had served time in prison for income tax evasion. Spiro Agnew, former Vice President of the United States, who became a close associate of Park's after he left office.

Because of Park's rumored ties to prominent Republicans the Justice Department and Congressional investigations have widened recently to explore the Korean's ties in the G.O.P. Particularly, these investigators are interested in determining whether the White House was aware of Park's activities during the Nixon and Ford administrations.

Robert J. Conkling

Perdue and Cummins had started looking into the life and times of Robert J. Conkling in February, 1977 after a friend of Perdue's suggested that he would be an interesting character to investigate because he was working for Tongsun Park, and had been a prominent Washington lobbyist, numbering the U.S. Jaycees amongst his clients. In addition, they knew Bob Conkling had served 17 months of a two-year sentence imposed after he had been found guilty on 18 counts of rape, sodomy, and other felonies, and later they found that he had a prior criminal record including convictions for arson and indecent exposure—although the latter charge which involved a minor, was reduced from a felony to a misdemeanor. On the other side of the coin he had been a National Director and Chairman of the U.S. Jaycees, and a member of the executive committee of the U.S. Olympic Committee, and had worked as a staff member on the Nixon campaign in 1968.

Considering his connections, there was a singular lack of information about Conkling, which struck the reporters as very strange. On February 4, 1977, Perdue found a telephone listing for Robert J. Conkling Associates, but there was no answer. He found a listing for a company called Urban Services, the name of a firm that Conkling had started to provide Washington representation for cities. The listing was for an Arlington, Virginia address, but the people there denied ever having heard of Conkling.

They went on a fruitless paper trail through the District of Columbia Superior Court building in search of Conkling's records, to find only an empty file. (The contents were never discovered.) They could get no information on Conkling from the prison authorities, or the halfway house where he had lived for a while after leaving prison.

Perdue called one of Tongsun Park's closest woman friends to ask if she had any idea what Bob Conkling might be doing for Tongsun Park.

"Why do you want to know? What are you going to do with the information?" the woman demanded in an angry voice.

Perdue explained that it was for a book and possibly for a news story.

"Well, you sure have got balls to be calling me about my friends, you stay away from my friends, you stay away from Bob, you hear? I'm going to call Bob right now and tell him that you're snooping into his life. You stay away from my friends!" The woman slammed her receiver down. Perdue was surprised by her reaction, particularly in view of Conkling's record of violence towards women.

Later, on April 13, Robin Moore was having a drink at Pisces in Georgetown, when he ran into Tandy Dickinson, a Washington socialite who invited him to her table. Tandy berated Moore for poking into the Tongsun Park story and asked him: "Why are you picking on poor Bob Conkling? He hasn't done anything wrong. He's my friend, he's a good guy."

"Well," Robin began, "I'd like to know how many people a person like Conkling has to rape and sodomize before he's not an okay guy in your book."

Ms. Dickinson's genteel southern facade disappeared as her face erupted in a rage that caught her friends at the table by surprise.

"Get away from here," she screamed at the top of her voice, "Get out of here! I'm going to have you thrown out of here!"

After Robin slowly and deliberately left the table, he told Perdue, "That's the first time I've been asked to leave the table since the time my mother told me to stop singing during a meal."

Research revealed that Conkling had been convicted

on the 18 counts of felony on March 4, 1975, and sent to Springfield, Mo. Federal Hospital Prison for observation. He was sentenced in June, 90 days later, and spent a total of a year at Springfield, undergoing therapy. He was then sent to the minimum security prison at Allenwood, Pa. Seventeen months after being found guilty of brutal assaults on three women, he was once again in general circulation. The reporters found that during the 90-day period, a Federal grand jury was considering Justice Department investigations into charges that Conkling had embezzled Federal grant monies under his control. That investigation was dropped because the prosecutor in the case knew that if Conkling had been found guilty of the embezzlement charges he would have been sentenced at most to five years in prison. But since the felonies for which he was charged in 1975 could have gotten him two life sentences, it did not seem worth proceeding on the embezzlement charge. The prosecutor was one of many who were floored by the two-year sentence which Conkling drew.

Perdue and Cummins found that mention of Conkling's name caused very strong emotional responses which ran all the way from fear to rage, but the impenetrable curtain of silence surrounding the man remained closed.

Then Cummins had a call from a former Conkling employee who helped fill in some missing information, and put Conkling into perspective, both as a former Washington lobbyist, and also as a close Park associate. The information provided by the former employee was corroborated by other sources.

Conkling's public relations firm Washington Consulting Group had been formed to handle corporate clients. In 1971 the Jaycees were considering getting Federal grants to operate self-help anti-poverty programs around the country, and Conkling reasoned that he could use his many political contacts to secure the grants which had been made in part during his time as a staff member on the Nixon campaign. The idea was that the Jaycees organizations around the country could provide the "warm bodies" to run the programs that Washington Consulting Group would create. There had always been some resistance on the part of the Jaycees to using Federal money to run their self-help programs, rather than private funds raised in the local communities. But Conkling was able to calm these fears, although at every national Jaycees' convention during the early seventies, this issue would be raised and hotly debated.

The first year Washington Consulting Group handled the Jaycees business, the firm landed five Federal grants totaling $1.3 million. Although the grants were awarded to the U.S. Jaycees, the Washington Consulting Group was to be employed as a subcontractor to administer the programs, the employees in the consulting firm constructing many of the grant proposals themselves and then handling the negotiations with the different Federal agencies involved in granting or not granting funds. In other instances, the Jaycees would design a self-help program, for example to combat poverty, venereal disease, alcoholism, or whatever the case might be. Washington Consulting Group would be called upon to put the proposal in the proper "grantese" language. The consulting firm could not, of course, receive fees from a Federal grant for having acquired the money for a client, but the firm, as the Washington liaison for the Jaycees was paid "for services rendered."

However, after obtaining the records of Washington Consulting Group transactions regarding Federal grants, and comparing expenditures and personal accounts, the U.S. Attorney's investigation uncovered nearly $10,000 of Federal money that Conkling was alleged to have converted to his personal use and approximately $1,000 of public money that one of his associates was responsible for. But then the matter was suddenly dropped, as we explained earlier, as a result of the prosecutor's expectation of a heavy sentence on the rape related charges. The prosecutor was aware at the time of Conkling's brushes with the law and his ability to always land on his feet after a fall.

"Guys like that are the fact," he said. "They make you angry because you look at them and you think, there is no justice. And that's true. There is no justice. We just try to come as close as we can.

"There's an old saying, 'You go to court to get the law. You get justice when you die.'"

After Conkling's conviction, Washington Consulting Group began losing its clients and Conkling saw that his business fortunes had been depleted. But when Conkling got out of prison Park gave him a job straightening out the affairs of a company Park had taken over, the Harper's Ferry Arms Company.

On April 5, 1977, Perdue received a call from one of his Conkling sources who wanted a meeting that afternoon. Perdue had previously set up an appointment that afternoon to meet with the publisher of a Korean-American newspaper who had been harassed by the K.C.I.A. for his opposition to the regime of South Korean President Chung Hee Park. Perdue wanted to ask the man several questions pertaining to Tongsun Park, and to ask if he would translate some of the documents that they had reconstructed that were written in Korean calligraphy. Cummins went to that meeting in Perdue's place.

Robert Conkling was linked by Perdue's source that afternoon to a Tongsun Park company in Los Angeles, Pacific Enterprises Inc.

On April 6, Cummins reached the manager of the company by phone. The manager explained that the company was related to the Hannam Company, another company that T.S. Park owned that was in the retail grocery business. The manager explained that Conkling was a personal friend of Park's and that he did not have any official title with Park's companies.

"I met Mr. Conkling last October when he was working for Pacific Development Inc.", the manager told Perdue, "Bob (Conkling) is doing pretty well with Mr Park's businesses in the Middle East. He has a lot of projects going."

One thing which struck Cummins as odd, especially

in light of the fact that Conkling had claimed that his position with Park was "minor and insignificant," and Spencer Robbins' claims of ignorance regarding Conkling's relationship to Tongsun Park, was what the manager said when Cummins asked him if he was in contact with Park frequently.

"I can't talk directly with Mr. Park. I have to go through Mr. Conkling. I don't have Mr. Park's telephone number," the manager told him. Conkling's importance in the Park organization was clear.

Conkling's name came up again the next day when the two reporters were trying to check out a new company that Park had set up, the American Pacific Trading Company.

Wendy Kramer who had been decoding the carbon paper typewriter ribbon found in the P.D.I. garbage, had come across the name of American Pacific several times, along with an Arlington, Virginia address. April 6, she had found a typewritten passage concerned with transferring accounts receivable from P.D.I. to American Pacific.

In April 1977, P.D.I. was under an I.R.S. lien and as such not free to do as it wished with the money that it received. Also, at the time, P.D.I. and Tongsun Park were strapped for cash because of the lien, and creditors were threatening foreclosure. Two weeks later, in a Jack Anderson column, Perdue and Cummins would report the story of the financial disarray within Park's organization.

But on April 7, the reporters were still unaware of the overall financial difficulties and the fiscal sleight of hand that was afoot to circumvent the Internal Revenue Service lien and siphon off the funds to another corporation.

The reporters learned that the top executive of American Pacific was a former vice president of P.D.I. The executive denied that either Conkling or T.S. Park had any connection with the company. The reporters would find out later that the head of American Pacific was taking his orders from both Conkling and Park. Cummins asked him about the accounts of Wilbur Smith and Associates that had been a P.D.I. account and had been transferred to American Pacific. (Wilbur Smith is a large, respectable consulting firm located in South Carolina. P.D.I. had been working with them on several multi-million dollar projects in the Middle East.) This was accounted for by the fact that the head of American Pacific had handled the Smith account at P.D.I. Cummins' knowledge of the transfer of the account elicited an admission that there was indeed a connection between American Pacific and P.D.I. The executive said,

"True, that account was mine at P.D.I. and has now been transferred to American Pacific. I am taking care of transferring the money to Seoul." (The corporate headquarters for T.S. Park's main company, the Miryung Group, is in Seoul.)

Out of the transcribed typewriter ribbon came Park's address in London (44 Green Street), but telegrams to Tongsun Park on April 7 and 8 and a telex on the 8th, asking for an interview, unsurprisingly went unanswered. The telex was sent to a number in Abu Dhabi belonging to Japan Lines, which Conkling had used in the past. The number for the telex had also been pieced together from the shreddings.

The Harper's Ferry Arms Company

The reporters had learned from several sources of Conkling's first assignment for Park upon his release from prison. It had been to straighten out the financial problems of the Harper's Ferry Arms Company, a small firm that Park had invested in heavily. They knew from a reconstructed telex that they had pieced together in March that Tongsun Park had been on the board of directors of that company and had resigned on February 17, 1977.

In addition, the name of the former owner, and then managing executive of the firm came up several times on the typewriter ribbon.

The two reporters managed to contact a business associate of Tongsun Park's who allowed them to view documents pertaining to Harper's Ferry Arms. The former owner was a former Army sharpshooter, who was stationed in South Korea for several months. He met Tongsun Park at a shooting match arranged between American and Korean soldiers. After getting out of the army, the former sharpshooter founded his own company, H.F.A.C., which manufactured replicas of classic weapons primarily from the Revolutionary and Civil War periods. The replicas were working reproductions. The owner of H.F.A.C. had always maintained his connections with South Korea, and he was having parts of the guns manufactured in that country.

H.F.A.C. began having financial troubles in 1976 and the owner began looking for rescue capital. According to informed sources, Tongsun Park heard of the company's plight through a contact in the South Korean government and in July 1976, Park contacted the owner.

Park's attorney at the time told Cummins in a telephone interview that the agreement which was reached called for Park to pump a considerable amount of money into the company and take care of all of the outstanding bills. The attorney said that Park hád put about $80,000 into the venture.

According to the documents and corroborating sources, things went smoothly for a few months until Park fled the country when investigations into his affairs began. At that time he stopped paying the bills for H.F.A.C., once again causing problems with the company's creditors.

The former owner, who had been employed to run the company after its purchase by Park, then began berating P.D.I. for not living up to its purchase agreement. (P.D.I. handled all of Park's affairs after he left the U.S.) The former owner tried to meet with a P.D.I. executive, but the executive did not show up at the meetings.

In February 1977, the former owner went on a visit

to South Korea to check on the company which had been manufacturing the stocks for his guns. The manufacturer had not been doing the job correctly, and a personal visit was required in order to settle the matter once and for all.

The former owner of H.F.A.C. left the Hopewell, Virginia location of the company on February 12, 1977, stopping on his way to the airport to confer with P.D.I. officials before continuing on to South Korea.

Two days after he had left on his trip, his secretary arrived at H.F.A.C. and found a P.D.I. employee already there. The P.D.I. employee had formerly worked for H.F.A.C. but she had been fired after being caught making copies of H.F.A.C. files for P.D.I. Ever since P.D.I. had fallen behind in meeting its financial obligations to H.F.A.C. the former owner of the company had been suspicious of Tongsun Park, fearing that he would not keep to his end of the purchase agreement. The firing of the employee had been a point of contention—P.D.I. claiming that the former owner of H.F.A.C. had no right to hire or fire anyone, while he asserted that as the top managing executive at H.F.A.C. he did have that right.

Next the P.D.I. employee demanded the keys to H.F.A.C. and ordered the former owner's secretary to leave. Instead she started listening in on all of the phone conversations at the company. When she overheard a person at P.D.I. telling the P.D.I. employee to copy all of the records and send them to P.D.I. she called the sheriff.

That afternoon, another P.D.I. secretary appeared at

H.F.A.C. Perdue and Cummins were familiar with the names of both the P.D.I. secretaries since their names had appeared numerous times on the shredded documents, and on the transcripts from the typewriter ribbon.

"Everybody was arguing over who was really employed here (at H.F.A.C.) and who wasn't," the former owner's secretary told Cummins. P.D.I. executives, including Robert Conkling, told the employees to leave. She reported that Conkling had told her,

"Now (name), we're very disappointed in you. (The former owner) stopped by here on his way to Korea and he knows about the change of plans and he knows you're not supposed to be here so why don't you run along like a good girl?" In addition the woman said that "Bob (Conkling) told me he had some people down here in Hopewell checking up on me." At that time she was in the midst of a divorce case. Then one day, a stranger called the school her six-year-old son attended and started asking questions about him.

"They scared the crap out of me," she said later. "I was just waiting for them to try something." She said after the phone call concerning her son, she started carrying a .357 Magnum pistol.

About noon on February 14, the woman heard the P.D.I. secretary calling a locksmith to have all the locks changed. But the sheriff arrived to arrest the P.D.I. employee before the locksmith came. However when he did arrive, the former owner's secretary went ahead and had the locks changed and kept all of the keys.

She had overheard a conversation from which it was

clear that a top P.D.I. executive would be arriving the next day to "take care of everything." In order to avoid a confrontation, she closed up and locked the office early in the day the executive was expected.

Several witnesses—one of whom called to alert her—told the woman that the P.D.I. executive, Park's attorney and an advertising man, together with three hired helpers arrived in a van around noon, entered the building through a window in the warehouse and carried out the guns. The attorney supervised while the guns were being loaded into the van. The entire operation, according to witnesses, took only 15 minutes.

The H.F.A.C. secretary said that according to an inventory she had made the day before, the group had removed almost the entire inventory. The guns sold for $200 to $350 each. On February 17, she filed a complaint in county court for the arrest of the P.D.I. executive on charges of grand larceny.

That day, the resignations from the H.F.A.C. board of directors for Tongsun Park and two others, arrived in the mail. H.F.A.C. would later get a letter from P.D.I. saying that the company had planned to sell the guns they had seized in order to recoup the money that they had put into H.F.A.C. before the purchase agreement had been cancelled by the resignations.

When the former owner of H.F.A.C. returned from South Korea on March 7, he had a warrant issued for the P.D.I. attorney's arrest on a charge of grand larceny.

Amongst documents obtained from Pacific Development Inc., the reporters found a telegram that the attorney had sent to H.F.A.C. promising that the guns would be returned if the former owner agreed to "drop all warrants and all future criminal prosecutions" resulting from the removal of the guns.

The attorney explained to Cummins that they were only "taking back property under the Uniform Commercial Code," and that the action had been legal. "The company (P.D.I.) was only trying to protect the property it had a security interest in," the attorney went on. "That's standard business practice. It happens all the time. It was Pacific Development's position that Harper's Ferry had breached their agreement. People were being hired and fired that had no right to be. The personal property was taken to try to pay off some of the obligations of Harper's Ferry."

However, the former owner of H.F.A.C. disputed the attorney's argument in a letter which alleges that the purchase agreement was invalid because all of the stockholders were not notified of the sale of the corporation and that P.D.I. first breached its end of the contract by failing to pay debts it had originally agreed to pay.

"We had no obligation to pay them until delivery of the assets," the attorney told Cummins, but he was vague on what he meant by "delivery of the assets." He said that the return of the guns was prompted when "they went and got a warrant for my arrest. I didn't want an arrest on my record."

At any rate, whatever the rights or wrongs of the situation, the guns were returned on March 21 at a service station on the outskirts of Richmond, Pa., where 66

Lafayette muskets and 24 Maynard rifles were delivered. P.D.I. is alleged to have kept one of the Springfield replicas.

The Harper's Ferry Arms Company was only one of dozens of companies that Tongsun Park was involved with. It presents an interesting light upon Park's business methods, and those of people that worked for and with him.

More Park Associates: Rosenbaum, Gallagher, Agnew

Francis Rosenbaum's involvement with Tongsun Park had not come to light until the reporters found his name in the transcripts made from the typewriter ribbon. On page 96 of the handwritten transcript, they found a January 31, 1977 memo to Francis Rosenbaum which read:

"Attached you will find a form 1099 (Miscellaneous income). For your record here follows an explanation . . . Total payment for (your) services $38,016.13—Total unpaid balance $13,483.87.—$51,500."

Initially, Rosenbaum denied any connection with Tongsun Park, but when confronted with the fact that the reporters had evidence that he received $38,016.13 for services rendered to P.D.I., Rosenbaum said that he could not talk about what the money had been earned for.

"Well, I think the money was probably earned for his role in helping to get the Moroccan irrigation project started," a former business associate of Park's told the reporters. Through many of the documents that they had pieced together, the reporters were aware that Park's people had been working on a multi-million dollar project for the Moroccan government. They had earlier learned that Robert Conkling was involved in the project, and that he had made several trips to Morocco to help coordinate it. They also learned that Park and his associates were only the middlemen in the operation, in charge of coordinating affairs between the Moroccan government and an Oregon company called IRECO—which would do the actual work. With Rosenbaum's involvement in the Moroccan business established, the pieces started to fit together well.

Park's former business associate also told them that "Rosenbaum was a close adviser and consultant to Park, particularly in 1976. Rosenbaum had a lot of international contacts and he was supposed to line up business deals on anything and everything. I think he worked on the Moroccan project for about six months."

With that information in mind, they called one of the top executives of IRECO. "If they paid anybody anything for lining up business with IRECO, they've thrown their money away," he said. "We haven't done one dollar's worth of business with Park's group. They're trying to get us some jobs in Arab countries and if they do, they'll receive a commission. If they don't, they'll get nothing." He added that the Moroc-

57

can project was the only one on which they had had any contact with Conkling.

"Bob Conkling, seemingly, has taken over as the official representative for Park's company overseas," said the executive of IRECO. "At least that's what he's told us." He said that when Conkling had first started working with IRECO he had hinted that he wanted to be given an expense account. "I hit that one over the head real quick," the IRECO executive said, "I told him, 'Look if you're looking for someone to pay for your traveling all over Europe, you can forget that right now.'"

The chief executive of IRECO said that he had known Rosenbaum "for many, many years" and considered him a good friend. He said that Rosenbaum had never done business with him nor represented his company.

Rosenbaum was the picture of legitimacy for the first 54 years of his life—the ultimate Princeton success story. He went to prep school at Hun, in Princeton, and then to Princeton University where he graduated with top honors, played championship tennis and was by every standard a success. He became a prominent and successful tax lawyer, an international business expert for Goodwin, Rosenbaum and Meecham, and developed many contacts in the banking communities in Switzerland and Liechtenstein. But in 1969, the facade of respectability crumbled when Rosenbaum went to prison for defrauding the U.S. Navy of $4 million.

Although it is clear that he was working for Park, it is not yet established exactly what work he was doing.

Cornelius Gallagher

Numerous reports had linked Gallagher to Tongsun Park in past business relationships, but none had been able to establish a current link. Both Park and Gallagher had denied to newsmen that there was any current link, and would not elaborate on the subject of previous connections.

However, in the garbage from Pacific Development, the reporters soon found current evidence of Gallagher's involvement. The evidence was not great—envelopes of mail addressed to Gallagher at P.D.I. and one telex—but it was enough to destroy the credibility of P.D.I. employees who had denied any connection with Gallagher.

During their evening conversation with Spencer Robbins at his home, Perdue had asked him, "Is Mr. Gallagher still receiving mail at the P.D.I. address?"

"No," Robbins had replied, "He has never received mail there. I don't ever recall seeing him at all. I don't know the man."

The previous night, the reporters had found an envelope, postmarked March 9, 1977, addressed to "Mr. Cornelius E. Gallagher, Pacific Development Inc., 1604 K Street N.W. Washington, D.C." The envelope had been opened and the contents had been removed.

Either Mr Gallagher had opened his mail, or someone at P.D.I. was opening, reading and discarding Mr. Gallagher's mail without his knowledge.

By March 9 they had also pieced together a copy of a telex to Tongsun Park from his assistant Bong Y. Lee. The message sent in July 1976, informed Park that the air cargo for Mr. Gallagher had been sent.

Numerous attempts to reach Gallagher for comment proved fruitless for the reporters. But they were later able to find two of Tongsun Park's former business associates who filled them in on Gallagher's relationships with Park's businesses.

Gallagher, a New Jersey Democrat was first elected to the U.S. House of Representatives in 1958 and served as a member of the House Foreign Affairs Committee. Ten years later, he was accused by the now-defunct magazine, *Life* of having close ties to organized crime in New Jersey. The *Life* articles, based on files Gallagher says were leaked to the magazine by the F.B.I., accused him of a long association with Bayonne waterfront leader Joe Zicarelli. The magazine article alleged that the two men had been involved in local police corruption and payoffs and in promotion of the still-controversial cancer cure, Laetrile. Gallagher denied all of the charges and denounced them as part of an F.B.I. plot to force him to resign his Congressional seat.

Four years later, Gallagher pleaded guilty to charges of evading more than $74,000 in Federal income taxes for the year 1966. The plea bargaining arrangement on December 22, 1972 allowed him to plead guilty to the tax charge, and in return the U.S. Attorney's office dropped other charges of perjury and conspiracy to cover up municipal kickbacks. Gallagher had maintained his innocence up until he finally pleaded guilty and had said that the charges were the result of a vast conspiracy mounted against him by J. Edgar Hoover and the F.B.I.

The charges related to more than $367,000 worth of municipal bonds which Gallagher had in his possession from late 1968 until he turned most of them over to the court in 1972. He denied owning the bonds, contending that he was only keeping them for the State Democratic party. The government prosecutors asserted that the bonds were the result of a conspiracy that Gallagher entered into with two Jersey City officials in a massive public contract kickback scheme. Gallagher, who denied owning the bonds during the trial, nevertheless claimed them as his own property after his conviction.

Secret grand jury testimony which was made public in 1973, showed that Tongsun Park cashed $16,000 worth of bonds for Gallagher in 1971 and that the transactions were made through a bank in such a way as to conceal the fact that they were owned by Gallagher.

Gallagher denied repeatedly that he had any business dealings with Park or any of Park's companies. He steadfastly insisted that he and the South Korean businessman were just "old friends." However, Gallagher's assertions were refuted by documents the reporters pieced together, and by information gathered in interviews with former Park business associates.

In late 1975, Gallagher urged Park to provide the seed money to back a pork slaughtering business for a long-time New Jersey friend, Anthony DeAngelis. DeAngelis had served seven years in prison for shortchanging his creditors by more than $175 million when his vegetable oil business collapsed in 1963.

It was widely reported in newspapers that Gallagher had received $250,000 from Tongsun Park for "a pork deal." But details were not available and Gallagher repeatedly asserted that he had had no business dealings with Park.

"We had two checking accounts for the project totaling a quarter of a million dollars," the former Park consultant told Cummins. "One for $225,000 and the other for $25,000. I wrote out the checks as I was instructed and they were countersigned by (Spencer) Robbins and then given to Gallagher."

To facilitate the pork deal, Park set up a company in Bayonne, N.J., near North Bergen, called Lambus. According to transcripts from the typewriter ribbon, the reporters found that Lambus was a wholly-owned subsidiary of Pacific Development. "Capital Investments," was the heading on the P.D.I. document. "Lambus, secured by two promissory notes No. 1 HOG-Amount, $225,000—December 26, 1976. No interest, principle due on demand. No. 2 HOG—Amount $25,000, January 2, 1976. Terms: No Interest, principle due on demand."

A later reference to Lambus in the same transcripts,

showed the reporters that the company was located at 599 Avenue C, Bayonne, N.J. and that the company was still active as late as February 1977.

According to a former Park consultant, Gallagher's part of the deal may have been that he received a commission from the profits. The source said "He worked on a lot of projects for Park."

According to another former employee of Park's, Gallagher traveled for Park on business.

"We paid hotel bills and airline fares for him to New York, the Dominican Republic, down to Florida and a bunch of other places," the former employee said. "And Gallagher would just travel all over the place and we would ask Gallagher, 'Well what's the deal here? Are you supposed to pay for this or is Park supposed to pay for it?' He'd say, 'Oh, I did that for Park. You pay it.' Then we'd ask Park and he'd say, 'Well, I don't know if he was doing it for me or not.' Shoot, I don't know. It might have been a wholesale ripoff as far as I can tell."

Spiro Agnew

Agnew is said to have met Park while he was still Vice President, and according to a close Park business associate, Agnew called Park "a jerk" and didn't want to have anything to do with him.

However, Agnew's attitude changed after he left office, and the two men quickly forged business bonds. Because of Agnew's attitude to the media, and Park's reticence about his business affairs, little solid information has surfaced. Although Agnew is involved with a Maryland import-export firm, Pathlight, when he is overseas, he conducts his business and accepts calls through Tongsun Park's organizations.

In the last week in May 1977, Tongsun Park is said to have tried to go to South Korea. He went to Hong Kong to await assurances that it would be safe for him to return home. With his assets in the United States tied up by the $4.5 million I.R.S. lien, and with his new company in London, Eastern Navigation, moving along rather slowly, it was natural that Tongsun Park would consider returning to his homeland. However, the attempt to go home carried with it a certain amount of danger. President Carter recently announced his intention to withdraw most of the American ground support in South Korea, President Park Chung Hee is in political trouble over the deteriorating relations with the U.S., and is said to be looking for a fall guy. Since Tongsun Park's role was to insure the continued support for South Korea in the White House and the Congress, and since he failed in that, he is a natural fall guy.

Whether assurances as to Park's safety from jail, personal harm or disgrace if he should return to South Korea, ever arrived, we do not know. Park's attorney has assured him that the I.R.S. lien will soon be removed by the courts and his assets and cash flow restored. The I.R.S. lien has been described as "nothing but harassment" of Park, engineered by the Justice Department. But at the time of going to press the situation remains unclear. It is still not known exactly what Park's status is, whether he did or did not violate his non-resident alien status. When that aspect of the case is cleared up once and for all, it will mean that the lien will be removed, or the I.R.S. will be free to collect $4.5 million in taxes.

The House Ethics Committee

The House Ethics Committee has subpoenaed the shredded material and the reconstructed documents rescued from oblivion in the P.D.I. garbage by Perdue and Cummins. The two reporters, together with Mintz, Sokolow, Kramer and Zullo started the ball rolling working twenty hours a day reconstructing the material, and it is now up to the Committee to unravel the rest of the story of the Korean Connection. At the time of going to press, a staff of twelve, expert in the restoration of historical documents are hard at work on the rest of the shreddings, which time and the Committee subpoena did not permit the young reporters to finish.

The fact that a team of young investigative reporters could unearth a story of such proportions makes the point once more of how fortunate we are in this country to have a free press, and how important it is that the press remain free and independent in order to expose the wrongs in our society. Congressional committees don't go down dark alleys at dead of night to dig through garbage cans to discover the truth, that is not their function. But investigative reporters are free to search anywhere and everywhere for evidence of misdeeds.

Although they wanted to be the ones to reconstruct the whole story of the Korean Connection, as good citizens Perdue and Cummins were glad to see the material they had unearthed in the hands of the Ethics Committee, whose business it is to police members of the Congress of the United States.

Over the July 16-17 weekend, as we were going to press, there occurred a series of explosions in the House Ethics Committee investigation of the K.C.I.A.—Tongsun Park alleged illegal lobbying activities in the United States and the investigation took on a definite Nixon White House Watergate hue. The Committee's special counsel, Philip A. Lacovara, 34, resigned after a stinging personal attack on his integrity and public questioning of his motives by House Committee Chairman John J. Flynt, Jr., a longterm Congressman from a solidly Democratic District in Georgia, President Carter's home state.

Lacovara, and his wife Madeleine, parents of eight children, were in London at the time enjoying a long delayed vacation marking their 15th wedding anniversary. He also hoped to covertly interview Park at his secret suburban London hideway, regarding the many accusations into South Korea's activities in buying off U.S. Congressmen with various favors.

Ironically, Flynt personally had picked Lacovara to lead the inquiry because of his reputation for ability and integrity earned as an assistant Watergate special prosecutor. Lacovara resigned that post in protest over then President Ford's pardon of Richard Nixon.

It now appears that Lacovara had dug too deep and was mounting serious evidence connecting key Congressional leaders, particularly older members of Congress on the Democratic side of the House.

On July 17, Sunday, ABC network news in a report from England, said it learned from an unnamed source close to the investigation that House Speaker Thomas O'Neill of Massachusetts and House Democratic Leader James Wright of Texas, both Democrats, have "reason to be concerned" about the investigation of Korean influence-buying. The network quoted its source as saying "it appears to be true" that O'Neill put pressure on the House Ethics Committee to slow its probe of South Korean favors, contributions and gifts to Congressmen over the last several years.

Flynt, O'Neill and Wright vehemently denied the report. In Georgia, Flynt, white with rage, told ABC-TV news "Neither House Speaker O'Neill or Majority Leader Wright have ever at any time put pressure on me about the conduct of this investigation."

Meanwhile, as the national news media continued to analyze the Washington Connection between the Korean C.I.A., Tongsun Park and important U.S. Senators and Congressman, Majority Leader Wright went on national TV and searched out the A.P. and U.P.I. wire services to defend himself, O'Neill and others and charging that the entire affair was just cheap Capitol gossip. "The whole thing is just a damn lie," Wright told United Press International. "This is an absolute and malicious lie."

The House Ethics Committee reluctantly began its investigation of its fellow members in the early spring of 1977 after press accounts in the fall and winter of 1976 specifically outlined a South Korean lobbying effort in Congress which showered cash, gifts, miscellaneous entertainment and women for sexual favors on key Congressmen in hopes of gaining their support for various kinds of foreign aid and shipment of food supplies, particularly rice.

In attacking Lacovara, Georgia Congressman Flynt accused him of charging unbelievably high legal fees ($75 per hour) and being "susceptible to temper tantrums and ego trips." He also accused Lacovara of "writing arrogant, self-serving, misleading and grossly inaccurate memos critical of the Congressional Committee's footdragging and deliberate attempts to paralyze the investigation."

Lacovara, in his letter of resignation, pointed out that "it is now evident that the relationship of mutual trust and confidence that must exist between lawyer and client no longer exists."

The story has now become so hot that it occupies the front pages of the Nation's major newspapers, is a key leading news story on radio and television and has even invaded the comic strips via Garry Trudeau's cartoon, Doonesbury.

One of the prime catalysts spurring Lacovara and his staff onward, was the revelation by syndicated columnists Jack Anderson and Les Whitten, *Newsweek* magazine and other news media that we had successfully collected and reconstructed from garbage found behind Park's Washington house much hard evidence that had been shredded and which provided linkage to Congressional payoffs.

Many Congressmen are now fearfully watching the unfolding developments with their eyes on the 1978 Congressional race and their ability to withstand attacks on their morals and ethics by an enraged constituency.

Lacovara, widely regarded as an up and coming lawyer with great perception and an innate ability to get to civil and criminal improprieties, reported that there was no way he could bend his probe to fit into the kind of a House Congressional whitewash desired by Congressman Flynt . . . "it was obvious that such a relationship could not continue . . . things have been difficult from the beginning. At virtually every substantive phase of our investigation, it has been an uphill battle to convince Flynt and some of his cronies to do what we thought was appropriate to conduct a professional investigation."

As evidence of the investigation's many problems, Lacovara cited Flynt's delays in approving a questionnaire to be sent to all members of the Congress regarding the acceptance of Korean favors and Flynt's House Committees' members unwillingness to disclose their own acceptance of favors from foreign governments.

Lacovara pointed out that "obviously, there is a reluctance by a few members to pursue what is the uncomfortable, unpleasant task of investigating their colleagues. This is an important investigation that ought to be pursued. From what I've learned, it would be tragic for it to be discontinued."

Some 30 junior Democratic members of Congress elected in the post-Watergate general housecleaning joined with leading Republicans in deploring Flynt's attacks on Lacovara and his subsequent withdrawal from the investigation. Bill Brock, chairman of the Republican National Committee and Peter H. Kostmayer of Pennsylvania, a leader among the more moralistic of the House Democrats, excoriated Flynt and renewed their demand that a special prosecutor take over the investigation of the South Korean scandal.

President Carter, however, in what may be the grounds for one of the first whisperings about the new administration's integrity, reiterated again and again that he had "no plans" to appoint a special prosecutor to investigate charges of South Korean influence peddling despite fresh demands for an independent probe.

Returning to the White House from a weekend at Camp David, Carter was asked whether he would appoint a special prosecutor to substitute for the ongoing investigation by the House Ethics Committee. "I have no plans to take such an action," Carter said.

Demands for a special prosecutor, in the Watergate fashion which Lacovara was pushing for, reflected intensifying pressures for someone outside Congress to investigate allegations that Congressmen took bribes and other favors from representatives of the South Korean Government.

Mr. Brock asserted in his statement that "Mr. Lacovara was forced to resign because of the vicious character assassination" by Mr. Flynt. He contended that Mr. Flynt's remarks about and attacks on Mr. Lacovara "were malicious and petty, and have resulted in a great victory for those in Congress who hope the investigation can be delayed until it dies or is simply covered up."

"By his performance," Mr. Brock said, "Congressman Flynt has shown that he is both inept and incapable of conducting a thorough and unbiased investigation. The investigation must be pursued by a special prosecutor."

Representative Kostmayer said that the departure of Mr. Lacovara "casts a lot of doubt as to whether Mr. Flynt should continue as chairman of the committee."

"Mr. Lacovara added a lot of credibility to their slow-paced efforts," he continued. "With his absence, I wonder whether others in the Congress or the people in the country can now believe that this committee can effectively continue the probe under Flynt's leadership."

When contacted about the various charges, Speaker "Tip" O'Neill said that he would not endorse efforts to make Mr. Flynt step aside. He also said that he would oppose the appointment of a special counsel or a select committee, contending that the ethics committee headed up by Flynt "could do the job." With the appointment of Leon Jaworski as special prosecutor, the furor died down, and the Ethics Committee regained its prestige once more.

About the Authors

LEW PERDUE was born in the Mississippi Delta town of Greenwood, and spent his early childhood in Itta Bena, a small cotton-economy town nearby. He attended public schools in Jackson, the state capital. While a student at Corning Community College in Corning, New York he became editor of the campus paper, and in 1969 he went to work for the Elmira *Star Gazette*. After graduating from Corning first in his class, he transferred to Cornell University in 1970. While still in college he worked for the Ithaca *Journal*—a Gannett newspaper, as was the *Star Gazette*—covering the police and city court beat. He was married to Shan Haley in June 1970. After several changes of major, he graduated *cum laude* from Cornell. He became consumer editor of the *Journal*, and started to do investigative reporting. He worked at Cornell as an instructor in magazine writing and mass communication law, and then headed the tourism department for the State of Mississippi. In 1974 Perdue became press secretary to Congressman Thad Cochran who represented the state capital. After a year spent working with Republican candidates in the 1976 campaigns, and editing a magazine for them, Perdue decided to become a fulltime writer.

KEN CUMMINS came to Washington in the Fall of 1976, after spending four years helping to found the *New Newspaper* for which he also wrote. He graduated from the University of Kansas School of Journalism in 1972, and then took a hitchhiking trip around the country, and worked on the McGovern campaign in Kansas, an experience which gave him first-hand experience of political life. He has also produced and directed video documentaries for KPTS Channel 8, the public television station in South-Central Kansas.

LEW PERDUE and KEN CUMMINS were assisted in their investigations by JIM MINTZ, who is a native of Washington. He is a graduate of Boston University and was the editor of *The News,* an independent newspaper serving the campus community, during 1975 and 1976. He has worked as an intern for nationally syndicated columnist Jack Anderson, and before working on this book, was employed by the Institute of Policy Studies to research the CIA role in Watergate.

DON ZULLO, 23, is a 1976 journalism graduate of Boston University. He also worked as an editor of *The News*, and is currently reporting for *The Newton Times*, a Boston surburban weekly newspaper.

RICHARD SOKOLOW came to Washington in November of 1976 to work in a reporting internship program for Jack Anderson. He attended the State University of New York at Buffalo where he worked as a news reporter for WBFO a public radio station, until his graduation in January of 1976. Since then Rich has worked as an organizer on a U.S. Senate campaign in Vermont and he has been a copyeditor for *Sport's Reporter*, a New York based gambling tout sheet, and has worked as a janitor.

WENDY KRAMER came to Washington in November 1976 to work as a reporter intern with Jack Anderson. Before that she attended the Evergreen State College in Olympia, Washington where she was anchorperson for the nightly news of KAOS-FM radio, and cover/feature investigative reporter for the *Cooper Point* Journal. In addition she covered the Washington State legislature for the Seattle *Post-Intelligencer*.

Congressional Abuse of Power

Congressman John Young
by Nick Rowe and Jane Rowe
Congressman Otto Passman
by Lew Perdue and Ken Cummins
Congressman Philip Burton
by Lew Perdue and Ken Cummins

"I don't find that there's anybody who's an innocent victim of anything. I mean, because they have a choice . . . I just don't believe that there's a victim. I think maybe people are used, but they also use in return."

Colleen Gardner

"Legally speaking you don't wound the Congressman, you either kill him or leave him alone. When they're wounded they're dangerous."

Justice Department Source

Congressman John Young—
by Nick Rowe and Jane Rowe
The background

On the evening of June 8, 1976 the phone rang at the McLean, Virginia home of Congressman John Young, Democrat from Texas. His wife answered and Colleen Gardner asked for the Congressman. Colleen, a former research assistant on his staff, had quit her $25,800 a year position in March of the same year and gone on unemployment. Within a few days of this phone call, she would be headlined in the New York *Times* in another "below-the-belt" blast at Congress. Elizabeth Ray had preceded her by three weeks and was well on the way to forcing Wayne Hays into premature retirement, thus setting the stage for a journalistic investigation of John Young.

Young's soft, drawling voice came over the receiver, "Hello."

"Hi, how're you doin'?"

"Fine. How's your Birthday party?"

"Pretty good," Colleen said. "My grandmother said you'd been trying to reach me."

"Yeah. Well, I think I need to tell you about these two fellows from the *New York Times* came over."

"Again?"

"Yeah. And Harry was on the Hill and Joe was

77

there an' the five of us sat down there an let me predi-cate the whole thing by saying they never got a gawddamn thing out of me. Now they do have their case pretty well documented."

"They do?"

"Yeah. I presume from information that (name deleted) has given them."

"What kind of information do they have?"

"Well, for example, at one point they said, 'Does the name, George Denton, mean anything to you?' An' I said, yes, it sure does. An' they said, 'Did you register under that name at the Pentagon Motel?' An' I said, yes, I sure did. Many times."

"Well, I don't remember ever telling (name deleted) anything about that."

"Well . . . so, they said, 'What was the purpose of that?' An' I said, well, I've had a running battle going on with the military with reference to my bases in Florida (sic) and so forth an' I'm gettin' very delicate information, to say the least, out of various people, and that they would lose their jobs if we met at the Pen-tagon or anywhere like that, so we had to meet clan-destine."

"Yeah."

"An' they said, 'Well, did you ever have anybody from your staff there an' (unintelligible) your staff?' An' I said, well, no. Not that I can recall, unless, pos-sibly, maybe somebody might have brought me some papers or books or somethin' at one time or another, but, uh, said, 'Well, was Colleen Gardner ever there?' An' I said, no, I sure don't think so, but it's possible she might have brought me some books or somethin'."

"Um, yeah."

"They said, 'Well, you seem to like the same, uh, the same room all the time.' "

"Wha, what room was that?"

"Well, I dunno. 1105 or somethin'. I said, well yes. Those are larger rooms and would accomodate more people."

"Yeah. Well, did you ever tell Colonel Woodward . . . anything?"

"No."

"Huh?"

"Negative."

"No?"

"No . . . no . . . no, no . . . no, no details whatsoever. An' of course . . . uh, apparently, they don't have any details."

"Uh huh."

"Other than, than I just assume that they got some from, from, from (name deleted)."

"Well, I don't recall ever tellin' (name deleted). . ."

"But you might have when you all were drinkin' or somethin'. I don't know."

"Well, I might have when I was drinking, but I doubt it."

"Well, of course, the thing about it is, I don't know, they could . . . there is, there're other ways they could have found out. They might have checked with a picture, for instance. They might have shown . . ."

"You think they might have checked with a picture?"

"Yeah. Might have shown a picture of me, but, but, uh . . . but they've never seen anybody but me there. I've been very careful to keep the other people that've been meeting with me as where they wouldn't be seen."

"Yeah."

"An' then they mentioned about the Skyline Tow . . . Skyline Hotel an' I said, yes, I could've, uh, it could, could be, uh . . ."

"You think they were just going around different hotels?"

"Yeah. I think they checked in, an' I said, uh, an' they said, 'for the same purpose?' An' I said, yes, for the same purpose. An' they said, 'What about the Channel Inn?' An' I said, well no, I don't recall, uh, registering at the Channel Inn under that name, but it could be, could possibly be . . . an' maybe some others around. I don't know. Well, and, uh . . . I showed them a lot of the material I had collected, uh . . . they didn't seem terribly interested in that, but, uh, but I said I can't divulge the names of the people because every damn one of 'em would be fired summarily for divulging this type of information to anybody, particularly a member of Congress."

"Right."

"So, uh, that was that. Then they asked me if I had any, uh, any nude pictures of any, uh, of women on my staff an' I said absolutely not! They asked me if I'd ever paid or offered to pay any members of my, any females on my staff for, for sex, an' I said absolutely not! Uh, I'm just tryin' to touch on all the points. Uh, of course, they, uh, we had a back an' forth about the salary scales and, uh, we're not worried about that. We can certainly defend that."

"Yeah."

"And, uh, then they asked me the direct question, uh, if I had had any, uh, any, uh, sexual relations with anybody on my staff. I said absolutely not, but I said, I'll have to tell you though, that if I ever did, I damn sure wouldn't admit it."

Young continues to fill Colleen in on the questioning. His pay scales were again challenged and he reasserted his confidence that Harry McAdams, his former Administrative Assistant who, despite a new job, still handled all matters pertaining to hiring, job descriptions and pay scales would be able to justify the wages. (McAdams was then employed by the Governor of Texas as the Director of State Federal relations), Young was assuming that a former employee had been talking with the reporters and requested that they be certain to check her story out thoroughly before proceeding to print. The Congressman appealed to Nick Horrock and John Crewdson to be "thorough, be frank and be accurate."

Later, in the tape recorded conversation, he continued with Colleen, "The reason I'm goin' into all this is that it's probably gonna be an ordeal that you're gonna have to go through and Christ sakes just . . . just deny every gawddamned bit of it an' if they quote (name deleted), just say, well hell, no way, she's just . . . erratic."

"Yeah."

"Ol' Harry's just . . . Harry was sure . . ."

81

"Was Harry upset . . . or?"

"Very upset."

"Really?"

"Harry thinks it's gonna . . ."

"Harry wha . . . I can't hear you."

"Oh, I'm sorry. Harry was very upset. He thinks it's gonna mean his job."

"Oh my God! Harry's job?"

"Yeah"

"What has Harry got to do with it?"

"Well, 'cause (of) his sec . . . she's been poppin' off about Harry havin' an affair with (name deleted) an' . . ."

"Yeah,"

"And, uh . . . uh, tyin' him in that way and, uh . . . uh tyin' in that Harry was runnin' the office and, uh, responsible for this . . . what they're playin' up, Colleen, is that this was an office policy . . . that's part of it . . . that when they came to work for us they had to uh . . . they asked the direct question, 'When girls came to work for you did you make them agree to have sex with the men here before you'd hire them?' An', of course, Harry and Joe both said, well jeez, that's just ridiculous. No way."

"Yeah."

"And, uh . . . they don't have a . . . they, they can't go with this thing unless they can corroborate what (name deleted) been tellin' them."

"Yeah"

"I don't see much chance of that. I know as soon as I hang up I'm gonna think of something else I ought to tell ya, but let me just emphasize that it was just absolutely negative."

"Um-huh."

"Uh, from the standpoint of their questions. Their questions were mean questions. An' I also want to emphasize what you already know is that, that, that, uh, these people don't have any authority to put anybody under oath and, uh, it's not like an F.B.I. man or the grand jury."

"Yeah"

"Uh, there's no, you're not obligated to tell them the gawddamned truth about anything."

"Well, what if the F.B.I. happens to come by. Then what happens?"

"Well, the F.B.I.'s reports would have to be, would be confidential an' then you cannot, you've gotta be damn careful about lyin' to the F.B.I."

"Yeah."

"When that happens, I, I would say then we better just take the whole gawddamned thing to the grand jury."

"Um. Yeah. Of course the grand jury is secret. Right?"

"Yeah."

"Yeah."

"But as far as these damn reporters go . . . and there have been no violations of law at all, Colleen, that the grand jury would be interested in . . . these, uh . . . these, uh, the peccability and, uh, pec-peccances of . . . of, uh, members, they've emphasized they're not interested in. It's violations of law . . .

what happened to Federal money when people on the Federal payroll . . . workin' for the money."

Colleen excused herself and went back to her birthday party. John Young went back to his lounge chair in the recreation room of his comfortable, ranch-style home, to ponder who the "deep throat" in his office was.

Young, an unobtrusive, ten-term veteran from the Texas Gulf Coast's fourteenth district, seemed an unlikely nominee for a Capitol Hill swordsman award. At sixty-one, he showed more mileage than did Wayne Hays at sixty-six. Neatly balding whiteness blends into a prison pallor gray face. Green, Coke-bottle-bottom glasses and a network of tiny, crimson veins across the nose are the only contrasts. Some scattered worry lines and smiling crinkles at the corners of his eyes add character. He's a moderately tall man with a troublesome paunch that requires a perennial promise to himself to go on a diet. Conservative suits, narrow lapels, white shirts and a bow-tie complete the image of, perhaps, a small college history professor or rural lawyer. Suddenly, however, he found himself targeted by the Washington *Post* and New York *Times* as an adjunct to the Wayne Hays' payrolled sex investigation.

What the 93rd Congress had accomplished during the Watergate crisis was backfiring on the 94th. Senators Sam Ervin, Howard Baker, Representatives Peter Rodino and Barbara Jordan, among others had distinguished themselves during the 1974 hearings and impeachment proceedings. Their performances cast a glowing aura of respectability and competence over the

House of Congress. On that final morning in August, 1974, when Richard Nixon boarded the White House helicopter for his last flight from the political trenches on Capitol Hill, the end of the imperial Presidency came with a whimper, not a bang. The victors, defenders of the Constitution, assured the nation that a new era of political morality and ethical purity was upon us. But that was the Fall of 1974, and the Spring of '76 was a bad one for a Congress that had yet to complete reasserting its power.

Watergate and its aftermath had elevated the role of investigative journalism from muckraking to a critical source of information for the electorate. Woodward and Bernstein achieved rare hero status and inspired the legions of investigative reporters who followed, although there were some stories of a superficial or purely sensational nature that resulted, instead of the more difficult-to-unearth revelations of a Watergate.

What had been a muffled tread through the halls of Congress became a stampede after Liz Ray opened her notebook on Capitol Hill's sex-for-pay games. More than a titillating, vicarious journey into the bedrooms of the powerful, it highlighted one facet of the dark side of life in a Congressional office. Wayne Hays became a symbol of arrogance in the face of privilege and trust and it was in this atmosphere that John Young found himself under suspicion of similar abuse.

Bob Woodward had been keeping a file on Wayne Hays since completing his Watergate investigation and was familiar with the tight-lipped staff that surrounded the man. When Marion Clark and Rudy Maxa of the

Washington *Post* were contacted by Elizabeth Ray, the flaw in Hays' armor appeared to be exploitable. Woodward turned his attention to other leads on the Hill and on Tuesday, June 1, 1976, he phoned Colleen Gardner at her Alexandria, Virginia apartment.

"I understand you used to work for Congressman John Young. Is that correct?" Woodward asked.

"Used to work for him?" Colleen verified the question, then answered tentatively, "Yeah."

"You quit about a month ago. Is that correct?"

"Yeah."

"Say, somebody up there on the Hill told me that there was some situation with him where you and another staff member had to take a gun out of his desk and throw it into the Potomac . . . and that there were some rather strange things going on in that office. Is that correct?"

"Who told you that?" Colleen queried.

"Oh, somebody who works up there."

"Somebody who works up there?" Colleen repeated.

"Yeah."

There is a pause, then Colleen said, "Well, I don't think I should talk to you about this on the phone."

"Uh-huh. Are you willing to sit down and talk? I tol . . . it was told to me in gr . . . in strict confidence and would very much like to sit down with you 'cause the story I heard seems to be a rather strange and bizarre one and it seems to indicate that Mr. Young is doing some rather strange things."

Colleen hesitated before answering, "Well, I think

this is kind of a strange, uh . . . who told you this story?"

"Oh, somebody. Somebody I know who's a source of mine on the Hill."

"Really?"

"Yeah."

"I can't imagine, you know, them telling you something like that. Really."

"Is it true?" Woodward persisted.

"Well, what am I supposed to say?" Colleen managed an embarrassed laugh. "You know, uh, I mean I'm right in the middle of studying and everything and I know all about, you know, the news about Betty Ray and Wayne Hays and I guess there's a general check on all the offices . . . but, uh, I don't know what to say, you know, on the phone . . . I, I really don't know if I should say anything . . ."

"Well, no, I think . . ."

"You know, I don't think I want to get myself involved . . ."

"Are you going to school now?" Woodward changed his questioning.

"Yeah."

"You are. Are you . . ." he went back to the main issue, "How long did you work for John Young?" Her protests were halted, at least temporarily.

"Oh, a total of about five years, but I left once before and then I went back."

"Did you . . . who was the other girl who quit the staff at the same time?" Woodward asked.

"Who quit at the same time?"

"Yeah"

"Uh, I don't think she quit at the same time. She . . . I think she quit a few weeks later . . . after I did."

"Where might I reach her?"

"To be honest with you," Colleen dodged, "I don't know. I haven't . . . you know, she hasn't, uh, contacted me in over a month. I don't know what she's doing or . . . you know."

"Does she live here in town?"

"I would assume she does."

"And her first name is (spells name). Is that correct?"

"But now what's going to happen? Are you going to print this in the *Post*? Now, I mean that's terrible!"

"Um, not until I talk to you. Why don't I come out and talk to you. Uh, could I do that this afternoon?"

"Gee, I don't know. God, you've really got me on the spot."

"Well, I'm not trying to put you on the spot . . ."

"I mean, I've just . . . you know, I just find this very strange that somebody would tell you something like that, you know. What are they trying to do get, uh, you know, try to . . . put some, uh, trouble on me. Is that what you're trying to do?"

"No, no," Woodward assured her, "No. I don't think anyone is trying to put any trouble on you. Uh, it's just, you know, that it . . . it seems to go a little bit . . ."

"You said something was stolen from his office?" Colleen asked.

"Yeah . . . or taken from his office."

"And that I had done it?"

"Well, that you were involved in it or knew about it."

"Jesus Christ! Somebody told you that?"

"Yeah. I give you my word . . . and also there was something . . ."

"Somebody in the office said something like that?" Colleen interrupted.

"That there was also his little black book . . . that was taken . . . and uh, you know, it listed some of his girlfriends or a good number of . . ."

"Was it somebody that worked on the Hill?" Colleen persisted.

"Yeah."

"I mean you're not lying to me about somebody that works on the Hill."

"I am not. I mean I just wouldn't . . . I wouldn't make up something like that, you know that."

"Gosh, that's unbelievable. I can't imagine somebody telling you . . . you're with the Washington *Post*?" Colleen hadn't realized who Bob Woodward was and made no association between him and the Watergate story.

"Yep." Woodward answered calmly.

The gentle probing continued as Woodward worked around the allegation that Colleen and another young employee had been involved in taking a pistol and "black book" from Young's office and that Colleen had thrown the pistol into the Potomac River. Colleen became wary, still not realizing that Bob Woodward was, in fact, an investigative reporter for the Washington *Post*.

Later, Woodward asked Colleen why she quit. She answered, "Well, that's very personal why I quit. I, really, I wanted to go to school . . . and uh, you know, the hours were pretty long and I decided . . . I'm trying to get my CPA and I've been going to school now it seems like forever and I've saved up some money and I just decided that I'd just dedicate myself this next summer and Fall to going to school at night and possibly finding a job just part time . . . you know, twenty hours a week . . . something like that."

"How did you get along with Mr. Young?"

"Well, I guess, on and off, all right."

Woodward questioned Colleen about her duties in the office and Colleen responded, "Well, several different things. I was a research assistant and I was appointed to this Joint Atomic Energy Committee and . . . occasionally, you know, we'd have some translations from Spanish into English, so I used to do some bi-lingual translations. I'm Spanish . . . well, I was born in Venezuela . . . and once in awhile I'd do some secretarial work, but I wasn't really classified as a secretary. I was supposed to have been promoted beyond that even though once in awhile they'd give me some secretarial work to do. But basically, it was taking care of the, you know, the liaison between the Joint Atomic Energy Committee and nuclear energy plants and my boss . . . and . . . so . . ."

"Well . . ."

"See I have a chemistry background. I had a couple of years of chemistry . . . physics, you know, math."

Finally, Colleen agreed to talk with Woodward at her apartment. He got her address and planned to be there by "about 2:30." Colleen still wasn't certain about him and Woodward had to convince her, particularly after she questioned whether or not he was a "spy for Mr. Young."

"Absolutely not!" Woodward chuckled.

"You probably are!"

"I am not!" They both were chuckling.

"Jesus Christ, that'd be a riot." She was laughing.

"You, you can check me out if you want. You want my number and you want to call me back at the *Post*?" Woodward volunteered. "To make sure."

"Yeah, I think I better," Colleen said, "Hold on a second." She left the phone to get a pad and ball point pen.

"Okay." She was back.

"What's the address there?" Woodward asked. Colleen gave it to him then he continued, "Okay. My name's Bob Woodward at the *Washington Post*. If you check in the phone book . . ."

"Bob Woodward?" Colleen confirmed, still unaware of who he was.

"Right."

"Washington *Post*?"

"Right."

"Okay. What's the number?"

"Uh, if you check in the phone directory, you'll find the Washington *Post*'s number is 223-6000, and, uh, ask for me and they'll hook you up. My extension's 7236. Could you call me right back 'cause I've got to run out?"

"Okay. I'll call you right back."

"Okay. Thanks a lot. Bye." Woodward hung up.

Colleen immediately dialed 223-6000 and got a *Washington Post* operator, *"Washington Post."*

"Extension 7236 please," Colleen said.

"Dial 223-7236," came the flat-toned reply, then a click.

"Uh . . . hello?" Colleen was talking to a dead line. She hung up and dialed the number.

"Woodward," he was immediately there.

"Yeah, I called the ext . . . you know, I dialed that number, 223-6000, and they said for that extension, I had to dial you directly."

"Okay, fine, but they can hook you up." Woodward reassured her.

"They can?" She asked.

"You sure . . ."

"They told me that I had to dial directly."

"Okay, but you, they confirmed the extension. Right? Or the number?" Woodward probably had not had such difficulty identifying himself in months.

"Well, I didn't ask for your name; I just asked for the extension."

"Oh, I see. . . . Okay, you, you check with them, you'll see that it's me. I assure you." Woodward must have wondered if this was a woman who subscribed only to out-of-town newspapers and had been out of the country during Watergate.

CONGRESSIONAL ABUSE OF POWER

At this point, John Young wasn't aware of the interest being focused on his office. He talked with Colleen shortly after her conversation with Bob Woodward and speculated that it was probably a general questioning of persons who had known Elizabeth Ray. Colleen asked Young if he had talked to anyone about the missing gun and books, then related that a "news reporter" had called her about the incident. Young attributed any leak to (name deleted) as well as presuming (name deleted) had taken both the gun and books.

Young's office was only hours away from coming under seige, but there was a tranquil air on that Tuesday morning. Room 2204, on the second floor of the Rayburn Building, is in a choice location with windows overlooking the Capitol and the baroque goose-foot intersection where Maryland Avenue, the Mall and Pennsylvania Avenue come together at the foot of Capitol Hill. The Rayburn Building, newest, largest and most elaborate of the three office buildings with its blocky architecture and over-imposing facades has been stylistically referred to as "Mussolini Modern," however, it contains the prime office space for Representatives.

The suite of rooms is somewhat spartan with General Services Administration desks, a pair of armchairs, a low table against the wall with guest book and a large, color-coded map of the counties in Young's 14th Congressional District on the wall behind the receptionist's desk. In the larger room to the left of the main door are long tables, in-wall recessed files, secretaries' desks and, on the wall above the files, a mounted sailfish, locked in a fighting arc as he strains against an invisible sportsman's line.

In the closed office directly behind the receptionist is Joe Pendergast, Young's Legislative Research Assistant and office manager. To the right is the door leading to the Congressman's private office. A few vases of flowers in the outer office add a touch of living color.

Young, sitting comfortably behind his massive desk, read to Colleen from the *Time* Magazine article on Elizabeth Ray, laughing as he came across passages chronicling Ray's escapades with various Washington figures, particularly her involvement with Wayne Hays. His relaxed, confident attitude was not reassuring to Colleen. She knew what was coming. Young commented on the potential spread of investigations from Hays office to others saying, "There's going to be a lot going on this other matter up here on the Hill, but I think that it's, uh, it's just gone so damn wild now that I wouldn't pay any attention to it. If anybody should come to me and ask me any questions pertaining to any employees, past or present, or about myself, I'm gonna simply take the position . . . I want you to pay careful attention to this . . . I'm gonna take the position, look, this is a matter of official investigation and anything that I say on this subject will be said to, to the official investigators, not to any media, anything like that."

"Yeah." Colleen was unconvinced.

"That's the way it's gonna be, because if the grand jury, uh, should want to look into anything pertaining to my office, I will give them a thorough run-down. I'll be glad to go over my personnel, present and past, my salaries, my salary schedules, my duty assignments and, and, and there won't be any damn question but that every damn body that ever worked for this office, uh, anybody who's workin' here now has more than earned their money. No problem."

"Yeah. Of course, it might look kinda odd . . ." Colleen offered.

"I don't give a damn what it looks like!" Young shot back. "I'm not gonna furnish any gawddamned, uh, anymore damn ammunition for the media to, to, to make a Watergate out of this thing with a front page headline every damn day. Yuh understand?"

Young emphasized that Colleen had no recent association with Elizabeth Ray and shouldn't worry about the media interest since Ray was their main target.

"Yeah. They're all involved in it apparently, but, but all that stuff was goin' on an' nobody over here knew a gawddamned thing about it, but that's what they're pursuing. And what I'm trying to be is helpful to you. Don't be offended by me. I'm just tryin' to 'emphasize that unless you had something to do with something like that, which I know you didn't, then you don't have anything to worry about. You understand?"

"Of course."

"Well, that's what I'm . . ."

"Well, what I'm . . . but what I'm saying is I wasn't, you know . . . I don't even know Wayne Hays or any of those girls that, you know, worked in the office . . ."

"True. True. So don't let your imagination run away

95

with you and worry about this gawddamned creepy-ass lawyer . . . that's tellin' you that you ought to go, go forth and, and, uh, and tell . . . and tell what you know, uh, well tell what? What do you know? I mean that's the important thing about it. You haven't had anything to do with that gawddamned bitch during this period at all."

Colleen's association with Elizabeth Ray went back to 1967, when they both dated a number of prominent men in the Washington area. Lawyer Sol Rosen, who had met Colleen in 1973, and become both legal counsel and escort, had encouraged her in late May 1976, after the Hays-Ray scandal hit the papers, to go to the U.S. Attorney's office with what she knew.

Going back to the Hays' investigation, Colleen remarked, "Isn't that strange that Wayne Hays would be having orgies? That's weird."

"Well, apparently takin' place right over there in the Capitol," Young said, "Accordin' to this article."

"God. He must have had quite a good time."

"Must have been . . . involvin' the Capitol police an' other members an' staff people an' . . . seem like they were havin' a good time ba . . . at the time," Young commented wryly, "I bet they've got second thoughts about it now."

"They mean all-out, real orgies? With everybody naked and in the same room?" Colleen asked.

"I guess so. I guess so."

"That's wild. That's strange."

"And that's down in the Capitol, right across from the dining room there." Young added.

"I'll be damned."

"Little private room. Mr. Rayburn used to have . . . used to have drinkin' sessions there with Lyndon an' all of us."

That afternoon, Bob Woodward visited Colleen in her apartment to expand on the morning's questions and lob a few more bombs. He arrived several minutes late and sat down for a brief warm-up chat. The apartment's living room is a splash of vivid colors: rugs, Spanish-influence paintings, large throw pillows and tiers of green plants in front of sliding glass doors opening onto a balcony. Mediterranean style chairs, a large couch and coffee table dominate the living room. The small dining area which adjoins the living room is crowded with a round table, four chairs, a partially-filled wine rack and, against the wall, a bookcase, its shelves filled with textbooks, novels, a stereo amplifier and assorted figurines.

He began presenting the allegations that had come from his Hill source. There were several accurate pieces of information mixed with allegations and assumptions, indicating that somehow he had a pipeline to the office. Woodward was accurate about a pistol and notebook being stolen from young's office. On February 27, 1976, a Friday evening, Colleen and a co-worker had gone back to the office after the others had left. The co-worker was distraught and had come to Colleen with her problems. In the course of the evening, the woman's anger turned to the Congressman and the two women went to the office, the other woman went through Young's desk and Pendergast's desk. The pistol, a souvenir-type weapon, a phone book with numbers Young had accumulated over the years, and a cash record book, went into their purses. Colleen had later thrown the pistol into the Potomac.

Beyond that, Woodward asked Colleen about allegations that she was having an affair with the Congressman, that she didn't do any work in the office and that she received special privileges because of her special relationship with the Congressman. He said he had heard that women in the office were under pressure to have sex with John Young. Woodward had obviously talked with other people, but beyond the pistol and book incident, he was on a fishing expedition. He blew any chance he might have had for communication by dropping a hypothesis on Colleen that she, working on the Hill and making over $20,000 with only a high school diploma, must be sleeping with someone.

In a call to Young after Woodward left, she fumed, "And then he confronted me with my salary and how was it I was making a certain number of dollars and not having an education and I asked him, 'Well, do you have a Ph.D? How much are you making?' And he said he was making twenty-nine thousand a year, and I said, 'Well, you have no Ph.D, so what are you telling me, why, you know, what's wrong with my salary?' " Colleen reacted strongly to the allegations and defended her education, her work and her salary as well as denying any pressures for sex on the women working in Young's office. She felt that after talking with her, Woodward has reassessed his allegations and wouldn't proceed with the story.

Woodward didn't get the confirmation he sought, but he did make more of an impression than he realized. During the conversation with Young, another woman on the staff was monitoring the call on an extension. After Young hung up, she and Colleen continued to discuss the meeting. Woodward, himself, came into the conversation, "Did he just come and knock on the door?" she asked in a whispery voice.

"Yes," Colleen boomed back.

"What'd he look like?"

"Very good-looking!" Colleen replied as both of them broke into laughter.

"What were you wearing?" came the shy, but curious voice.

"Just my blue jeans . . . and my sweater," Colleen answered, then became serious again, "I was, you know, studying . . . and I told him, I said, 'You know I'm going to tell my boss about our conversation.' He said, 'You are?' And I said, 'Of course.'"

Colleen did call John Young and he thanked her warmly for her staunch defense of the office. Young mentioned that he'd had his first encounter with the press that afternoon when Dick Lyons, of the *New York Times*, came into the office. Lyons questioned Young about allegations that he was having sexual relations with three women on his staff. Young called Jim Woodward, his projects and research assistant, in to witness the exchange, then categorically denied the allegations and stated he had no comment for the press; rather, he would say anything that needed to be said to a grand jury. Young noted that Lyons also mentioned the pistol and notebook, relating the allegation to Woodward's questions to Colleen. Young surmised, "Of course, they (the *Times*) work closely with and I think maybe . . . maybe they're owned by Washington *Post* or vice versa. I know they both work together."

In both of these cases, Young and Colleen managed to thwart potential stories before they were written. Woodward's memo following his interview with Colleen reflected a young woman who worked full hours in Young's office, went to American University at night and was within a few credit hours of attaining her degree; hardly the image of another Liz Ray—an image Colleen desperately wanted to avoid. Nevertheless, there was some consternation among Young's staff members with big guns like the *New York Times* and Woodward poking around.

In the June 1, calls between John Young and Colleen, the allegations to which each of them had answered clearly indicated the areas of media interest. Young realized that an investigation of his pay records, job descriptions and salary increases would reveal no violation of Federal law. The generous limits of Congressional power afforded a Representative in personnel matters provides virtually unrestricted control over the above functions so long as the annual total staff employment allowance of $255,144 (November 1976 data: relative to Colleen Gardner) is not exceeded. The only other significant limits (Nov. 1976) were a maximum of 18 staff members and a maximum single salary of $39,600. Further, the Legislative Reorganization Act of 1970, specified in section 472, paragraph (e): "Each member and Resident Commissioner may, by written notice to the Clerk of the House, establish such titles for positions in his office as he may desire to designate."

In addition to the privileges Congress allowed itself, by law, in staff and salary matters, John Young had another trump card. Harry McAdams, during his tenure as Administrative Assistant, had been responsible for all matters pertaining to the hiring, firing, pay scales, pay increases and job descriptions. After he left the office, Young retained him, on salary and still designated as "Administrative Assistant" while McAdams continued to handle personnel matters. He was carried with that title until the July 1 to December 31, 1976, Report of the Clerk of the House. Young was confident that McAdams could respond to any questions directed to him by official investigators regarding use of Federal funds. McAdams continues to serve on Young's staff, but is now designated as "clerk."

During the next three days, *New York Times* reporters Nick Horrock, John Crewdson and Lucinda "Cindy" Franks pursued leads relating to allegations they had turned up. Young's prime suspect as "deep throat's sister", was contacted by the *Times'* investigative team. Nick Horrock contacted former Young employees, in Los Angeles and San Francisco, and John Crewdson made the rounds on the Hill. This team of reporters seemed to have a crystal ball and detailed knowledge of incidents, personalities and associated dates that caused growing concern in the office.

Colleen, in calls to and from John Young, related the progressing search for facts in which she was being trapped. Young had warned his District Office Managers in Texas, after the Woodward interview, of a potentially damaging news story even though Colleen had handled him well. Young laughed about the allegation that he had three mistresses on his staff, "One, maybe; two, not very damn likely; but, three . . . preposterous!" Young felt that stories based on gossip and rumor could be bad, publicity-wise, but an investigation of his payroll would reveal no criminal offense. Nevertheless, on June 2nd, he began to review Colleen's work record and staff responsibilities, mentioning to her the work she had done on the Rules Committee and Joint Committee on Atomic Energy, both assignments which Young held.

The indication that Colleen might be sought out by the press because of her prior association with Elizabeth Ray was of minimal concern to Young. The chance that she might say something which would be detrimental to the office was a remote possibility. Young told Colleen on June 2nd, "If I can't trust you, I can't trust anybody." Referring to Bob Woodward, Young said, "I can't help, but just say again I thought you just stood up to that bastard just beautifully. The idea of that son of a bitch tellin' you those damn lies to try to break you down. Isn't that somethin'?" Woodward had told Colleen that Young mentioned to another Congressman that he was in love with her and the word had been relayed to Wayne Hays. Young denied this emphatically to reassure Colleen he had said nothing to outsiders about the office.

Young related to Colleen that her salary had been rigged to the Rules Committee although he never put her on the Committee payroll, "I was just checkin' up on the Rules Committee to see what they're payin' . . . wha, what those salaries are an' they're all on the high side."

"How much are they?"

"Well, the, uh, the assistants, of which you were one, but I never did put you on the payroll because you had not only the Rules, but also the Joint Committee on Atomic Energy. But, uh, the salaries range from 18,600 to 24,600, and, uh, I'm getting a list of all of them which I will have, uh, I guess before the day's over, but they told me that they were all on the high side."

"Well, how much, like (name deleted). Was she making . . ."

"Oh, she'd make more than that. I'll have to find out what she's makin', but she . . . she's not under tha . . . in that category. She's probably makin', uh, 25-30 thousand. But she's not one of the . . ."

"She's like a director."

"Yeah. She's, she's, uh, she's a staff person. These others are just on the individual members' staffs."

"Do you know that guy that had that girl there, that cute girl that you thought was attractive? Was she making what I was making?"

"Uh, I don't know. I'll try to find out. She's still there an', of course, they just come an' sit like zombies

103

in the room. I wouldn't anymore have anybody . . . have that goin' on than anything." Young commented.

"I know. Wasn't that interesting how she just sat there. Maybe he didn't want her to . . ."

"All of them do," Young said. "They just come an' sit an' occasionally they'll come over an' hand the boss a note, or the boss'll give them an errand or, uh . . . it, it's . . . it's absurd; besides they're takin' up valuable space."

There seemed to be no basis for undue concern on Young's part although an incident in his office on Saturday, February 14, 1976, grew in importance. That Saturday was the first day of a three-day, long weekend commemorating Washington's Birthday. Young went into the office even though it was a holiday weekend and found one of his women employees there also. According to the woman's account, Young forced himself on her while they were alone in the office. She repeated her account of the incident to Colleen and others on the staff; therefore, Young suspected that if reporters were to question her, the same allegation would be made.

In the June 2nd conversation with Colleen, Young discussed the matter:

"I really can't hold it in my . . . in my heart to hold any meanness toward, uh, (name deleted), 'cause I honestly don't believe that girl's in her right mind," Young said.

"Yeah."

"That's the thing that worries me about what, what she would say or do to a close and devious, uh, in, uh, interrogation such as that guy put on you yesterday, I'm afraid that she just wouldn't have the mental capacity to stand up to it."

"Right . . . yeah. That's what I'm a little concerned about too," Colleen said.

"An' if she's foolish enough to fall for that then of course . . ."

"Of course," Colleen interrupted, "You know, the thing about it is, like, nothing may come of it, you know . . . but the fact, if in the event they happen to subpoena her, I'm sure she's going to, uh, I mean she's not going to lie . . . about what happened."

"Well," Young answered, "If it gets down to subpoenas and grand juries, we all have to, we'll have to get our heads together and regroup."

"Yeah. Because, uh, I just couldn't believe it anyway when, you know, that you would . . . I don't know . . . that you'd have . . . you know . . . anything to do with (name deleted), knowing what a nut she was."

"Yeah, well, (she) wouldn't have even been there if it hadn't been for your good, charitable feelin' to save her. That part of it was unfortunate, but at the same time, I appreciate your kindness in that respect, because her butt was gone." Young said. He had been on the verge of firing the woman at one point, when Colleen interceded on her behalf.

Colleen continued, "Well, it's a good thing you know, that nobody knew you were in town."

"That's true," Young said. "That's a good point too, because, uh, there's nothin' . . . in, in an accusation of this type, alibi is somethin' nobody can argue with. Particularly since I was off with my wife."

"Yeah."

"If indeed, in fact, that's what she's . . . that's the time she's talkin' about. I don't really know. She's such a gawddamned screwball. But I guess so."

Later in the same conversation, Colleen said, "I just wish that you hadn't had anything to do with (her)."

Young replied, "Well, the thing about it is, I wish I'd never seen her . . . uh, an' I don't care what she conjures up, because she's not going to tell the truth about anything anyway and uh . . ."

"Because, like you said, she said, 'Well, I don't need a rubber, 'cause I have birth control pills,' you know. Sounds . . . for somebody's being raped that's certainly . . ."

"Well, she's eager . . . nothin' but eagerness all the way 'round, you know. But I don't know what, uh, I'm not, uh . . . course I don't admit a damn thing about that." Young said.

"Well, I don't blame you. I wouldn't either." Colleen agreed.

"That's all her imagination an' . . . an' if there ever was an aggressor, she was it, an' . . . an' I just wouldn't have anythin' to do with her anyway."

"Right. Well, and plus there's, you know, she's got no proof of anything. You were the only two people there . . . who knows what went on. You know what I mean? And you might not have even been there."

"Well, as far as I'm concerned," Young answered, "I wasn't. And she wasn't supposed to be there. It was a holiday weekend an' she just got her damn dates mixed up if she picks that date . . . but she wasn't even in the office, the office was closed."

"Well, did you tell her not to come into the office?"

"No, I didn't tell her anything, one way or the other. I didn't know she had the duty or anything about it. I didn't expect anybody to be there. Because we never, uh, you know, when we have . . . the Saturday preceding a long weekend, uh, it's been our inviolable, uh policy to close up, you know."

"Yeah. Well I know you were surprised to find her there. I couldn't understand what she was doing there so late." Colleen said.

"Yeah, well, I'm beginning to think now she must have been goin' through my things an, and if I'd come in a half hour earlier, I might have caught her in the act, you know." Young speculated.

He dismissed the possibility of the woman's story having any major effect, saying, "I have an idea that if they run (her) down, she'll come up with that hard-core, gawddamned preposterous rape story an', and that won't involve anybody but me an' I'm just gonna add that to that business of having three mist . . . three un-named mistresses on my payroll. I'll say it's just about as gawddamned factual as that an, uh, say, again I say, whatever I've got to say, I'll say to the grand jury on it."

Nevertheless, the thought of grand jury testimony brings this remark from Young, "Now if this thing does get to where it's gonna have to be a grand jury matter, then I think we better, we all better, you an' I better compare notes on it. Because there's one place that you do not want to have a divergence of stories, you know."

"But, I mean. I don't understand. How would we divert (sic)?" Colleen asked.

"Well, I mean as, uh . . . whatever is said has to be absolutely the truth, you know." Young replied.

"It does?" Colleen asked.

"Well, it does," Young answered, "Or you'll get in trouble if they prove otherwise. You understand?"

"Oh . . . then I'd have to admit that . . ." Colleen asked.

"Well . . . uh," Young broke in, "We, we'll talk about that. Huh."

"God." Colleen muttered.

"Well, we'll talk about that."

"And then, but, uh, that wouldn't be public. . ." Colleen asked.

"No." Young said, "No, it's secret."

Finally, the alibi comes up again after Young asserts that "nothin' really happened. It's just her gawd-damned imagination." He said, "She's gonna have to be damned careful about the, bout, bout her specifics because there's one absolute defense against this an' that's alibi . . . particularly when you're out of town an' with your wife."

"Right. Wha . . . you talked to Jane (the Congressman's wife) about that then, huh?" Colleen asked.

"No," Young responded, "But will."

"But the thing about it is if they check it out, the

plane. Won't they have your name on the plane or what?" Colleen asked.

"Right, but I, I didn't go to the office. I stayed at home until . . ."

"Oh, I see. Yeah. Right."

"And, uh, the plane got in about noon. I didn't go to the damn office . . . I wasn't in any hurry to get there. Didn't get to the office till about 2:15." Young said.

"Right."

"An' was surprised as hell to find anybody there."

"Uh-huh . . . so . . . well, Jane . . . I mean, didn't you have to explain to Jane . . . something like that? You know what I mean?" Colleen asked.

"Didn't I have to?" Young asked, "Or wouldn't I have to?"

"I mean, wouldn't you?"

"Oh yeah. If it gets down to that, of course I will. Just, just, but it'd just be . . ."

"Whoa-a . . ." Colleen interjected.

"No, no. It'd just be a one on one basis. Uh, if that happened that's all it'd be is just . . . I'd just tell her the damn facts about that particular incident."

"Yeah . . . well I . . . ooh, that's not very good for you . . . that's going to really hurt Jane."

"Yeah. Yeah." Young agrees.

"I don't think you ought to tell her. Really." Colleen suggested.

"Well, I'm not going to unless I, unless the little bitch gets me to the point where I have to. But, of course, that's absolutely preposterous, you know that? Her version of that thing." Young said.

"I know it is," Colleen agreed, "but still, you know, I mean, the fact that you'd have to tell your wife . . . that's awful."

"Well, I don't know that I will. I'll cross that bridge when I come to it. I'm not goin' to worry about it right now . . . cross that bridge when I come to it. But I don't want a lot of adverse publicity about the thing . . . I'm, I'm about half, as you well know, I'm about half fed up with my service here anyway, and, uh, wouldn't take anything . . . I don't want to quit under fire or anything like that, but I . . . I might not be long for around here."

Young obviously trusted Colleen and confided in her. His estimation of her loyalty was raised by her handling of Bob Woodward and he contrasted her ability to deal with a difficult press interview with his doubts that the other woman employee could fare as well. He had been unable to contact the other woman and, because he felt certain there was no leak from within the office and trusted Colleen, the other woman was the logical source.

Colleen had talked with (name deleted) on June 2nd, and learned that John Crewdson of the *New York Times* had called her the day before. While Bob Woodward of the *Washington Post* was hitting Colleen with allegations about incidents in Young's office, Crewdson was terrifying (name deleted) with the same line of questioning. Two competing newspapers had virtually the same information. The question was: who was or who were leaking the stories?

Colleen's principle concern was the allegation about

the theft of the gun and notebook since it had, in fact, happened just as Bob Woodward had said. Colleen was afraid that it could mean criminal charges against her for theft and she challenged (name deleted) demanding to know if she had told the reporter. (Name deleted) denied talking to anyone about the incident, although she had told someone about the theft in a phone call the very night it happened. Young had the matter reported to him shortly thereafter and it became common knowledge within the office.

The other woman, on the other hand, was confronted with the question, "What did Young do to you on St. Valentine's Day?" Crewdson handled the question as delicately as possible, but he stated that he understood she had submitted to Young's advances and asked if she would confirm it. She denied it, but more allegations followed, with only the request for her to confirm them if she could. The amount of information Crewdson had, indicated to her that someone close to the office, with detailed information about her and Colleen was talking to the press.

(Name deleted) first suspected Bill Gardner, Colleen's ex-husband, primarily because he knew and had been in touch with Elizabeth Ray. The woman knew Colleen had confided in her ex-husband and that he did have knowledge of a number of incidents which occurred in the office. Young also had mentioned Bill Gardner as a possible source of the allegations. The woman considered Colleen suspect because the phone number Crewdson had obtained from his source was known only to a few people, one of whom was Colleen.

(Name deleted) was everyone else's prime suspect as the leak. So far, however, everyone was denying everything.

Young realized the necessity of presenting a united front against the reporters' questions and called Colleen frequently to keep her apprised of the developing investigation. On June 4th, Colleen was still focusing attention on the June 1st Woodward interview and Young continually reassured her that there was no story in the material Woodward had gathered. A rift had developed between Colleen and another Young employee when Colleen learned that office gossip had gotten to Woodward, possibly through the other employee. Young cautioned Colleen, "I hope you didn't get ahold of (her), because, really, course, you're the best judge of this, but, uh, I would think this would be an awful time for you to have a fallin' out with (her) . . . because, if I get the story right, she's been strictly on your side an' on the side of the office."

"Yeah."

"Granted, that, that, that all that, that it's unfortunate that gawddamned loose talk got over there to this (name deleted) through (name deleted), whatever her name is, but, uh, there's nothin' you can do about that; that's done an' I'm sure, I feel quite sure it wasn't done maliciously . . . I think it was just done gossiply (sic), gossipy, you know."

"Yeah," Colleen said, "because the story he had was that, you know, that you had been pressuring me for sex and that I had been having sex with you and that in the last few months you and I had been fighting over it and that, uh, I had decided to quit because of that, and because of something that had happened to (name deleted) . . . so . . . you know, I mean, what I'm saying is that we did start fighting about that sort of thing . . ."

"Well,' Young responded, "Of course, you, you an' all that damned ol' unfortunate thing about the books and the gun an' all that crap . . . but anyway . . ."

"See . . . and that's the thing that gets me is, that the girls noticed that you and I were fighting a lot, you know . . ." Colleen said.

"They never got it from me."

"Well, they saw my face when I came out . . ."

"Could be. It could be," Young admitted.

"I looked pretty drained," Colleen finished.

"Yeah. It could be, but of course, that still is their ima . . . that still is their presumption an' conclusion, but, uh, but you can't make any gawddamned story out of that."

"Oh, I know," Colleen agreed, "but what I'm saying is that he seemed pretty accurate, you know, about the fact that you and I had been fighting and, uh . . ."

"Well, I have no doubt that he's picked up somewhere something about the office that has some thread of, of, uh, reality to it, but, uh, of plausibility . . . but, but, uh, he's not goin' to be able to do anything with that unless he can get some confirmation or something that has something to do with, uh, that's a hell of a lot more concrete."

The conversation turned to the key issue, salaries. Colleen said, "Then I know that he said that all the salaries in the office . . . but mine was the highest of the women, you know, like the third highest, or something, and that you had increased everyone's salary in the last six months of 1975, a considerable amount, and he named it; you know, each person and how much their salary had jumped . . . and I was really surprised."

"Well," Young retorted, "He's, course, he's got that off the pay records, is what he's got off of . . . an', uh . . ."

"Cause like he mentioned that (name deleted) had gone from 14 thousand to 21 thousand . . ." Colleen began.

"Yeah."

". . . something like that; in a short period of time and that (name deleted) had gone from 16 to 21 and that (name deleted) had from 12 to 16, or something like that . . ."

"17," Young corrected.

"And that I had gone from 18 to 24."

"So theirs went up a hell of a lot more than yours did!" Young blurted inaccurately.

"That's right," Colleen agreed.

"Their's went up a hell of a lot more than yours did and, uh, and, uh, uh, tha, uh, yours is thoroughly justified," Young said. "If he wants to go over my salary records with me, I'd be glad to get Harry out here an' get the records out an' go over every gawddamned bit of it. If anything, you were underpaid!"

"And then he said," Colleen continued, "you know, what . . . he said I was the only one, that Legislative

Research Clerk, or something like that, and that the others, that, that (name deleted) was secretary, caseworker and . . ." her voice drifted off.

"Well, Harry, Harry, uh, uh, always puts that job description on there, and . . ."

"Yeah, well how come Harry, Harry made mine so different from everybody else's?" Colleen asked.

"Well . . ." Young hesitated, "Uh, what do yuh mean, different from everybody else's? You were doin' different work than anybody else was."

"No, I know it, but, you know, like you were going to transfer me off your staff . . ."

"No," Young denies.

". . . and into, was he trying to get rid of me?"

"Oh no. No, no, no. What he was doing, he was, he was rigging your salary to the, to the committee, uh, uh, staff level, so in case we ever decided to do that . . . that in case we needed the, more room for more salary, then we could transfer your salary to the Rules Committee. That was that in a damn nutshell."

"Um, yeah."

Young went on, "And he's got these, uh, he's got, uh, employee position and title, . . . Harry, uh, Harry does that very carefully," Young explained, "and, uh, an' he does it for a purpose."

Meanwhile, John Crewdson of the *New York Times* had called (name deleted) during the evening of June 2nd, and informed her that one of their reporters was on the West Coast at that moment, talking with two former Young employees who had been with the Congressman for over five years apiece before leaving their positions. The *Times* was pursuing all possible leads to obtain corroboration or denials of the allegations and (name deleted) found herself confronted with detailed material given Crewdson by an unknown source or sources.

So the *Times* reporters did have a source or sources who were providing a great deal of information not only about (name deleted), but about many facets of Young's office routine. Nick Horrock had traveled to Los Angeles to contact a former employee. He had her address and left a note in her mailbox asking her to call him when she returned from work. She did return his call, but declined to comment on any of the allegations.

There was an unwillingness to discuss matters relating to the newspaper probe by former members of Young's staff which was frustrating to the reporters. Corroboration by several members of the current staff or former staff members would be required to force Justice Department to act through legal channels. Even with that, there would have to be sufficient evidence to convince a U.S. Attorney that he had a good chance for a conviction. Young was correct in his assumption that there was little in which a grand jury would be interested. Particularly if the reporters ran into a stonewall with his staff.

There were a variety of reasons for members of Young's current staff to deny allegations, refuse to comment or, as Young had advised Colleen, realize that there was no legal requirement to be truthful with the press, and mislead them.

CONGRESSIONAL ABUSE OF POWER

In a June 6, 1976, conversation-for-record with Colleen which Young, himself, was tape recording, he commented at length on Bob Woodward's assumption that Colleen's salary was out of line, based on her academic background. Afterward, he commented on the salaries of the other staff members:

"Well, of course, Colleen, you understand, the reason I'm asking you to put this on record is 'cause they're (the allegations that Young was one of Liz Ray's 13 congressmen) totally untrue and I do want to be able to demonstrate both this man's attitude toward the employment of women and how they go about badgering a person to try to get statements out of them . . . and, uh, with regard to, nobody knows better than you with regard to you, to your sca, salary scale, as well as the other girls in this office, that everybody in this office earns their living and more."

Young continued, "May I ask you this question? Do you consider that you earned your salary when you were here in the office, by working, by the work you did for the office?"

"Yes." Colleen answered. "I believe I did."

"Well, I certainly do too. If anything, I think you were underpaid, uh, and I say that because I read just in this morning's Post, that article where the lady, uh, woman columnist said there were, uh, of all the twenty thousand dollar jobs on the Hill, only 27% of them were held by women, uh, and . . ."

"Well," Colleen said, "we were very fortunate in the office to be getting paid as well as we were."

"Well, I think so," Young replied, "Because, you see, I have six jobs here in this office that, that, that are paid more than twenty thousand dollars a year, and of those six jobs, four of them are held by women."

"Yeah."

"And for somebody to take the attitude that, that women can't hold a job more than twenty thousand dollars or twenty-five thousand dollars a year without sleeping with somebody in the office is a terrible injustice to women," Young declared, "an', an' an' it, uh, it, it, it's such, it's the sorta situation, I'm giving you my viewpoint, that will, will discourage anybody from paying women, particularly nice lookin' women. Uh, if they're shapely and so forth and good-lookin', uh, then immediately somebody like this reporter, Warren Woodward, uh, Bob Woodward, uh, assumes that she must be sleeping with somebody to draw that money; so, so, what . . . just a minute, please (Young excused himself, then continued:)

"I wonder what (name deleted) has to say about all this?" Colleen asked.

"I didn't discuss it with her," Young said, "because, uh, uh, she has, as well as the rest of the staff, they just, they, it, they just don't like to talk about it, Colleen. And, uh, and they think it's a very unfortunate thing and, of course, uh, as you well know, I haven't, I've been thinking for some time and, uh, uh, not stayin' on here in Congress cause I been here twenty years and, uh and I'm faced now with goin' into some more intricate work with the Joint Committee on Atomic Energy and so forth and so on an' so I don't know whether really I want to take it on an', an' I think it's gonna be a terrible injustice to them, like (name deleted) buyin' a house an' (name deleted) is buyin' an apartment, uh, a condominium, I think, an' things like that an', an', an' I doubt if they'll ever be able to get, get, uh, get employed again an' certainly not at the salaries that I paid 'em. It's gonna be hard on them."

Certainly the opinion that his female staff members could find no other work if he left office was overstated; however, it is reasonable to assume that they would not find work at comparable salaries. Young boasted in several conversations that he hoped that he "paid the highest salaries on the Hill," and, within the discretionary powers granted him, as a Congressman, he did his utmost to reach that goal. In a very cordial conversation with Colleen on June 5th, Young commented on the women, the probe and their salaries:

"Well, sweetie, I don't know what you're gonna do about your plans, but I . . ."

"My plants?" Colleen asked.

"Your plans. You know, like you're sayin' like you might travel or somethin'."

"Um-hum."

"I'm gonna fight this son of a bitch, an', an', an' I'm gonna come out of here swinging. Now, gawddamn that son of a bitch may beat me cause they buy ink by the barrel, you know." Young declared.

"Whose this guy you're talking about?" Colleen asked.

"I'm talking about the newspaper reporters."

"Oh. Uh-huh, yeah."

"They buy, they, they've got that ink by the barrel and I don't, but gawddamn, I'm gonna get my say somewhere an' there'll be some newspapers will print my say-so, too. The papers at home will," Young said.

"Right," Colleen agreed. "Well, that's what's important, is the papers at home."

"Well, it's not too important to me because I'm not that crazy about stayin' here." Young replied. "The most important thing to me is that I get these women to understand that if they don't get up and fight, gawddamn it, there's nobody gonna be able to help 'em. If the son-of-a-bitch is willin' to give sixty per cent, sixty-six and two-thirds of his twenty thousand dollar year jobs to women and a gawddamned piss-ant reporter, a scavenger, comes in and accuses, accuses anybody who's giving six, uh, twenty thousand dollars a year to any woman that doesn't have a Ph.D., of havin' to sleep with somebody to get it, then gawddamn, their case is hopeless."

Colleen offered an alternative. She said, "Okay, well, I was thinking about some things that you could do. You know, for the women on the Hill and everywhere. You could put in some, like, regulations, you know. As far as written . . . you know what I mean, 'cause right now there really isn't any. You know, they could be working and they have no protection. What you should do is have the Congress have like little, like they have with the Civil Service."

"You can't do it, honey," Young declared. "There's, it's inherent in, in an office, a Congressional office and that's why I'm so anxious to pay more than anybody downtown or anything like that.'

"Well why can't you do that?" Colleen questioned. "You don't think the Congressmen would agree to set up like the Civil Service?"

"No, no, honey. There's no way that you can run an office, a Congressional office, and not have the staff directly beholden to the mentor. There's no way you can do it. This is a bad way to run a railroad, I understand that, but there's no other way; how, visualize for a minute, how would we be doin', runnin' this office here, if, if half of those people out there didn't, didn't have to, uh, didn't have to depend on me? If they were Civil Service, you know?"

"Yeah, but what I'm saying is, like you would still be able to, you know, review their work and this and that; but what I'm saying is, for example, after a certain period of time, they'd have automatic pay increases according to their work and they would have, you know after a certain number of years, they would have certain number of increases and vacation days and sick leave, and if they got real sick and were sick for two or three months, that they would still, you know, have compensation and still be paid. You know, like they do in a lot of other places."

Young, who had been interjecting periodical, "Yeah's," during Colleen's proposal answered, "Well, of course, you're right. There ought to be something like that, but at the same time, I like to think of myself as being a fair type of equal employment, you know, equal opportunity employer. So, that, that, I hope that

I have the highest salaries on the Hill, and just right when this guy starts makin' something' of it, about these salary increases, I'm gonna announce another raise."

"Um-hum"

"I'm gonna announce another raise, right in the middle of the son-of-a-bitch." Young declared.

"Well that's probably good, but that might also look kinda strange," Colleen added.

"I don't care whether it looks strange or not, honey," Young said. "Really. I mean, I'm mad."

"Yeah."

"I wanna fight!" Young cracked. "You wanna fight?"

Colleen laughed and replied, "Oh goodness, I guess I'll have to take lots of vitamins and, and get lots of rest if I'm going to have to fight."

"Yeah" Young chuckled.

"So, uh . . ."

"I hope you do, darlin' ", Young continued, "And understand one thing, that you sure got a gawddamned friend; I'll tell you that. I think you know it though."

"Oh, I know I have a friend."

"And you thought, you were quakin' in your boots, thinkin' how I was getting mad when you told me about that grand jury. Why hell; if you'd a told me, it might'a been a little helpful here, but hell, I don't blame yuh. Shit, I wouldn't do it either. I just think it's terrible that some son-of-a-bitch got you dragged in there though," Young said referring to the 1973 subpoena Colleen received requiring her to be interviewed by a

U.S. Attorney. "I, I just can't believe that anybo . . . must . . ."

"Well, it was supposed to be coming from your office and they wouldn't tell me who," Colleen said, referring to the complaint which preceded the subpoena.

"Well," Young said, "Isn't it odd that they never said a word to me about it?"

"Who never did?"

"The grand jury, anybody else."

"Well, evidently, they had no way of proving anything." Colleen said.

"But, it looks to me like they would've brought me in and asked me about it . . . or somethin'," Young said.

"Well, maybe they didn't feel that they had any reason to, cause they couldn't substantiate anything."

"Did you actually get a subpoena?" Young asked.

"I certainly did; a U.S. Marshall or whatever. I got an actual subpoena."

"But you weren't working at the time."

"Nope. I sure wasn't," Colleen verified.

"Uh-huh."

"I sure wasn't."

"That's interesting, you know it?" Young mused.

"Christ, if I'd been working there, it'd been even worse."

"Yeah, but at least I'd have known about it." Young said.

"Yeah."

"But that's so interesting to me an' how you were able to keep that all to yourself all this time."

"Uh-huh."

"You're pretty close-mouthed, you know it?"

"Well, I guess about certain things I am. You know," Colleen agreed. "But then I always felt that you cared about me, an' I was confused quite a lot, you know, and I didn't want to hurt you . . . so . . ."

"Didn't want to get run off," Young joked.

"You wouldn't have run me off, would you?"

"Course not. Hell no," Young laughed. "No more than now."

"Right."

"You always did your job!" Young said, "an' you did a gawddamn good job an' I can remember one time when you cried on the phone an' said, all I did was come to work there wantin' to be a good employee, an' then, by God, you were; an' you earned every gawddamned nickel you ever got paid and a hell of a lot more."

"Yeah."

"And I can say that everybody in this office," Young declared, "in my judgment, is underpaid, including me!"

"Yeah," Colleen agreed, "You sure are. You sure are."

"Well, I hope that sometime you'll get relaxed enough to where we can visit, or somethin'."

"Yeah."

"But I understand the problem."

"Yeah," Colleen said, "Well, you know, it, I just

think it's kind of, right now I don't want to be in contact with anybody 'cause I don't know just how far this has gone."

"Right. Right. And my evaluation would be that there's a pretty good chance that there'll some more of it too."

"Really?" Colleen asked.

"It might just be written up in the way, like, 'bout a lot of offices . . . all thrown together, you know, with a high, uh, the high salaries and the rumors and all that go with it." Young explained.

"Well, Christ. If you're going to give everybody another raise, they're going to be ecstatic." Colleen said laughing. "They've really benefitted all the time haven't they?"

"Well, I planned to give them a raise the time that (name deleted) quit, but when she got so gawddamned crazy, then I just canceled the whole goddamned thing."

"Yeah."

"I was goin' to give them all an 1800 dollar a year raise, so I'll just do it now." Young said.

"Uh-huh."

"I think all, except the brand new ones here. Now I told you there's a girl comin' Monday."

"Uh-huh."

"I won't give her a raise, you know," Young said.

"Well, she's already going to be getting a pretty damn big raise from what she was making before," Colleen said.

"From ten-five to sixteen thousand," Young finished. "That's right."

"The other girl, that Latin, went from ten, ten-five to fifteen-five."

In another tape, Young remarked that another woman employee had been making $8,000 a year before coming to work for him, asked for $9,000 to start, he gave her $10,500 to start, and she currently was making over twice that amount. Raises, tied to standard Federal increases, cost of living and other factors, also were given to cover the cost of a second mortgage, to offset the expense of a vacation or whatever reason might occur to the Congressman. There was no question that John Young's salaries would be hard to match anywhere else.

The other alternative for the staff denying the allegations would be that they were, in fact, untrue. In this situation, the Congressman is at a distinct disadvantage as it is much easier to disbelieve a politician and his staff than to accept what they say as the whole truth. Denials of wrongdoing roll from the mouths of politicians even after a verdict has been rendered and the past performances of some of John Young's contemporaries did nothing to raise the odds on Congressional veracity.

While the reporters dug into pay records, questioned members of the House Rules Committee staff and Joint Committee on Atomic Energy, John Young continued to talk with and confide in Colleen Gardner. It is evident that there was a particular relationship between the two of them, one that went beyond the limits of professional association. Young repeatedly asked Colleen in their conversations, if she could meet him. She declined because of the ongoing investigation. Young continued to discuss with her, the source of the reporters information and to shore up what he felt were weak points in his position. Nothing of major importance happened until the afternoon of June 8th.

Nick Horrock and John Crewdson had done their work carefully, even in the face of potential cover-ups and reluctant staff members, and felt that they had sufficient material with which to confront John Young. They called beforehand and made an appointment. Young was waiting, unaware of the information that had been gathered.

The allegations came out, one after another. John Young denied everything. He was positive he knew who was the leak. He knew the reporters needed corroboration to make the story stick and knew his justification of salaries would stand the test of a grand jury investigation. He knew his staff would back him and Colleen was a proven veteran under fire; she had turned back Bob Woodward.

Then on June 10th, the day before the story made headlines in the *New York Times*, John Young placed his last call to Colleen. (Name deleted) was obviously working with the *Times*; that Young had expected, but there was a new, very disturbing question on his mind.

The call came at 6:30 in the morning. Colleen wasn't out of bed yet.

"Hello," Colleen muttered.

"Hi! How're you this morning?" Young said brightly.

"Uh," Colleen managed.

"Listen, honey," Young began, "Hello."

"Yeah"

"Uh, uh, I do deeply apologize, but I wanted to talk to you before everything got started . . . Can you hear me all right?"

"I'm half asleep."

"Well, kinda wait a little bit," Young offered. "How was your party?"

"Oh, it was okay."

"Just went on and on, didn't it," Young said, then went to the main point, "Listen, honey, I, I do want to ask you something' an' I want you to be candid with me and just completely honest with me."

"Yeah."

"I've gotta know what to do," Young said. "Have you been puttin' this information to any of those reporters or anything?"

"No," Colleen answered, "But (name deleted) called me. She told me that, uh, I think the *New York Times* had contacted her."

"Hold a minute. Just hold the phone a minute." Young left the line, then came back, "Yeah . . ."

"So . . ." Colleen began.

The Congressman asked her where the press could have gotten certain information.

"Well, I don't know where they'd find out about that," Colleen said. "But I never said anything about that to anyone."

"Well, I'm so glad you're telling' me because, you see, the thing about it is, I can, I can, uh, I can stand up to 'em as long as I know you haven't talked to 'em. You know?"

"Yeah."

"Because the only gawddamned way in the damned world that they would ever be able to do anything like that would be, is if, would be if you threw in with 'em, then, of course, my goose is cooked," Young declared.

"What now?"

"I say, if you threw in with 'em and then, corroborated whatever, wherever they're getting this stuff, then, then it wouldn't be any point in my holding out any longer. You know?"

"Yeah."

"So you would tell me, wouldn't you, honey, if you had talked to any of them?" Young asked.

Young felt his case would be hopeless if the reporters were getting the information from Colleen and was relieved at her denial. His relief was short-lived. When the story broke the next day, he learned that Colleen Gardner had been in contact with the *New York Times* reporting team since late May and had made available to them tape-recorded telephone conversations she had made of Congressman Young, and others involved in the investigation. Colleen Gardner, his "favorite," had blown the whistle.

Colleen Gardner

Robin Moore became interested in Colleen Gardner's case in June 1976, after the story had appeared in the *New York Times* and other papers around the country. He contacted her and inquired about the potential for her story being made into a book. Initially, it was to be an entire work based on her material and experiences. His representative in Washington, Clancy Isaac, continued talking with Colleen after Robin had made contact and eventually, in August of the same year, Colleen agreed to allow access to her tapes in order that an evaluation might be made of them to determine whether or not a story actually existed.

After lengthy and involved negotiations, Colleen was satisfied with a letter of agreement which she drafted and contained only minimal changes by Robin. For $3,000, Colleen agreed to allow an individual or individuals designated by Robin to listen to and evaluate the tapes.

In September 1976, Nick Rowe and his wife, Jane Carolline, met Clancy as old friends of Robin's and on purely a social basis. Nick had just completed his second book for Little, Brown, a novel entitled, *The Judas Squad*, and was preparing a research program for his next book. Robin, Clancy and Nick discussed the stalled *Washington Connection* and, when the discussions ended, the Rowes were assigned to the Colleen Gardner story as well as a multitude of other leads which had been developed concerning abuse of power in the Capitol.

The first step was to meet with Colleen to determine whether or not the three of them would be compatible. They met that same month and began the long process of developing a factual account of Colleen's experience.

I had only vague recollections of a blonde, sobbing sometimes incoherently into outstretched microphones, streaked mascara and reporters' questions pounding incessantly from behind each microphone. With only that impression, meeting Colleen Gardner was a surprise.

She was seated comfortably on the pastel striped couch in Clancy Isaac's stylish, walk-up Georgetown apartment, sipping a bourbon and ginger. Jane and I were late, as usual, and there was already relaxed conversation in the room. My initial reaction was probably identical to John Young's when he first saw her across the floor from him at the Top of the Town Restaurant, back in 1970. She was a fully-clothed Playboy centerfold; the kind of figure Raquel Welch paid thousands of dollars for and even then missed some of the curves. Her close-fitting jersey dress didn't down-play any of those attributes.

After that, bonuses weren't really necessary, but she had them. She was more attractive than any of the photos I remembered. Her platinum blonde hair was cut shorter than the below-shoulder length she'd worn on the Hill; a definite improvement. She had hazel eyes that locked on and didn't shift until she had seen what interested her; a gaze that was curious, yet understandably guarded. There was the wide, full mouth, curving easily in a smile as we were introduced. It was all very relaxed, very natural. The only flaw was a brittle hardness about her features, like a too-heavy coat of make-up, obscuring the real face beneath. During the evening, I couldn't decide if I was really talking *with* Colleen or just getting a recorded message.

We sat around the coffee table chatting for an hour or so before going across the street to the Georgetown Inn for supper. Conversation was flowing and new impressions were formed. Her voice was soft and well modulated with a trace of a Virginia drawl; very easy to listen to. She had a natural, quick laugh and didn't suppress it when something struck her as funny.

She was articulate, obviously intelligent, apparently open in her answers to gentle questioning, but, as we talked, a curious mixture of toughness, or worldliness, became apparent, and yet there was an underlying naiveté. There appeared to be a little girl who wanted to trust, inside a woman who had learned that trust brought pain and disappointment.

She is an easy person to like, and Jane and I found that a basic rapport had been established. Jane and Colleen agreed that they would work together as Jane listened to the tapes, a monumental task. There were over sixty hours of recorded conversations to be evaluated before we would know whether or not there would be a book.

CONGRESSIONAL ABUSE OF POWER

We began work that week and while Jane and Colleen set up a schedule that would accomodate Colleen's study and class schedule at American University, I proceeded to follow up other leads that had been gathered prior to my coming on the book.

For the month of October and part of November, I met with alleged sources who will remain anonymous, not merely because of the First Amendment, but because they uniformly established the fact that "checkbook information" is overpriced. The word had gotten out in Washington via the *Washington Star*'s "Ear" column and disco-grapevine that Robin was in town, looking for material on the sexual proclivities of the powerful. Aside from one or two individuals who led me to cases of potential abuse of power, most cost me the price of a meal, related gossipy tales of musical bedrooms, dropped names of prominent individuals and waited to learn if their material had been accepted. They are still waiting.

We all learned early in our "mistake-making" phase that to chronicle the sexual escapades inside the beltway alone, would require several volumes, and would serve little purpose except to sensationalize a common, very natural, if not strictly moral occurance. The issue was one of greater importance: the abuse of power by elected officials in which human dignity, the taxpayer, or the interests of this country suffered.

While I was trekking about Washington, Jane was discovering that Colleen's moods had more daily ups and downs than the elevator at the Hyatt Regency House. In order to brief me on the tapes she had heard, Jane was taking notes; later to be read to me. Unknowingly, Jane was creating minor chaos with Colleen. The agreement she had drafted specified that the tapes could be listened to, but not transcribed. It was becoming an impossible situation since there were only a few hours during three or four weekdays when Colleen's schedule permitted Jane to sit with her and the tapes. At the rate they were going, it would be mid-1977 before we knew whether or not there was enough to go on, and unless I sat and listened with them. I got only what Jane could remember. It was difficult for us to understand, but as we learned more about Colleen, her hesitancy to fully trust anyone seemed more justifiable.

Colleen was born in Venezuela: her mother, a Venezuelan national, her father in the U.S. Army, assigned to the embassy. Her parents divorced when Colleen was still young and the break had a profound effect on her. She fended for herself during the difficult years of adolescence and was only fifteen when she married for the first time. She had a child at sixteen, in 1964, and separated from her husband in mid-1968, with a divorce following soon thereafter. At twenty, she was alone with her child and no substantial background to qualify her to support either of them.

In 1969, she met Bill Gardner while she was working in the Washington area and they were married in July 1970. Prior to that she had met Elizabeth, then Betty, Ray and the two of them had dated some of the same men in Washington. Colleen introduced Betty Ray to Bill Gardner—who promptly sold her an insurance policy. Betty Ray called him regularly during the time he and Colleen were married and she still keeps in touch with him.

Colleen has several mental pictures of Betty Ray. She always refers to her as Betty. The first is Betty Ray, vintage 1967, prior to having her nose bobbed and cosmetic surgery to tidy up the image. The second is Betty Ray during their period of friendship which included a party on a then Congressman's houseboat, when the Congressman had arranged for Betty Ray to entertain a Senator one evening and asked her to get another girl for him. Betty had called Colleen and the four of them met at the marina. Once aboard, the party quickly progressed and, according to Betty Ray, she took the Senator up to the flybridge, at the Congressman's insistence, and made love to him. This liaison was ostensibly to secure the Senator's support, on the Senate side, for a pet project of the Congressman's.

The Bill in question passed both Houses without noticeable help from the Senator and has become a still incomplete, multi-million dollar burden to the taxpayer. The Senator has denied any sexual relationship with Betty Ray although Colleen corroborated her account of the incident.

Colleen's final picture of Betty Ray was during and after the explosive Hays' disclosures. That image is one that Colleen fears will be attached to her. Even though there are similarities between the exposés, even with the Young story breaking as a follow-on to Wayne Hays', Colleen hardly fits the Betty Ray mold. She's an enigmatic young woman with intelligence, motivation, goals and achievements well beyond those of Miss Ray.

Colleen Gardner has pursued her education with an intensity marred primarily by interrupted studies, as various crises have arisen or her major has changed. Colleen has logged almost seven years of part-time and full-time college credit hours. She's been in undergrad programs for science, medicine and, finally, accounting. There were thoughts of a law degree in the interim. At this writing, she is within three months of receiving her degree in accounting.

Before her marriage to Bill Gardner in 1970, she worked for him at the Life Insurance Company in Virginia. Prior to that, she had modeled, worked as a dental assistant, been a receptionist for a Washington-based engineering firm, and done a brief stint as a Bunny at the Baltimore Playboy Club. Aside from this erratic employment background, Colleen could, in fact, type and take shorthand.

A new manager replaced Bill Gardner in the insurance office. Colleen remained for a short time, then was fired. She was making $113 a week at that time.

John Young had come on the scene only weeks before Colleen was fired. She went with a friend to the Top of the Town Restaurant, an Arlington dining and drinking spot looking over the Iwo Jima Memorial into Washington. The manager, whom she knew, approached her and mentioned that the Congressman and his friend were interested in having the young women join them for dinner and a drink. They declined, but did sit at an adjacent table, chatting with Young.

During the conversation, Colleen indicated that she

spoke Spanish and Young displayed interest, commenting that his district had a large number of Spanish-speaking voters and there was space for a linguist on his staff. He asked if she was looking for a job. At that time she wasn't, but after being fired, she reconsidered. In late February 1970, she submitted a resume to Harry McAdams and was hired.

Meanwhile, she and Bill had purchased a home in Burke, Virginia, adding mortgage payments to the already heavy monthly payments. The position in Congressman Young's office saved them financially. She went from a final salary of $5,400 per year at the insurance company to an $8,500 starting salary on the Hill.

She entered the Congressional domain bewildered and awed by her surroundings. Suddenly, she was inside the Washington power circle, seeing and coming in contact with Congressmen and Senators whom she had only before seen on TV or in newspapers. Her salary allowed her, for the first time, to begin to catch up with back bills and hope for a bit of financial security. Then there were the parties, the lunches, the perks that went along with being a Hill secretary. It all looked good.

Less than two years later, in December 1972, Colleen left Young's office. She was making $12,500 a year, but found herself unable to continue working for the Congressman. Her reasons for leaving are clouded. There were problems with her school work, problems in the office, and problems with her marriage. She separated from Bill Gardner in 1973, went back with him and, finally, was divorced.

In her application for unemployment after leaving the office, she stated on the standard form that she left the office due to "sexual pressures." A duplicate form which is routinely forwarded to the former employer for comment came back stating that she had been released due to a staff reorganization. When queried by Unemployment Bureau personnel about the discrepancy Colleen asked if she'd draw unemployment benefits either way. Assured that she would, Colleen decided not to push matters. Paramount in her mind was the reality of her dependence on Congressman Young for a favorable recommendation should she find another job. A bad recommendation could knock her chances of getting a desirable position.

Meanwhile, she had met Sol Z. Rosen, aggressive and outspoken attorney, who is well known among his contemporaries and reporters at the District Courthouse. Rosen is a dynamic, well-read man, enthusiastic about the practice of law.

Colleen didn't realize at the time, the part Rosen would later play in her life. She did find an immediate need for his assistance when she received a subpoena from the Office of the U.S. Attorney to attend a hearing and give testimony. Rosen agreed to help her and arranged for a private hearing with Attorney Lester Seidell.

The hearing involved a complaint against Congressman John Young that had come from his office, alleging that he exerted pressure on members of his staff to have sexual relations with him. Named as potential witnesses to corroborate the allegation were Colleen

Gardner and another woman, both of whom had left Young's employ.

Colleen made a statement in which she claimed to have had sex with the Congressman on a number of occasions, but principally on weekends when she drew what was termed, "the Duty." This was an organized requirement in which one staff member would be assigned weekend duty on a rotating basis. Colleen stated in the interview that she had drawn the duty approximately once every five to six weeks and, on the days she was in the office, the Congressman would come in and she would then submit to having sex with him.

When asked if she had proof or substantiation of any kind, Colleen said, "no." It had never occured to her to attempt to document the incidents. There was an important factor here. Colleen mentioned later that it wasn't unusual for a boss to attempt to have sex with her. It had happened before and was almost like an accepted work hazard. In most jobs, the pay wasn't so high that she couldn't just quit, but in the Congressional office, the salary was high and getting higher. It was paying the bills and giving some hope for the future. She admits the decision was one based on financial desperation and the realization that in the Congressional office she had the opportunity to continue her schooling, work in the exciting environment on Capitol Hill and establish some chance for advancement.

When there appeared to be a dry well with the Young allegations, she was asked if she had knowledge of any kick-backs, bribes or similar wrongdoing. Colleen related her account of the houseboat incident in answer to the question.

It was evident that there was going to be no further action because of lack of any substantiation. The probe ended without an investigation being conducted, beyond Colleen's interview. John Young was unaware either that Colleen had listed "sexual pressures" as her reason for leaving his office or that she had appeared before the U.S. Attorney. Later, when Colleen made other job applications, Young gave her a high recommendation.

During this period of time in 1973-1974, Colleen had been living with her grandmother and depending on unemployment benefits to meet her bills. She attended Northern Virginia Community College, taking courses in shorthand, secretarial procedures and administration, and modern college algebra. Finally, the financial bind was crushing in and Colleen went on job interviews. Young's recommendations were consistently favorable and she called to thank him.

Young greeted her warmly and asked her to return to work in the office. In May, 1974, Colleen went back to work for him. The best salary she had been offered during her off-period was $160 per week, $7,680 per year. Young started her at $17,000 per year. She was aware of the situation in the office, but felt she could handle it. She was undergoing therapy, she'd been away for almost a year and a half and she needed the job.

In July 1975, Colleen began tape recording conversations between herself, Congressman Young and others on his staff as she talked with them over the telephone in her apartment. She continued taping past the time she left the office in March 1976. The tapes are significant because they relate incidents and emotions as they occured. The exchanges are frank and revealing although there are instances of Colleen interjecting leading questions in certain of the tapes.

It seemed that there would be a good working relationship with Colleen to examine her side of the story while researching Congressman Young's position. Colleen interrupted the process when she began to have second thoughts about another venture into public view. The memories of the first incident with the *New York Times* was still vivid: they had met with her, she gave her side of the story, they wrote the article, the explosion came and there she was, alone . . . the reporters had moved on to new stories and she was left with canceled credit, notoriety and nothing accomplished.

With this book, she saw a potential repetition and began to draw back from all of us. She had rejected proposed first person stories in the *Washingtonian* Magazine, *National Enquirer* and others during the first episode. There had been offers of $3,000 and up, for her story and she gave it to the *New York Times* for nothing . . . she never even got the dinner the reporters promised to buy her after their story broke.

Colleen was thinking ahead to the time she would have to live with whatever came out in print and felt there wasn't any price worth what she had been through before. In December, 1976, she met in

Clancy's apartment with Clancy, Robin, her lawyer and a potential investor. She pulled out her pocket calculator, did some figuring and had her lawyer inform the gathering that she was out. She wanted nothing more to do with the project and looked forward to quiet anonymity.

The next months were an experience in frustration for Clancy, Jane and me as we attempted to bring Colleen back on board. Robin remained steadfast in his desire to obtain the tapes and develop the story that would grow out of them. We had heard enough to realize the insight that was available into the psychology of a Congressional office.

We had known Colleen long enough to recognize the ambivalence which dominated her decision-making, not only with this project, but apparently in most of her general associations with other people. There were two factors which remained constant throughout the other fluctuations. One was a love for and dedication to her child, an unusually close and mature acceptance of one another by the two of them which translated itself into trust and understanding in the face of a sometimes hostile world outside.

The second factor was Colleen's singleminded determination to obtain a college degree, to finally have the accepted documentation which would qualify her as an accountant, a professional qualification rather than her previous bag of heterogeneous job skills. There wasn't a conversation that any of us had with Colleen that didn't involve some talk of her exams, the studying she was trying to cram in or the grades she'd made.

We began to think of the studying and exams as convenient "outs" for Colleen when she didn't want to talk.

But we were wrong about the studies. She was committed to the completion of the required courses and had, on other occasions in the past, been forced by circumstances to drop courses and otherwise interrupt her curriculum. The scandal that broke around her in June 1976, after the New York *Times* printed its story on her involvement with John Young, was totally disruptive and she was attempting to keep herself in a low-key role, at least until she had the diploma in hand. Perhaps longer.

It reached a point where Colleen felt badgered. Almost the same feeling she'd had in June 1976, when Nick Horrock and Sol Rosen were talking to her about the need to tell her story. Both men were convinced of the truth of Colleen's story and were determined that if enough material could be gathered to substantiate the allegations, it had to be printed. The reporter's interest was in a timely and extremely pertinent follow-on to the Wayne Hays' case. Colleen, however, was suffering from the ambivalence that made her detest what she had experienced and want to see the abuse of power ended, while, at the same time, feeling a twinge of conscience when she realized the strain that would be placed on the Congressman and his family when the story came out. On one hand, she hated the Congressman for "using her," while simultaneously considering the benefits she had received in his office while working there and the relationship that had existed between

143

them. She desperately wanted to believe that John Young had felt more than a physical interest in her. Young had been her "benefactor," her financial "crutch" in times when things were tight. But what the experience had done to her, psychologically, her feeling of having been used like a prostitute, made her want to see the abuse stopped. There were always other people who were advising her about what was best—"When I say no, then there are ten thousand people who come around to tell me to say 'yes.' "

We found ourselves in the same roles. We were trying to advise Colleen based on our personal viewpoints, not realizing, that for her, it was a nightmarish replay of her experiences during the time when the story first appeared. We had only begun to hear the story that her tapes told about the office, the people in it and their interrelationships. We hadn't begun to analyze and compare the hours of conversations, finding bits and chunks of fact in one tape that appeared in a different tape with different people, checking dates and incidents against documents and written records, listening to poignant outpourings of emotion, not in retrospect, but at the time the incidents were occurring.

We knew the material was there and we had begun to know Colleen. It was a matter of trying to understand her feelings and fears, to give her the best picture of what might result from the courses of action open to her and hope that she would agree to let us tell the story.

Finally, in the Spring of 1977, Colleen agreed to let us use the tapes. Jane had been instrumental in maintaining contact with Colleen and keeping the lines of communication open. There had been a couple of false starts when Colleen seemed ready to let us use the tapes and then changed her mind. It had been a roller coaster ride on Colleen's emotions as we did our best to refrain from pushing her, yet tried to make her aware that the tapes were critical in the presentation of the story. There was no other way to objectively chronicle events unless we could go back to the time the incidents occurred and listen to the voices and thoughts of those involved.

Were we to depend solely on the statements of individuals connected with the story, we had to be concerned with the potential for inaccurate, misleading or forgotten information. To cover the alleged activities of Congressman John Young in the same manner as the *New York Times* would only replow ground that had since been packed solid. It had to be the story of an investigation, as it happened, with the reactions of the principles involved and the facts as they emerged. To be fair in dealing with Congressman Young, we had to look at the manner in which he was investigated and how he reacted to that investigation. Finally, we had to follow-up the major allegations to determine where, in fact, the truth lay.

Colleen, still with some reservations, met with Robin and completed the arrangements for total and unrestricted use of the tapes. She did begin to contribute to the developing scenario of her years in the Congressman's office. There were points, however, that we had investigated on our own that deviated from the initial image Colleen had given us. For the most part, she has worked with us in absolute frankness; revealing material which must have been, at best, embarrassing to remember.

I can't say that I believe everything Colleen told me. Some of the material she initially gave us was not entirely accurate. There was a question of the image she wanted to convey versus the image that would emerge naturally. I do, however, accept the basic truth in what she has said. There are those who will sharpshoot her and question her motives. Only she knows what they really are. I have my opinion, but it will remain just that. What does remain is that she walked away from a $25,800 a year job on Capitol Hill, knowing that she was going on unemployment and would have to scrape each month to meet expenses; yet choosing that and the thought of independence a professional degree would give her over remaining in a position she could no longer tolerate.

There are others at this time who are in the same position in which Colleen found herself. Since beginning this book, we have received reports and documentation which implicate other members of Congress. Colleen Gardner's case is not an isolated incident.

This particular story deals with Colleen, however, and the readers will have to understand the complexities of her experience, her outlook, her goals and those things which are important to her in understanding the abuse of power on Capitol Hill and one example of how it occurs. To complicate the matter, there is no clear indication of a single victim. Colleen in one tape

said, "I don't find that there's anybody who's an innocent victim of anything. I mean, because they have a
choice. . . . I just don't believe that there's a victim. I
think maybe people are used, but they also use in return." This can apply to Congressmen as well as those
associated with them.

John Young

Our first encounter with anyone in Congressman
John Young's office came on a bitterly cold winter
morning. Clancy Isaac and I walked to the Rayburn
Building from the Ivy Street parking lot, across from
the Rotunda Restaurant. The inch-thick ice sheet that
had been on the ground for nearly two weeks was reflecting brilliant, frigid sunlight. We turned into the U-
shaped drive leading to the Rayburn entrance,
anticipating the shelter and warmth of the building.

Once inside, I opened my briefcase for inspection
and we passed the uniformed guard. The elevator took
us to the second floor and it was a short walk to the
end of the hall where we found room 2204. It was an
unusual experience as we entered. I had a preconceived
picture in my mind of how the office would appear. I
knew the staff by name and verbal description, but had
seen none of them before.

We were greeted by a receptionist who fit none of

the images I was carrying in my mind. No matter how objective I had tried to remain, the initial exposure to Colleen and the tape recordings had shaded my perspective. The young lady was conservatively dressed, though a very nice figure was evident. Her hair was neatly and attractively arranged and her manner was cordial, professionally correct, yet warm enough to make us feel welcome. I speculated who she might be, but came up with no immediate answers.

She informed Young's Legislative Research Assistant, Joe Pendergast, that we had arrived and walked into the adjoining room to get a cup of coffee for me. We signed our names in Young's guest book although it was debatable how long we would remain guests.

The door behind the receptionist's desk opened and Pendergast came out. From the expression on his face, it was clear that he had not come to greet us, rather, to put up with us as long as was absolutely necessary and then return to the important matters facing him.

I called him ahead of time to arrange this appointment and had prepared a list of questions. They had arisen from our conversations with Colleen and from material contained in the tape recordings we had heard before Colleen broke off the working relationship. Most were designed to give me more insight into policies and practices in the office which could be related to the situations Colleen had described to us.

We sat down in his office after Lewis Perdue, another member of the writing team and an experienced investigative reporter on the Hill, joined us. It was an overloaded three-on-one situation which added nothing to the already politely hostile atmosphere.

Joe Pendergast is a modish young man with a well-trimmed moustache and unflappable air that serves him well. He could be a middle-level young business executive or a salesman. He has a convincing style and does enough homework to stay reasonably well ahead of the game. But that, amongst other things, is what he's paid for.

We hadn't gotten to any of our questions, having no more than taken our seats when Joe fired an opening volley, "I'm stating at the outset that I'll deny any and all allegations that Colleen Gardner may have made," he said. "They're totally without basis in fact."

That was too big a statement for me to accept all in one breath. Lew got up and walked out. Clancy looked up at the ceiling and then at me. Then Pendergast threw his first counterpunch, mentioning that word had reached him concerning a remark I had made, or was supposed to have made, about the Congressman's similarity to King Farouk and a comment about some of his staff members being emotional cripples. In reviewing quickly in my mind any possible references to the statements, I realized that I had mentioned that opinion to an individual who was later to relate it to Pendergast. There *was* reason for his hostility, although the tapes would later reveal the accuracy of one of my early opinions.

At that point in time, Pendergast hadn't heard the tape recordings, so he had no way of knowing what, in fact, the Congressman had said to Colleen Gardner.

Nevertheless, he had been assigned the task of assembling material for the Congressman's pending suit against the *New York Times*, Sol Rosen, Colleen Gardner and others.

Pendergast was a recent graduate of the International School of Law in Washington, D.C., and was diligently pursuing his task. Because of this, he did have a good deal of information that aided us in screening fact from mere allegation. On occasion, Joe blew a little smoke, just to check what we knew, or perhaps to take us off on a non-productive path. Whatever, I wrote it all down to sort out at a later date.

One thing that interested me was the use of job titles in the office. Pendergast was the Congressman's senior assistant in the office, drawing the highest salary among the staff and acting as the office manager or chief of staff. His title for pay purposes was "Legislative Research Assistant." I realized that a Congressman has the freedom to designate positions within his staff in any manner he so desires. If he should want to number his staff members rather than giving them titles, it is his perogative so long as he submits to the Clerk of the House of Representatives a written notice of the designation. It's hard to tell the players without a program and particularly when there is no standard format for positions.

Harry McAdams, long time Administrative Assistant to Young, had left the office, but remained on the payroll for retirement purposes, listed as the Administrative Assistant, until the July 1, 1976-December 31, 1976 Report of the Clerk of the House. At that time, his title was changed to "clerk." In the majority of Congressional offices, the Administrative Assistant is the highest ranking and highest salaried member of the staff. When I questioned Joe Pendergast about this, he replied that Congressman Young had several "Administrative Assistants," one of whom had been Colleen Gardner.

I asked him to explain the designation. "Colleen," he said, "was the Administrative Assistant for Committee Affairs," in that she handled the Congressman's liaison work with the committees on which he sat. This was even more confusing to me since the Report of the Clerk of the House listed Colleen as "Legislative Research Clerk, (Stenographic)." The official record had no one else listed as anything even closely resembling an administrative assistant, but Pendergast was certainly knowledgable and I didn't see any reason for him to mislead me on a simple point like that.

I asked, "Who determines pay levels for the employees?" Joe answered, "Harry McAdams;" then qualified his statement by adding that the Congressman has the final word on all matters pertaining to office matters. Harry McAdams continues to handle Congressman Young's payrolls, salary scales and position titles even though he is no longer in the office. His principle employment at this time is with the Office of the Governor of Texas.

Clancy took several minutes to explain to Joe the purpose of the book and what we were looking for. A mere sexual relationship between a Congressman and someone other than his wife is a matter for family resolution. However, when such a relationship affects the judgement or performance of official duties by an elected Representative, or tends to abuse the rights and/or dignity of another person, then it is of interest to the electorate. This is particularly true if a misuse of Federal funds is involved. Another related area was the use of Congressional position to achieve favors and/or rewards that would not otherwise be available.

There was an abuse of power that concerned Pendergast and he took the time to elaborate on his views of journalists who hid behind First Amendment freedoms to viciously attack public officials, particularly Congressmen. There was an insinuation that our project fell into that category.

After clearing the issue of what constitutes abuse of power, we went back to a somewhat more relaxed exchange. I asked what, in Pendergast's estimation, since he had been an immediate supervisor, were Colleen's qualifications for an annual salary of $25,800?"

"Five years' experience on this staff." was his immediate response. "She knew the Congressman's district."

"How many of the Congressman's staff, at the time Colleen was here, were actually from the district?" I asked, thinking of other Congressmen who choose staff members from their districts for that very reason.

"I don't recall," Pendergast said.

Naming other staff members I said, "You are all from outside the district; in fact, none of you are even Texans," I mentioned.

"I don't recall," he repeated.

We went onto Colleen's capabilities and Pendergast

explained the duties that Colleen had performed during her first two years in Young's office, from 1970 through the end of 1972. There was no question that she had done substantial stenographic work during her first tour in Young's office. In addition to her office work, she had been carrying an academic load in night school. Pendergast noted that rather than not having work to do, Colleen, at times, complained about the heavy load she was carrying.

Colleen had readily admitted her typing and shorthand skills. She was capable of doing basic secretarial tasks in a competent manner although the full extent of her work hadn't been clear until our conversation with Pendergast. He made a point to tell us that examples of her work would be presented in court and at the proper time.

We learned why Pendergast had been waiting for us with both barrels loaded. He was a veteran of the June 1976 blitzkrieg and after going up against the *New York Times* and various and sundry other professionals, he had just about had his fill of people looking into the affair.

After more than an hour of questions and answers, we broke the session in order that he might return to business. It was a good starting point for us because it opened communications that were necessary to balance and analyze the results of each new gleaning of information.

Just before we left the office, the Congressman, who had been unavailable during the conference, happened to walk through his anteroom and greeted Clancy and me.

Young appears soft, even pudgy, on the outside; the smiling, gentle-spoken, long-term representative of a hard-core, Texas Democratic district. The paternal figure inspires confidence and trust. With a wife and five children, Catholic background, a career as a County Attorney and County Judge before entering Congress in 1956, he has obviously merited the approval of his constituents and special interest groups in his district.

Although not a highly visible Congressman, on the scale of a Les Alpin or even a Robert Drinan, Young is, nevertheless, not an underachiever either. Young is one of the remaining members of the old Sam Rayburn-Lyndon Johnson "after work sippin' and talkin'" group, the men who are now Texas' senior Congressmen.

Young has been characterized, in one of the few available comments about him, as "one of the old school, pork-barrel, district representatives," who, in a strong Democratic district, would remain in office until they chose to retire. His projects for the district include "Harbor Island," the first proposed deep-water port in the Corpus Christi area. This is the centerpiece of Young's legislative career, should it be completed. The Choke Canyon Dam is proposed for construction on the Frior River to provide for future water needs in the Corpus area.

There has to be a tough, shrewd individual inside that deceptive exterior to have survived politically for as long as John Young has, to move his projects through committee with any degree of success and to produce satisfactory results by winning skirmishes rather than fighting all-out wars.

Tough, politically shrewd, yet pleasantly understanding and concerned where his constituents are involved; these are two facets of Congressman John Young. Was there another side, a lecherous, abusive man who took advantage of his position and power to inflict himself on his female employees? Was there a misuse of government funds in the salary scale established by Young and Harry McAdams for members of his staff?

Our meetings with Pendergast on April 4, 1977, and on May 24, 1977, filled in many of the blank spots in the picture we were developing. There was a balance that began to emerge and Colleen's statement about people being used, while at the same time using, began to take on more significance.

The Three Faces of Colleen Gardner

Colleen's role in the feeding of John Young to the investigative lions wasn't one she wrote for herself. There was a great deal of prompting going on and what might have appeared to be a calculated sell-out was, in fact, the result of her indecision.

There were at least three separate and distinct Colleen Gardners during the two weeks of investigation and siege which began in late May 1976. Not one of the three Colleens agreed with the other two and it was the fragmentation of personality, of outlook and of intent that produced the inconsistant and irresolute young woman in the spotlight.

Her hours of tape recordings do exist and were made during the period July 1975 through June 1976. This is significant because she had returned to work in Young's office in May 1974, over a year before the date of the first tape. If her intent from the outset had been to incriminate the Congressman, it would seem that the tapes should begin in November 1974, or earlier. Her written log of motels, room numbers and dates goes back to the notation, "Nov. 11, 1974; 801; Quality Inn; George Denton; 8 P.M. approx." (George Denton was an alias John Young admitted using.). Then follow:

November 23, 1974; room 1103; Quality Inn; 2:30 P.M.

November 30, 1974; room 1235; Quality Inn; 11:30 A.M.

George Denton.

December 21, 1974; room 1205; Quality Inn; These continue through the final entry:

March 24, 1976; room 603; Quality Inn; 7:30 P.M.

Each of the handwritten entries represent a meeting with John Young in motels from the Pentagon Quality Inn and Channel Inn to the Holiday Inn in distant Gaithersburg, Maryland. A number of the taped conversations between Colleen and Congressman Young correspond to the motel meetings. The Wednesday, July 23, 1975, tape is one of these:

"Hi. How're you doing?" Colleen asked.

"Just great! Just great! Yuh feelin' good?" Young responded.

"Yeah," Colleen said. "I'm just tired."

"Did you get any rest when you got home?"

"Huh? No. I just got home." Colleen answered.

"Oh well, I'll be here a little while longer anyway, so. . . ."

"Oh, you will?" Colleen asked. "Okay. You want me to call you right back?"

"No. Why? I thought I'd call you when I'm ready to leave here." Young replied.

"Oh, okay."

"Okay?"

"Uh-huh."

"Bye, bye."

"Bye." Colleen hung up.

A short time later Young called back:

"Hello," Colleen said.

"Hi!" Young answered.

"Hi."

"I, I'm, uh, uh, ready to go on over there an' I'll call you from there," Young said. "Do you want me to, uh, to give you the number an' all, do you want me to order you a good steak?"

"Yeah."

"An', an' some beer?" he asked.

"Okay."

"Fine! Everything all right, darlin'?"

"Yeah," Colleen replied.

"Good. Well, I'll call you from there an' give you the number."

"Okey-doke."

"Bye, bye," Young said as he hung up.

Later, the phone rang again and Colleen answered:

"Hello?"

"Hi-i-i," Young intoned.

"Hi-i," Colleen echoed.

"Me-e-e, eleven-oh-three-e-e," Young chanted.

"Okey-dokey, pokey."

"Get yuh a good steak an' some beer," he reassured her.

"Okay."

"Bye."

This conversation corresponds to the July 23, 1975, note: room 1103, Quality Inn, George Denton.

This relationship between Colleen Gardner and Congressman Young was known to Bill Gardner, members of Young's staff, Sol Rosen, and Colleen's psychiatrist, among others. Rosen had accompanied Colleen to her 1973 interview with the U.S. Attorney and had acted as her legal counselor from that time forward.

After the *New York Times* article appeared and there was local TV coverage on network stations, more requests came to Colleen, including a June 15th call from Bruce David of *Hustler* magazine. Sums in excess of $20,000 were offered for a story with photos. Colleen rejected all of the offers.

Next, Colleen was advised by her attorney, for her

protection, to tape all phone calls during the investigation by the *New York Times*.

Finally, her attorney was in contact with the U.S. Attorney's office during the course of the *Times'* investigation and advised Colleen of the potential for legal action against the Congressman.

Colleen's ambivalence is evident in her conversations with the opposing factions during this period of time as well as her conversations with other members of Young's staff.

In conversations with Young, she was the loyal mistress, defending him, the office and herself against the inquiry by Bob Woodward. With the *New York Times'* reporters, she was alternately helpful, fearful and remorseful. The latter was later coupled with an unwillingness to procede and to do injury to Congressman Young and his family. With her attorney she was concerned about the legal implications of her actions, angry with him for fostering her involvement with the reporters or, conversely, in agreement with him about the correctness of her actions. With her former co-worker, she was an injured friend who had been exposed to scrutiny and interrogation by the press as a result of leaked information involving both her and the former co-worker. Several times, Colleen challenged the other woman, insinuating that she had been responsible for the information getting to the press.

During all of these exchanges with Young and other members of the staff, it was Colleen who was supplying the information to Horrock and Crewdson with which

they confronted former Young employees, and, ulti-
mately, Congressman Young.

After the June 1st call from Bob Woodward, Colleen talked with John Crewdson:

"They asked me, they said that they had heard that
I was involved with taking a gun and something out of
the office with (name withheld). How would they
know about that?" she asked.

"I don't know."

"They said they got it from a Hill source."

"That's very interesting," Crewdson said. "Who
called you?"

"Uh, Bob Woodward," Colleen said innocently.

"Oh Jesus!" Crewdson laughed.

"Who's that?"

"Bob Woodward," Crewdson explained, "Is half of
Woodward and Bernstein; the guys who broke the
Watergate story."

"Oh Jesus Christ," Colleen exclaimed.

"Pshew, wow."

"So, what do I do?" Colleen asked.

"Well I don't know. What'd you tell him?"

"Well, I just, you know, just laughed and I denied
it."

"You denied it?" Crewdson asked.

"Well, you know, I didn't deny it and I didn't say
yes either."

"Yeah."

"I just said that I was shocked. I said what, somebody trying to make allegations to put me in jail? You
know? And, uh, you know, I just sorta covered myself.

I don't know, I mean, everybody in my office knows about that," Colleen explained.

"Is that right?"

"Yeah."

"Well, obviously they've been poking around and somebody's told 'em about it," Crewdson said.

"Either that or Sol Rosen said something," Colleen said. "Do you think he would do that?"

"I don't know, Colleen. I just don't know."

Colleen mentioned that Crewdson, Rosen and her ex-husband were the only people whom she told about the incident with Young's pistol and notebooks, although it could have come from anyone on the staff.

Crewdson discounts the staff as unlikely and they settle on (name deleted) as the probable source. Crewdson advised Colleen not to deny knowledge of the incident, but rather to refuse to talk with Woodward, to make no comment at all.

After talking with Crewdson, Colleen met with Woodward and then called John Young and related the entire encounter with Woodward. She listed the allegations and her denials, the challenge to her salary and her defense of the work she was doing. Young was extremely pleased with his former assistant's performance and reiterated his confidence in her.

Colleen's next conversation was with Sol Rosen:

"Okay. You're on tape," Colleen begins. "I hope I'm not washing anything off."

"Thank you, dear. I hope not," Rosen replied.

"You're now being taped, my dear."

"Okay," Rosen said, "I'm not going to say anything obscene."

"Yeah, but that son of a bitch, Bob Woodward, he said, 'very mysterious, very strange; you have to (unintelligible) sex with your boss. You're making twenty-seven thousand a year.' And I said, look, how much are you making? And he said, twenty-nine. I said, do you have a PhD? And he said, no. I said, all right, well then, why are you accusing me? I said, I have four years of college. I may not have a degree. . . ."

"You should have asked him if he was sleeping with Katherine Graham," Rosen quipped.

"And I asked him, are you sleeping with your boss?"

"And what'd he say?" Rosen asked.

"He said, naw, he kinda laughed and I said, well, you know, let's face it. . . ."

"All right, now look," Rosen changed subjects, "Here's what I think happened with (name withheld). You know, there's always the, I think I told you Sinatra's classic comment about Judith Campbell Exner, 'All you need, anytime you have a hustler with a literary agent, you got problems.' Now I seem to think maybe (she) may have, probably blabbed to everybody."

"She has," Colleen confirmed.

"All right, now, what (unintelligible) happened, somebody gave her the great idea of selling her story to the *Post*. You see? Because if you'll notice, the first person who called me and I spoke to, and of course the only reason that I spoke to you, that it was the

New York Times and these reporters are very responsible. You can see the way they spoke to you and the way handled it. There was no sensationalism, there was no pictures. You know, I mean, they didn't just run into a story and call up Young right away. You know what I mean?" Rosen's rapid fire diction tumbled words over one another.

"Yeah."

"And try to, you know, what they wanted, they wanted to find out facts. They wanted names. They wanted to try to investigate this the right way."

"Right." Colleen said.

"You know what I mean? I mean you could see their approach and their demeanor. They didn't have photographers there ready to photograph you and ask you for the lurid details of everything that happened. You know, it was really a professional way and the only other writer that I suggested about getting money from was the *Atlantic* Magazine because I know Sandy Unger. He's won a Pulitzer Prize, he wrote two books, number one on the best seller list including one book right now on the F.B.I., and he's a top-knotch investigative reporter. And the *Atlantic* Magazine is a, it's a first rate magazine."

"Uh-huh."

"Now I seem to think (she) probably sold somebody a bill of goods." Rosen said.

"You think so?" Colleen asked.

"Yeah! There's no doubt about it, because it just wouldn't be, you see, somebody indirectly . . . let's assume . . . let's assume you told your mother your experiences. It wouldn't be logical for your mother to call up a newspaper and say, 'hey, you call this girl, you can get a good story.' "

The speculation was that (she) had been paid by the *Post* for her story and through her, Bob Woodward had gotten to Colleen.

Later in the conversation, Rosen discussed the tapes and their purpose:

"I seem to think Young is going to call you soon and, you know, once what's his name is in the paper, once the questions are out there," Rosen said, referring to the potential story by Bob Woodward, "You know, we make a request not to say anything and not to talk or something like that."

"Yeah."

"So, uh, that's about all I can say. And you know, if you can get a tape of that, you know, this is just mainly for, whether you ever give it anybody or use it, this is really for your own protection," Rosen explained.

"Yeah."

"You see, and that's what you have to be concerned about when. . . ."

"Well, I'm not interested in any kind of publicity," Colleen interrupted, "You know, I want just to eliminate it."

"I understand that. I'm not saying that you should, but what I'm just teaching you now and why I gave you that coil is that you have to protect yourself."

"Yeah."

"In other words," Rosen said, "Let's assume, always

assume the worst. Let's assume Young is questioned; let's assume he does admit it was stolen; let's assume that it does come out that he admitted he did have relations with a couple of the girls. Next question: then he calls you and has a conversation. What do you have in the way to protect yourself?"

"Yeah."

"You see," Rosen continued, "If he calls you up and makes certain admissions or allegations, at least you've got him on a tape and you can prove what you said, you can prove what he said."

"Yeah."

"Doesn't have to come down to a one on one anymore," Rosen said.

"Yeah."

"You see, that's why I'm saying if you're taping this, fine. This is my advice to you."

"Right," Colleen agreed.

"If (she) calls you, you gotta tape her, at least, as John said, my God, that tape of (name deleted), that was precious. Because at least you have down her feelings, her emotions and her own admissions."

"Yeah."

"So, put that in the safest place you know of and just keep it there. Because this is to protect you and if we can keep you out of trouble, that's all I'm concerned. I don't care about Betty Ray, I don't care about (name withheld) or any of these other dingbats. I'm concerned about keeping you out of trouble. You don't want publicity. . . . I don't want to see your picture on page one of the *Post* going into the Courthouse with a subpoena or being on Television or what-not." Rosen was prophetic, although neither of them realized it at this time.

Colleen, using the cassettes Rosen had given her and some of her own, recorded conversations with virtually all callers during the June 1, 1976 through June 10, 1976, period. Despite the school schedule she was maintaining in the midst of the investigation and intrigue, she managed to talk with Young at least twice on most of the days between the first and tenth, with (name deleted) for extended conversations on several days, Sol Rosen almost daily, and John Crewdson more frequently than any other reporter.

Young, in his conversations with her, was obviously confident of her loyalty to him and warned her against outside advice that might increase her involvement in the Hays-Ray scandal. Colleen, in her conversations with Young, had painted Rosen, her legal advisor into the role of a minor ogre. In a June exchange, Colleen returned one of Young's calls to her and complained that,

"Well, you know, it's just that, this guy, you know, this Sol Rosen, he's gettin' me worried now."

"Yeah," Young replied, "I tried to head you off from that, but . . . okay, what's he tryin to do, sweetie?"

"Well, I don't know, he's, like he's trying to get me involved, you know." Colleen said.

"Of course he is!" Young said. "You know why? He wants to get you involved so. . . ."

"He's trying to scare me and tell me that if I don't say something, the grand jury will subpoena me and that my name'll be in the paper and, uh, my picture will be in the, you know, I'm, an' it's really scary." Colleen said.

"Well honey, you, you, uh, I, I just tried my level best to head you off from that son-of-a-bitch. I could tell that's a creep if I ever saw one," Young fumed.

"I think so too," Colleen agreed.

"An' what he's tryin' to do," Young continued, "Is to get you involved so that you'll be indebted to him, you know. That's all that son-of-a-bitch is gonna do; he's a busybody and a goddamned nut and, uh, you don't have anything to go forward with. What in the goddamned hell do you have to go forward with? Just let that son-of-a-bitch . . . let me tell you one thing. Whatever, whatever, I've just got to keep harpin' on this, you don't have anything to hide from those gawddamned bastards and if, uh, don't talk to anybody except official people. I'm talkin' about grand juries or F.B.I. or something like that."

"Now if I were subpoenaed," Colleen asked, "Do I have to say, can't I plead the Fifth Amendment?"

"Well, you'd have to have an attorney to do, yeah, yeah, the answer is yes, you can. But the thing about it, what the hell do you have to hide? Just don't go talkin' to any gawddamn newspaper reporters. The matter is under examination by the grand jury and by the F.B.I. and the Federal District Attorney. It would be most inappropriate for you or anybody else to make any comments to any newspaper reporters. That's the only way your name'd get in the paper. Those grand jury proceedings are secret. You haven't read anybody's name's been before that grand jury have you?"

"Have I done what now?" Colleen asked.

"Have you read anybody's name's been before the gran . . . ?"

"No."

"Well, hell no you don't," Young said, " 'Cause those are secret an' they won't even let the gawddamned reporters get on the same floor with them . . . but that's the creepiest son-of-a-bitch I ever heard of, that you're dealing with there."

"Yeah," Colleen agreed, "I think so too. I think he's just tryin' to. . . ."

"He's tryin to get you involved so that you. . . ."

"So maybe he can get some glory or something," Colleen added.

"Either that or so that he can work his way into your affections and things like that, you know. Which, apparently, he's not been able to do in the past," Young was speculating. He went on, "Oh Jesus, I hate to see you take up with that son-of-a-bitch. Now gawddamn, I tried to tell you, darlin' . . . I'm an old prosecuter. I can spot these creeps . . . uh, it's bad of me to fuss. I don't mean to be fussin' at you."

Young later asked Colleen if she'd gotten any studying done and she replied,

"No, not at all. Well, I studied a little bit last night, but, I've just been, uh, you know, he's (Rosen) been calling me up and, you know, I've been really concerned because, frankly, you know, I just want to get away from all the stuff, I just want to go to school and

I just want, you know, to get ahead and, I don't know
. . . what they're trying to do is, I think they're just trying to get lots of big stories about everybody and everything, because this is a big thing now."

"Sure! That son-of-a-bitch wants to wa . . ." Young
began.

"Anything perverted or distorted that they can get,
they want to do. You know?" Colleen said.

"Yeah," Young agreed. "For Christ's sake, don't
talk to that son-of-a-bitch and don't talk to anybody. If
you have to talk to anybody, talk under subpoena. You
understand what I'm talkin about?"

"Yeah."

"And then remember one thing, Colleen, don't vol-
unteer anything; when they ask you something, tell the
gawddamned truth. You understand?" Young said.

"Yeah."

"And, if I understand what the situation is, you
don't know any . . . you don't have a gawddamned thing
to come forward with anyway. You didn't even know
that gawddamned, you haven't had anything to do with
that gal since she's been with ol' Hays."

"No," Colleen confirmed.

Colleen took Young's advice about Betty Ray, but
she was certainly not following it with regard to his office. On June 2nd, she was already discussing her tapes
with John Crewdson and on June 3rd, she asked if he
would like to hear the set of tapes. Crewdson was obviously interested and made a date to come up to her
apartment. Colleen called Rosen immediately after
talking with the *New York Times* reporter and told

him that she had agreed to let Crewdson listen to them. Rosen indicated that the decision was entirely up to her, but he would be available to come to her apartment when the reporters were there in case she needed him.

That night, Crewdson and Lucinda Franks came to Colleen's apartment and stayed until the morning hours, listening to the recorded conversations. Colleen, upset and sipping beer with them, had faded shortly after midnight. It was impossible for them to hear all of the conversations, but specific ones regarding Young's relationship with Colleen, their visits to motels, and the picture of office routine that emerged were of immediate interest. The tapes gave concrete leads for further investigation and provided, in (name deleted) case, information about her that now even she knew Colleen had.

Through Colleen, the *Times* reporters reached two other ex-Young employees, confronting each with information which indicated they had a source with indepth knowledge of the office and its personnel. Colleen then talked with each of them, one daily and the other on June 4th and 10th, allaying their suspicions about her.

The unusual point in the early skirmishing, was Bob Woodward's call and subsequent visit to Colleen. This caught her completely off balance and became the dominant topic of her conversations for the next week. Colleen knew she was the source for the *Times'* investigation, but who was Woodward's? Speculation ran to all kinds of people. Or perhaps Woodward had come up with another "deep throat," and his knowledge of the situation was the final factor in Colleen's decision to provide full information to Horrock and Crewdson.

In Colleen's changing pattern of relationships, she constantly sought advice from Young on the proper manner to handle the Woodward matter, never hinting that she was, at the same time, harpooning him through the *Times*. Young's attitude toward Colleen was one of trust and confidence as he discussed the expanding investigation with her and explained his defense against the press. Young expressed confidence in his ability to withstand a grand jury or a House Ethics Committee investigation, but he had his office drawn into a tight circle of wagons against the attack by the media.

By June 7th, the *Times* reporters had done most of their groundwork and were preparing to confront Congressman Young with the allegations. Young, in a June 6th conversation with Colleen, focused on his prime contention.

"The real question is did you earn your money here, or were you hired as a mistress?"

"Of course I earned my money!" Colleen answered. With that assurance of support from her, Young was secure in his plan to confront the investigators with an authorized and justifiable salary scale. There was sufficient evidence that she had done stenographic and research work to dispel any charges of this being another Betty Ray situation. In her first two years in the office, 1970-1972, Colleen had done basic stenographic work and some research on petroleum imports and exports. During the last two years, she began with research work, some simple statistical analysis, and a variety of duties in no specific category—helping the Congressman with the preparation of his speeches, correcting other staff member's work, and some translation of Spanish-language letters. During her final eight months, she had been given the role of liaison to the Joint Committee on Atomic Energy, of which Young was scheduled to take over the Chairmanship in 1977.

Colleen was responsible for setting up a filing system for Young's Joint Committee work. Nothing organized had existed before she took the responsibility of establishing and maintaining the files. She dealt with letters and brochures which regularly came to Committee members and kept Young aware of Committee business.

Young also indicated that Colleen was his staff representative to the House Rules Committee, on which Young is a ranking member. Her salary was "rigged" to the Rules Committee although he had never put her on its payroll, according to Young.

When the investigative team checked with the Rules Committee, a slight misunderstanding occurred. Greg Nicosia, then Chief Counsel to the Rules Committee, was asked if Young had a staff assistant assigned to the Committee. He answered, "No."

"Who in Young's office do you deal with on Rules Committee matters?" He was asked.

"Joe Pendergast," Nicosia replied.

"Do you have anything to do with Colleen Gardner?"

"No."

"Do you know her?"

"No," Nicosia replied.

After this conversation, Nicosia called Congressman Young and related the incident to him. Young immediately pointed out that Colleen had been gone for two months, and Nicosia wouldn't, therefore, have had anything to do with her. Young told Nicosia to call the reporters back and clarify the point.

Young contacted the then Assistant Minority Counsel, and had her call the same reporters to explain her association with Colleen on Rules Committee matters. In a June 8th conversation, Young told Colleen of the Assistant Minority Counsel's verification of her Rules Committee duties. Colleen asked,

"So if they ask me, what did (she) say I did on the Rules Committee?"

"Well she just said that she took up all the Rules Committee business that she had, pertaining to the Rules Committee and my office, she took up with you. Like, uh, uh, wha . . ."

"But see, yeah . . . 'cause (she) hardly ever even called me," Colleen said.

"Well-l-l," Young said.

"I need to know if she says she talked to me about anything in particular. . . ."

". . . and so, she said, that you handled my Rules Committee work in my office and whenever she had anything pertaining to Rules, she called up and talked to you."

"Uh huh," Colleen said.

"And such things as askin' me if I wanted to handle a rule or asking me, telling me what's up for that day or just anything about it, and she said, if they had people who wanted to talk to me about a rule, that they'd send 'em to see you an' that sort of thing." Young said.

"Uh-huh."

"Which, if you remember back, honey, that's precisely what happened too."

"Yeah," Colleen said, "I just don't remember. You know."

"No, it's hard to," Young agreed. "Because you had so damn many other things to do an' I can remember on that immigration bill, comes to my mind just off hand, and there were many others, but on an immigration bill when this fellow came in; it had to with making the employer responsible for seeing that the fellow he hired was an eligible worker. And the church was supporting it and they must have come to see you two to three times about that."

"Yeah, but I think they just came to ask me questions about what you were going to do," Colleen said.

"Sure. Right. So you, in other words, you represented me and kept me from havin' to meet with 'em. You know? And that's the function of it." Young explained.

"But you did talk to them," Colleen said, "Remember? When they were there?"

"Sure, but after you talked to 'em and then you briefed me on what they wanted and so then it didn't take me two seconds to tell 'em. You know?"

"Yeah."

Shredded material secured from garbage cans from rear of Tongsun Park's Pacific Development Company.

Shredded material sorted out into separate plastic bags.

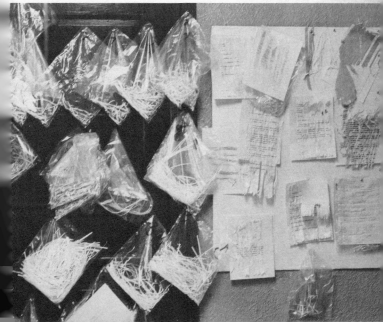

Jim Mintz, one of the investigative reporters sorting out shredded material. *Photo by Lew Perdue*

Shredded material painstakingly re-created, strip by strip. *Photo by Lew Perdue*

(From L. to R.): Ken Cummins, Wendy Kramer and Richard Sokolow reconstructing the shredded documents.

Photo by Lew Perdue

(From L. to R.) Lew Perdue, Jim Mintz and Richard Sokolow sorting out the shredded material.

Photo by Lew Perdue

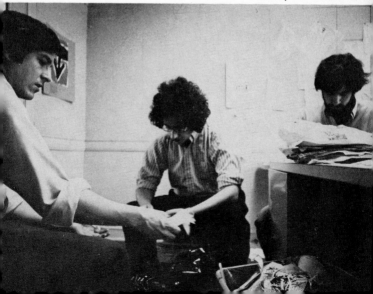

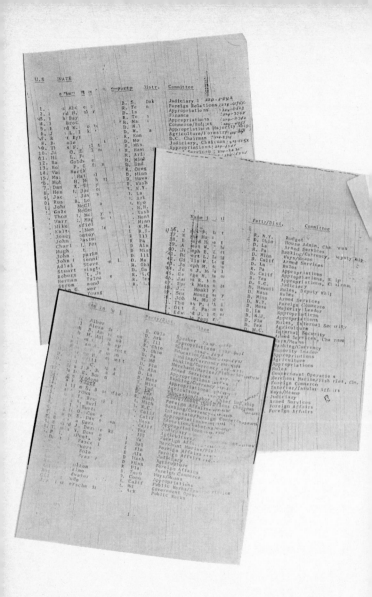

Sample pages of re-assembled "shredding" listing many
U.S. Representatives and Senators.

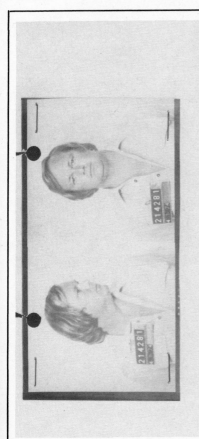

THIS SUBJECT IS: ROBERT CONKLING, W/M/36, DOB 5-16-37, LIVES AT 1411 35th STREET NORTHWEST, SUBJECT DRIVES A LATE MODLE LINCOLN CONTINENTAL, SILVER IN COLOR, HE'S 6'2", STOCK BUILD, APPROX. 200lbs, PALE BLOND HAIR, HE LOOKS THE SAME AS THE PICTURE AS IT WAS TAKEN APRIL 1, 1974.

A "mug shot" of Robert Conkling from the local Washington, D.C. Metropolitan Police File.

Colleen Gardner, former aide of Rep. John Young (D–Tex.) She alleged that part of her duties was to have sexual relations with him. *Photo by U.P.I.*

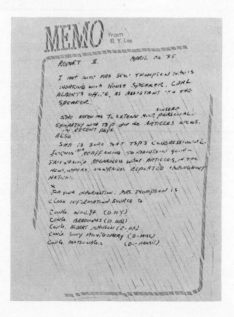

A memo about Mrs. Suzi Park Thomson, former aide to former Speaker of House, Carl Albert (D–Okla.), reconstructed from the shredded material.

"Sheer poppycock," said Rep. John Young (D–Tex.) to allegations of sexual misconduct made by Colleen Gardner.

Photo by U.P.I.

Sen. Henry M. Jackson (D—Wash.), Chairman of the Investigations Sub-Committee, administers oath to "Seven Sisters" oil company executives called to testify about the energy shortage. (From L. to R.): Roy Baze, Exxon; A. M. Cord, Texaco; Z. D. Bonner, Gulf; A. E. Murray, Mobil; T. M. Powell, Standard of California; Richard Leet, Standard of Indiana; and Harry Bridges, Shell.

Photo by U.P.I.

"But, of course, another thing that is good is that while your salary was (unintelligible) and rigged to the Rules Committee scale, you were not on the Rules Committee payroll. Which is a damn good thing, because now they'd make a hell of a lot of that, too; that while you were on the Rules Committee payroll, most of your work was on Joint Committee, you know?"

"Uh-huh."

"So, the only connection you really had with the Rules Committee, other than handlin' my work in connection with it, it was the salary comparison. Because your major work for the committees was the Joint Committee work and it was major, Colleen. Hell, those gawddamned people drove yuh nuts back there. You came. . . ."

"I just hope they don't start askin' me about any details, you know," Colleen said. "I really don't know that much about it."

"Well, that's a long time ago," Young said, referring to the period less than five months prior, "And if you want to do it, you can just bring 'em on back down here an' go into the files with 'em. Or whatever, you know? But, if it ever came to that, and it's not gonna come to that. What they're lookin' for is a Betty Ray . . . that was doin' nothin' and will tell them she was doin' nothin'. You know? That's what they're lookin' for. Hell."

In a conversation with a former Young employee, a different perspective of Colleen's Committee work was revealed. The woman was asked by John Crewdson about Colleen's Rules Committee work, she responded,

"That's a bunch of shit! I said, look, I did the office filing for that office for almost a year. I said, never, ever did Colleen get any Rules Committee stuff. I said, Rules Committee was always given to Harry McAdams or Joe. I said, Colleen never got Rules Committee stuff. I said, she got nuclear energy information. I said, we were told to put that on her desk."

Meanwhile, Rosen had been in contact with Robert Ogren, head of the Justice Department's Fraud Division, concerning the potential for Federal investigation of the Congressman based on the material which was being turned up. Colleen had given her tapes to John Crewdson in order that they might use leads and material in the tapes. She was upset to learn that Crewdson had read (name deleted) transcripts of a conversation she had with Colleen describing her repulsion of the act and contempt for herself after submitting to Young's sexual demands in the office on February 14th, 1976.

Before that, she had talked to Colleen at length about the necessity for her keeping her job in Young's office. It was, according to the woman, a situation where she would have to put up with whatever was demanded in order to keep the position and salary. February 14th was obviously a shock to her and her sobbing conversations with Colleen after it, reflect the intensity of pain she felt. Two months after the incident she left her job in Young's office and attempted a new beginning. The investigation swept over her and she became a unwilling victim, then a willing participant in the effort, affirming and reaffirming her willingness to stand by Colleen in whatever comes of the impending story.

After Horrock and Crewdson confronted Young, McAdams and Pendergast with the accumulation of allegations on June 8th, giving the Congressman an opportunity to rebutt the charges, they proceeded to put the story together. Colleen was bewildered and frightened, feeling that she'd gotten in over her head and the process had gone along, with her in tow.

She complained to Rosen that the *Times* had promised that no story would be printed without her consent. Now it seemed that she had no control over it at all. It appeared to Colleen at the time that Rosen had become as suspect as the reporters in using her to get a story. Rightly or wrongly Colleen felt that Nick Horrock had been the source of greatest pressure to her with his seemingly unsympathetic push for hard facts. In an exchange just before the story was released Crewdson asked Colleen:

"How did it go with the U.S. Attorney?"

"I haven't gone yet," Colleen responded.

"When are you going to go?"

"Well, I'm supposed to be meeting Sol in about 20 minutes."

"You going to go this afternoon, then?" Crewdson asked.

"Why, I, I don't know."

"You're not going to go, are you?"

"Well, it's not that I'm not going to go."

"What is it? You got somebody there?" Crewdson asked.

"No. I don't have anybody here, it's just that I didn't think I had to go."

"You don't have to go. We thought you were." Crewdson said.

"You mean and make a complaint," Colleen asked.

"Well, not make a complaint. Just be interviewed by them. I mean, we thought Sol had arranged an appointment with them," Crewdson said.

"No. No, it's because I keep backing out of it."

"You backed out again, did you?" Crewdson asked.

"Yeah. I've just gotten really scared."

"Why?"

"Well, I was readin' what the girls were saying on Capitol Hill about Betty Ray. Saying that, you know that she's guilty and she's a prostitute and that women don't have to do that sort of thing. They can always say no. I just think it's gonna be pretty, uh, I mean, they're just gong to laugh at me . . . an' everybody else. You know, people just don't understand some sort of pressures you know. They don't understand why people do what they do.

"Yeah, okay, good. See you later, Crewdson said.

"You still want me to come by? Colleen asked.

"If you want your takes, yeah, you might as well come and get 'em."

"Allrighty, Bye."

Shortly after the gentle probing by Crewdson, Horrock called:

"I understand you had an appointment with the United States Attorney today," he said.

"No, I didn't."

"Oh, I see. Okay. Well then Sol may be misunderstood or we didn't make clear what he was saying.

"No. I, Sol told me that if I wanted to get immunity, you know. In other words, they just don't give you immunity for no reason. You have to give them a reason why you want it. And he said if I wanted to go to the U.S. Attorney, and I just got very paranoid last night and we never did make an appointment, you know. So. . . ."

"All right," Horrock snapped, "Fine. I meant, you know, we've done our good deed for the day. We were told about crimes and we asked you to report them to the government and you didn't report them. That's your business. I can't help on that, but I did want to be clear because it appeared to us that Mr. Rosen had gone to government officials and told them that he had a witness and so forth and so on. So I thought, it seemed to me that kinda left it up in the air, but I take it it's your impression he never went to the government at all."

"Well," Colleen said, "I think he did go. I think he discussed it with them and I think, the impression he gave me, was that the man didn't feel that there was any criminal. . . ."

"Well, I told you, I . . . we went yesterday. We're going to do a piece on this probably anyway, because the Department of Justice tells us that there's a serious investigation of this matter and, uh. . . ." Horrock paused.

"That there *is* an investigation?" Colleen asked.

"Yes, certainly," Horrock replied, "And we're going to be going ahead with it. . . ."

"Of Mr. Young or of . . . ?" Colleen asked.

"Of Mr. Young and of the allegations that you . . . as we understand it, you've made to us and that he's characterized to the government, and . . ."

"*Who*'s characterized?" Colleen demanded.

"Sol. Mr. Rosen's been talking to the government for two years about this case or when. . . ."

"He has?" Colleen asked incredulously.

"Whenever you went to him first," Horrock said, "So, uh . . ."

"Well, see, I. . . ." Colleen started to explain.

"I never, you know I'm sorry, I just," Horrock blurted, "I've done a lot of work in this field. I really have and I don't make stories. I'd just as soon go back and finish my coverage of Ronald Reagan, but you have reported to me felony crimes. We've talked to other people, whose names suggested, who've confirmed felony crimes and your lawyer, you've empowered your lawyer, and he tells me and he may be putting me on, but he tells me he went to the chief United States Attorney and the Deputy Attorney and outlined these allegations. I've confirmed independently through senior Justice Department people that, in fact, such a witness is known to exist and to be in contact with the U.S. Attorney's office and the allegations will be put under investigation . . . and I don't understand how you get to walk out, back out on that. I'm not complaining, but I would think that he's going to have to do a lot of explaining to them."

Colleen, by this time, was understandably shaken, but she responded, "All right. It's going to be very difficult to prove that Mr. Young forced anybody to do anything. And it's going to end up looking like a bunch of girls that were greedy; who wanted a good salary. You know what I mean?"

"I didn't, I'm not trying to tell you what to do," Horrock said, "I'm saying you have seen and have been a part of a crime in commission and you've told me this yourself; you've told John Crewdson this and all we said is that when a citizen has this happen to them, their obligation is to report it, and. . . ."

"Well, I reported it once already," Colleen said referring to the 1973 interview with the U.S. Attorney's office.

"I see. Okay."

"Didn't I?" she asked.

"Well, I don't know," Horrock said. "You know, they didn't conduct an investigation of it at that time, uh. . . ."

"Well, they didn't obviously think it was of any consequence."

"All right. Well," Horrock said, "You know, you've got to make your own decisions in life and I'm not gonna make them for you, because I'm not empowered to nor do I take that much interest in personal life, but I think that you're on the edge of between whether you're. . . ."

"Well," Colleen interrupted, "(Name deleted) saw the crime; (Name deleted) did, and neither one of them have done anything about it."

"All right. Well, listen, uh, I don't have any medals for heroism, Vietnam or anywhere else, so I'm not going to go around putting people down. You may be doing the right thing and I can't tell you that you're not. I do think that the damn thing may snap back now and jump at you without, you see, without your being able to control it anyway; and, uh, six months ago, I suspect you could say, well look, I'm going to forget this. It was just silly and Young is going to make a fool out of us and so forth. I don't know if you can do it anymore. So, maybe when they come to you, if they do, you can just be honest with them at that point. But, anyway, I was confused and I think maybe. . . ."

"Well, I'm just going to, I'm supposed to be meeting Sol right now to have lunch before I go to the unemployment," Colleen said, "And I'll just have to ask him, you know. Because, when he talked to me about this whole issue, he said, and I have it on tape what he told me if you want to hear . . . it's not that I'm making up stories. . . ."

"No. I'm not saying you're making up stories," Horrock said.

"And the impression he gave me was that there are an awful lot of loopholes in it as far as the Justice Department was concerned and that from, you know, if I wanted to come down and talk to them and fill in the gaps and give them what I had, that was fine, but they still didn't know whether they had any case or not."

"He told me that Sunday night (June 6th)," Horrock declared. "I told him that I've been in this business seventeen years and I heard a felony accusation made and it was clear to me and I can read and I can count."

"Yeah."

"And if Mr. Ogren doesn't want to talk to you and you want to get in touch with some other lawyer in this city, I'll give you the names of lawyers who'll take you to Justice Department officials who'll listen to your allegations. They are serious allegations. They are very serious allegations and Mr. Ogren or no one else can make that decision without hearing the evidence and I don't believe they've heard the evidence and even Sol imparting it to them second hand does not adequately set out. So they have made no decision whether they're going to prosecute this case or whether they're going to investigate it or whether they aren't because they haven't heard it yet. And that's what, you know, whether Mr. Rosen decided he doesn't want to do this anymore, I don't know. All I'm saying is, that anybody who tells you that the Department of Justice says it's not interested in it, is putting you on, because they haven't made any decision. If I ever catch them not interested in investigating felonies allegations in this city, we'll do a story about that. Because that's quite a different matter and I don't believe that Mr. Rosen is empowered by the U.S. Attorney to tell you that they're not going to investigate that crime. And I don't believe that they've made that decision and whether the guy says 'antsy-pantsy' about whether he likes this or he doesn't like that, what I'm talking about is, once they've heard your evidence and they say, 'look, we don't see a crime committed here,' fine . . . but, if the reverse is true and they go ahead and investigate it, but after you've made the presentation. I'm not going to get in the boat of telling you what you should do. What I'd do, if I were you, if you don't like the lawyer you've got, then hire somebody, Colleen, that you have regard in. If that guy says, 'Don't go to the United States Attorney. Don't report this crime, whatever,' then do whatever he says, but I don't think any lawyer can tell you that. Most of them are supposed to tell you to report a crime when you see one happening. It's not only this; it's the question of (name deleted) too, which is a very clear-cut case, which she's told you about."

"Yeah. I know."

"Well. You talk to Rosen. If he wants to give me a call, that's fine, but we, you know . . . you've got your own decision to make. I think that this thing has gotten far more confused, you know. I think you're just as vulnerable in your present position as you'd be if you walk in there and set out what you've told us to the government. You're just as vulnerable right now. so, in any event, if you're going to have lunch with him, then let's find out what he wants to do and what he thinks. He's supposed to be your lawyer and you're retaining him to give you advice, legal advice, and not to tell you stories about whether the government thinks whatever you had to say, secondhand, is interesting. Until you've been talked to by the F.B.I.; given a complete statement to them or to a U.S. Attorney; taken down in writing; signed as being your account of the things; and they evaluate that and investigate it and then tell you they're not going to prosecute the case. That's a valid handling of a government case. It is an invalid handling of a government . . . Miss Ray's charges may not be true, but the government is absolutely committed to investigate charges of misuse of government funds, misappropriation of funds, extortion and the other things which are suggested by what you told us. They just are."

"Yeah."

"It's their basic obligation and I, and all this stuff about whether the Assistant U.S. Attorney, or whoever the hell this Ogren is, is interested or he's not interested, or he had a good morning this morning or he liked his breakfast food, is a put-on. As a matter of fact, our very next question, in fact, if nothing is done, we're going to go ask the government why anything isn't done, because Mr. Rosen had imparted enough for them to have a strong suspicion that a crime had been committed."

Rosen, however, had already told Colleen on June 7th that in his conversations with Robert Ogren there was doubt that criminal conduct or criminal intent could be established. Young, characterized as a "shrewd old geezer," could fall back on the unlimited discretion given him with his staff salaries and simply state that Colleen's salary was in keeping with his policies.

Colleen had never denied doing work in the office. Young was authorized to pay her whatever he chose as long as it was under $39,600 and above $1,200 per year. With evidence of work that she had done, no matter how inconsequential, and absence of any kickbacks, there would be little hope for an indictment.

There was some thought of possible bribery on

Young's part with sexual compliance by staff members in return. Colleen, in discussing Horrock and Crewdson's attitude toward the situation, told Rosen,

"Well, the *New York Times* lawyers evidently felt they had a case. I suppose they felt Young was bribing and was getting kick-backs . . . sexual kick-backs.

"Well, that's right," Rosen agreed, "But the technical end of the law only deals with financial kick-backs. I think it says, remuneration.' "

"Well," Colleen asked, "Remuneration. Is that *only* monetary?"

"Well, that's how the. . . ."

"Remuneration is anything in return," Colleen declared.

"Anything of value," Rosen said.

"Well, sex is not of value?" Colleen asked.

Rosen pointed out that the Justice Department was inundated with complaints that were, perhaps, valid; however, the concern of a prosecutor was not merely getting an indictment, but obtaining a conviction in court of law. The Betty Ray case was a classic example of a defense lawyer's dream. She had no corroboration and Hays had defenses open to him in court that would have made him an odds-on favorite in a trial.

In Colleen's case, she had evidence of a sexual relationship between herself and Congressman John Young; there was corroborative evidence from (name deleted); yet, Young could claim that their salaries were paid for the work they did and sex was merely a by-product of their attraction to him.

Wayne Hays was brought down by the publicity sur-founding Betty Ray's allegations, not by prosecution in a court of law. Because Colleen and (name deleted) *had* done work in the office and could not establish that Young had given them an ultimatum of "submit to sex with him or get fired," there was no technical violation of the law.

Colleen was discouraged at this point. It seemed that there was no recourse open to her and she hadn't intended for there to be a public disclosure unless it would result in Federal investigation and legal action. Horrock and Crewdson, however, were prepared to confront Young with the list of allegations in order to obtain confirmation or denials, basing their story on conflict between Young's responses and what they knew to be fact.

Colleen panicked at the thought of her name being used in the confrontation and having the subsequent story released without her approval. She had understood from the reporters that nothing would be printed without her consent, but Horrock, during his visit to her apartment with John Crewdson on the afternoon of June 7th, indicated strongly that they weren't playing games. They had put a lot of time on the story and felt it was substantial enough to pursue. Crewdson was less severe with her, exhibiting more understanding of her feelings, yet urging her to consider what good might be accomplished by her story coming out.

Horrock stated that he understood Colleen had no objections to them confronting Young with the allegations. In conversations with Sol Rosen that same day, Colleen clarified that her name would not be used and agreed to the meeting between the *Times* reporters and Young. The pressure she felt, particularly from Nick Horrock, terrified Colleen. The situation was far out of her hands and she began to feel as if she had been used.

The reporters, on the other hand, were dealing with a source who was running very hot and very cold. They had devoted substantial time to the leads which Colleen had given them, obtaining information which led them to question the soundness of and justification for the salaries Congressman Young paid members of his staff. Horrock, in particular, had dealt with the Washington scene for a number of years and was sensitive to areas of Congressional hanky-panky, as well as punishable acts. His approach was direct and left Colleen little room for vacillation. (Name deleted) had begun to confirm Colleen's account of the situation in the office and added her own encounter with Young as substantiation of his relations with staff members. The tape recordings gave a clear picture of (name deleted) reaction to the February 14th sex act with Congressman Young in his office. She had been read excerpts from that recording and realized that her repulsion and feeling of guilt afterward were known to Crewdson and Horrock. Colleen told her on June 7th, that she had given the tapes to the *New York Times* and that (name deleted) was on them. From that time forward, (name deleted) was willing to support the facts of the case.

The reporters were also told that in the February 27th visit to Young's office, (name deleted) and Colleen after talking about what they might obtain in terms of evidence against Young did more than take his gun and notebooks. The other woman, in addition to taking the phone book and financial record book and putting Young's pistol in Colleen's purse, xeroxed contribution checks, letters and related material that she found in both Young's and Pendergast's desk. None of this evidence, however, is known to have surfaced.

Horrock stressed to Colleen that events were moving along without her volition. Their responsibility as reporters was to pursue the story, based on the allegations made to them and to confront Young with them so that he might have the opportunity to answer them. Even with that, Horrock assured her that they would not print a story quoting her, without her permission. There was a chance, however, that when Young heard the allegations, he would suspect Colleen of being the source and would make a statement involving her. Horrock told her that should that happen, they would call her for a statement. The next afternoon, they walked into Young's office and laid the entire presentation before him.

Colleen began to have a strong feeling of remorse for bringing the storm down about Young's head. She still wasn't certain that a story would be printed and began to hope that all the furor would die down. The realities of her situation were clear: she was facing the prospect of appearing like another Betty Ray while having to think about getting a job, finishing school and supporting her child. There was doubt that anything would be accomplished in a legal sense and, therefore, she would have made a futile effort at great expense to herself. She speculated that John Young would remain in Congress at $47,500 a year, continue whatever extracurricular activities he chose and generally ride through the experience. She, on the other hand, would have stepped forward, told her story, been ridiculed and condemned and lost what ground she had gained since leaving Young's office.

On June 9th, Colleen and (name deleted) met with the *Times'* reporters and taped a final conversation with John Young. (name deleted) was determined to support Colleen and see that Young was investigated and his abuse of female employees ended. Colleen had made phone calls the day before to see if she could gather support from other women. The only person she was certain of was (name deleted), who encouraged Colleen to go through with it.

On Friday, June 11, 1976, the *New York Times* carried the story headlined, "Congressman's Ex-Aide Links Her Salary to Sex." On June 12, 1976, the Washington *Post* carried the story. On June 15, Colleen turned her tapes over to the F.B.I. and made a full and complete statement of the entire episode. (Name deleted) refused to support Colleen after the stories appeared.

On August 19, 1976, the *New York Times* carried an article stating, "U.S. Investigation Clears Representative Young."

CONGRESSIONAL ABUSE OF POWER

A subtle abuse of power

Colleen Gardner was a young woman who found herself involved in a situation which highlights one of the hidden abuses of power on Capitol Hill. An abuse that occurs because of the irrational and fiscally irresponsible system of staff salary payments that exists in the Congress of the United States. It is a system that lends itself to abuse because of the extremes of latitude that are granted in the entire spectrum of personnel management in Congressional offices.

This is not to say that there are no Members of Congress who use their staff salary allowance judiciously. There are more who respect the trust placed in them by the public than those who abuse that trust. Nevertheless, the lack of standards of performance, aside from those imposed by the individual Member, the lack of related salary levels for particular positions and skill levels, and the lack of any job protection for staff members establishes what Washington Channel 7's David Schoumacher called in a special report, "Capitol Hill: the Last Plantation."

The attraction is salaries, with the glamor and excitement of the Hill as a bonus. There is a tremendous amount of work done in Congressional offices; survival of the Member in the next election depends on it, but there is also a percentage of positions which draw salaries disproportionate to the amount and type of work done.

In this case, Colleen Gardner quit while making $25,800 per year as a "Legislative Research Clerk (Stenographic)." Joe Pendergast explained that Colleen was actually an "Administrative Assistant for Committee Affairs;" however, the official, bi-annual Report of the Clerk of the House failed to reflect the title.

Her primary duties in the Congressman's office were with the Joint Committee on Atomic Energy, of which Young was in line to assume Chairmanship in 1977. Colleen was responsible for establishing a filing system for material relating to the Committee and its work and for processing correspondence from nuclear associated corporations. In addition, she kept the Congressman informed of Committee schedules and business.

Colleen, however, did not have the required security clearance to be a paid Staff Assistant on that committee, so her duties were, by necessity confined to unclassified paperwork. Young spoke of future requirements and grooming Colleen to assume a position heading a separate office for Joint Committee work after he became Chairman. This planning and preparation would have proven unproductive because the Joint Committee on Atomic Energy was dissolved in 1977.

Colleen was also associated with Young's Rules Committee work. Greg Nicosia, then Chief Counsel of the House Rules Committee, told reporters that all Rules Committee work that he transacted with Young's office went to Joe Pendergast. Nicosia had been on the Rules Committee for several years and had dealt with Harry McAdams before Pendergast. This is factual and relates to major Rules Committee business.

Young, when called and informed that Nicosia had denied dealing with Colleen, told him the Colleen had been gone for two months, therefore, Nicosia wouldn't have been in a position to contact her. Nicosia had been the Majority Counsel for the Committee in 1975. There was ample time for him to come in contact with Colleen Gardner if she had, in fact, dealt with matters of significance.

The then Assistant Minority Counsel, contacted the New York *Times* and stated that she did deal with Colleen Gardner on occasions. In this committee, as in some others, it is not unusual for a Minority staff member to contact the office of a Majority member with routine matters. The Assistant Minority Counsel had been on the Rules Committee for a number of years and knew Congressmen on both sides. Colleen recalled infrequent calls from her. Young, in recorded conversations with Colleen, has difficulty in explaining specifically what her duties were.

Again, her duties were of clerical importance, yet Young repeatedly stated that her salary was "rigged to the Rules Committee level." She was not on the Rules Committee payroll, however.

Colleen assisted the Congressman in preparation of some speeches, did translations from Spanish to English on correspondence, and, on occasion, corrected or assisted in other stenographic work. Her skills as a stenographer were praised by Pendergast in conversations with us and on tape by Congressman Young. Her background in statistics equipped her to do several analyses on helicopters and related subjects.

For these duties and associated types of work, Colleen Gardner was receiving $25,800 per year. In examination of Research Assistant position in the private sector, those openings which offer in excess of $20,000 per year, generally require a minimum of a Master's Degree. In this case, nevertheless Congressman Young was within the bounds of his salary allowance for Colleen Gardner.

Colleen's position was so well defined that during the first two weeks of March, just prior to Colleen leaving the office, Congressman Young, in conversations with Colleen assured her that he had explained to the rest of the staff exactly what Colleen's program was. Apparently there was some question about Colleen devoting full time to familiarizing and acclimatizing herself with the nuclear program in order to prepare for the task of heading up Young's proposed atomic energy office.

How can this be so loosely controlled when it requires a budget in excess of $100 million annually to pay for it? Congress simply makes its own laws and has legislated itself conveniently out of all the employment and Civil Service type controls and protections placed on the private sector. The Congressional Handbook prepared by the Joint Committee on Congressional Operations in November 1976 listed the following limitations and guidelines for staff allowances:

1. Total allowance for staff employment provided to each member by the Clerk of the House is $255,144 per year.

Limitations on use of allowance include the following:

a) number of staff which can be employed, a maximum of 18.

b) Total monthly payroll for the staff cannot exceed one twelfth of annual allowance.

c) Maximum salary for one staff member $39,600 per year. Minimum salary for one staff member $1,200 per year.

d) Use of allowances for staff only employed in washington D.C. or District Offices of Members.

e) Staff appointments should not be made for a period of less than a month. Exceptions permitted only by the Committee on Staff Administration.

f) Multiple employment of one staff member by two or more members is allowed. Minimum salary is $1,-200 per year for each appointment; maximum salary for one staff member is an aggregate salary of $39,600 per year.

g) Employment of relatives is not permitted by law under the staff allowance. (With the new pay hikes the new salary for the House of Representatives is $57,500. And the top employees in a Congressional office are now eligible for a maximum salary of $47,500).

The Legislative Reorganization Act of 1970 provides that a Member of Congress may establish such titles for positions within his office as he may desire to designate. He may give them functional position titles: Administrative Assistant, Legislative Assistant, Secretary, Caseworker, Receptionist, District Office Manager. He may list his entire staff as clerks and differentiate only by salaries. If the Member chooses he may number or letter his staff members. There are no job descriptions required.

With this system which lends itself to abuse, we get to the bottom line, what is the corrupting factor? (Name deleted) in a July 18 1975 conversation with Colleen Gardner said: "I'm just so disillusioned with everything. Every aspect of life, that this Mr. Young is just . . . I wasn't even surprised that I feel this way. I never thought that I could ever work for anybody that I really didn't respect. I never thought I'd be able to do it but my father was so right when he said, 'We are so corrupt money does everything for us' and that's the only reason I'm in that job Colleen so that some day I can quit that job and I can do what I want to do. I don't know what it is yet but I won't be strapped and I am strapped to that job. I wouldn't want to lose that job for anything Colleen and so in that statement I have to accept the way things are going to be."

Colleen amplifies this in a June 8 1976 conversation with Sol Rosen, discussing her feelings about John Young and the progressing investigation. "Even now I think what I lost you know, how he was willing to come over here, put my mirrors up, you know, put my paintings up on the wall for me, he bought little marble stuff for my plants and he bought me some liquor. You know since I've been gone from that office he's really gone all out to try to do something nice for me. You know and then I really feel like a goddamned heel now, you know after all this to turn around and say, you know . . ."

"Yes," Sol Rosen replied, "But the point is was he really being nice for the purpose of being nice, or did he want some other ulterior motive."

"Well, who is nice without an ulterior motive?" Colleen asked.

"I am," Sol replied.

"Oh come on Sol, you know everybody has a motive. Okay, his motive was that he wanted to have sex with me and I think most men have the same attitude. That's behind everything they do when they're with a woman. That plays a large part of what their motivations are, and all night, last night and last evening, I was beginning to feel terribly guilty because I thought, my God, a great deal is true about Mr. Young pressuring people for sex and what not. When I come right down to it though, as much as I've gone through I've really accomplished a hell of a lot. I couldn't have done it otherwise. I mean no way would I have what I have now."

"You mean moneywise?" Sol said.

"Well," Colleen asked, "What is there Sol? I've got everything else. I mean I've got my sanity. I've got my health, and the thing I was always lacking was having some furniture for me and my child. Having some clothes you know. And at least now that I have it, for me to turn around and you know, after I was totally in agreement on the whole thing. Sure I tried to get out of it. I wanted to have the salary and not have to do anything for it. But that was the price I had to pay. But for me now to turn around after I've accepted all these things, I really feel pretty damned rotten about the whole thing 'cause I mean I have no intentions of doing anything like this to that man. As angry as I've gotten, as upset and as many . . . sure he's hurt me but then I've gone along with it. I didn't have to accept that abuse. I accepted the abuse because I liked the money."

"Uh," Rosen grunted.

"Well, why else would I have Sol?"

"Look I understand the situation."

"You know," Colleen explained, "I mean I didn't have a husband. I didn't have anybody that I could depend on and I was clearing a decent enough income to afford . . . and I have the freedom, you know, that I was getting cash. You know some people buy you this or they buy you that, but it's much better when you have you know, cash where you can do what you want with it. And I thought about this and I thought this last night and all night and I just couldn't sleep."

"Uh-huh."

"You know," Colleen said, "Because I'm not innocent of all this stuff that's gone on. I mean for me to take . . . sure I was victimized because of my circumstances but at the same time I fully participated in it and I understood what the problem was. I understood that this was part of the deal, really Sol. You know it's like the kettle, what is it?"

"The pot calling the kettle black," Rosen said.

"Sure, when I first went to work there," Colleen continued, "I was under a lot of pressure and everything that happened to me was very innocent. . . . Oh I wouldn't say completely innocent you know. Everybody plays a certain role. . . . All the girls involved get involved because of the money, because they figure what the hell . . . like we discussed before."

"Right," Rosen agreed.

"I mean Christ this is not such a terrible deal. It's not the greatest deal in the world, but it's not the worst. And then of course after they get caught into it they want the money but they don't want to pay the price."

"Right," Rosen said.

"And when their turn comes, the fact that they have to pay the price, and of course everybody gets all upset."

"Yeah."

"And I think that this is one of the reasons I think that none of the girls has said anything before, because they've all condoned it."

"Yeah."

"And no one has come forward and complained because they frankly have been a great participant in it, you know and they've encouraged it."

Colleen Gardner was making $25,800 a year when she left her position with Congressman John Young. In May of 1977 Colleen Gardner, having applied for a Civil Service position at a G.S.9 level for an Accountant, Auditor or I.R.S. agent submitted the required Form 171 and statement of scholastic achievement. In these she listed her former employment responsibilities and salaries on Capitol Hill. In addition she had credit for her degree in accounting which she will receive in August. In a return notification from the Washington D.C. Civil Service Bureau, Colleen Gardner was informed that she was not qualified as a G.S.9. She has resubmitted hoping for an entry level as a G.S.7.

Were he an executive in a profit-oriented organization and paying salaries comparable with those in his Congressional office, John Young would find himself answering to the stockholders. Young, in recorded statements, indicated to Colleen Gardner that there were at least two former members of his staff one making $14,476 and one making $19,517, earning well over what they were worth.

Young prided himself on having the highest salaries on the Hill. One employee to whom he referred as "emotionally unstable" and spoke of in other derogatory terms in conversations with Colleen Gardner nevertheless was well enough qualified to earn $17,170 per year. These salaries are at the discretion of Congressman John Young, the controls on him are minimal. If there are errors in his judgment there is no recourse so long as he stays within the bounds of applicable legislation. The system lends itself to abuse. To discourage the abuses there have to be one of two alternatives: correction by the House itself prosecution by the Justice Department, or exposure by the press. As one Justice Department source stated, "Until Congress changes the law giving it complete control over salaries and jobs there is no legal recourse."

As of this writing, Sol Rosen has filed suit against Congressman John Young for defamation. Congressman John Young has filed suit against the *New York Times,* New York *Times* News Bureau, John Crewdson, Nicholas Horrock, Sol Rosen, and Colleen Gardner for libel and defamation.

Colleen Gardner is within two months of getting her degree in accounting. Good luck Colleen.

Note:

In the recent vote to save the 29% pay raise Congress allowed itself by default February 1977, one hundred eighty one members voted against the pay increase, 241 voted to keep it. Many congressmen waited until they were certain the raise would pass before casting their pay votes. The Democratic leadership had shrewdly tied the $12,900 congressional pay boost to salary increases for 20,000 upper grade Federal workers and congressional staff workers thus making it more difficult to vote for pay rollback without hurting many Federal and Hill workers in the process.

The House leadership had prevented a vote earlier in the year, realizing there would be a good chance the pay raise recommended by the Federal pay commission

201

would be rejected. Under the system adopted in 1967, the recommendation by the Commission is subsequently transmitted by the President and automatically takes effect should it fail to be vetoed by either house within 30 days. By merely avoiding a vote, Congress backed into the 29% pay raise.

The furor in the media and from constituents which followed this lack of action caused serious second thoughts by members who represented districts that reported median incomes well below the old congressional pay scales. Rather than face a revocation of the raise, the Democratic leadership forestalled a vote until the new ethics code could be written and the additional 6.3% cost of living increase scheduled for October could be rejected by both Senate and House.

Nevertheless, it will still be difficult for some members to explain this congressional generosity towards itself to those tax payers who are paying for it without the benefit of cost of living increases and benefits in the face of unemployment, inflation and the pressures of Federal, state and local taxation.

John Young's district has a per capita income of less than $6,000 with only 13% of the constituents making over $15,000 per year while 15% make less than $3,000 per year. Young employed no staff members from his district in the Washington office; thus depriving a number of capable workers of jobs with extremely high salaries. Joe Pendergast's salary was at the top of the legal limit of $47,500 per year.

Pendergast, in one of our conversations, stated that it was difficult if not impossible to get office workers from the District; thus the congressmen had to "compete" with the private sector for local office workers. This was given by Pendergast as a reason for the high salaries. The fact is that private industry and business in the Washington metropolitan area cannot compete in the salary range that Young offers.

Currently research assistants in the private business positions can expect to be making in the $17,000–$21,000 a year bracket if they have the prerequisite bachelors or masters degrees in the area of research interest and several years of experience in the field. Colleen Gardner as a legislative research clerk without benefit of degree or background which would give her specialized knowledge of either Rules Committee or Joint Committee on Atomic Energy work, was drawing $25,800 per year.

This is the twilight zone between unethical and provably illegal, a zone created by Congress for its own convenience in creating and maintaining staff to serve the constituents. There can be no basis for the common complaint of equal pay for equal work until Congress permits some regulation of its salaries, job standards and basis for hiring and firing of personnel. In February 1977 John Young transferred $25,000 from campaign contribution funds to his personal account. In March 1977 the new ethics code prohibited such transfers. Young stated in a press release at the time that he had transferred the funds "to accomplish the fiscal flexibility needed to meet increased expenses both in the office and at home." He complained that congressional salaries had not kept pace with the increased cost of living. Later, Young admitted that the funds were to be used at least in part to offset the legal fees he was incurring in his suit against the *New York Times*, Sol Rosen, Colleen Gardner, *et. al.* and in his defense against the suit filed against him by Attorney Sol Rosen.

Epilogue

On July 13, 1977, a muggy, Wednesday evening, Jane Gallier Young wrote her own tragic sequel to over a quarter century of marriage to Congressman John Young. With a single shot from a .22 caliber pistol, the 55 year old mother of five children took her life.

John Young returned to their McLean, Virginia home at approximately 7:00 P.M. and found his wife alive, but unconscious in a bedroom. She was rushed to a nearby hospital where she died at 9:15 P.M., never regaining consciousness. The Congressman's most loyal supporter and helpmate was no longer beside him.

The quiet, unassuming Mrs. Young rarely appeared in the public eye, her accomplishments, talents and potential eclipsed by the office her husband held. As required by political doctrine, a public mask obscured whatever private unrest existed . . . until this ultimate statement betrayed the depth of her despair.

In this book, the examination of John Young's relationship with Colleen Gardner, the 1976 revelations and media investigation, and the insight provided by the tape recorded conversations were focussed on the principle characters. References to Congressman Young's family were deleted from transcripts and treated as privileged information. The only exception was mention, by the Congressman himself, of a family member in conjunction with his inter-office relationships. Some material was of a sensitive and personal nature. Anyone having access to the tape recordings would be privy to information not intended for outsiders or perhaps even those mentioned in the conversations. Yet, in Washington, the private life of a legislator is regarded as fair game. Privacy is forfeit once an individual accepts elective office, part of the price of admission.

Where appropriate, defensive hypocrisy protects the public image. Whatever inner conflict may be raging, the image must be maintained if the office holder is to survive the next campaign. Public confidence in him must be sustained as a matter of course. Throughout John Young's ordeal in the press, Jane Young remained steadfast. In her only public comment during the 1976 press coverage of Colleen Gardner's allegations, she said, "John and I have had 26 fine, good years together, and we're not going to let something like this disrupt our relationship." In a telephone interview with the Corpus Christi *Caller-Times*, she laid blame for the furor to Washington, with its pressures and responsibilities, to the press, and to the women on Capitol Hill. Asked about the allegations she replied, "Her allegations don't concern me. What does concern me is that anyone would take her word and report it."

Thinking back on the conversations we had with various people during the months we worked on the story, I recall Colleen saying, how much she truly liked Jane Young. How ironic to like a person while contributing to the erosion of everything she holds dear, even if the situation is not of one's own creation. I wonder how Jane Young actually regarded Colleen? Was anger or frustration or hatred a result of the relationship that existed between the Congressman and Colleen. . . ? Or because it had been made public? We, as uninvited observers, empathized with Mrs. Young, for she was more the victim than any of the active participants. She had less opportunity to influence events as they occurred; yet bore the greatest burden in the aftermath.

"Washington has changed," Jane Young said in the *Caller-Times* interview. The Youngs had arrived for his first term in 1957, to a different political climate. "It's harsher and there are more pressures to deal with," she continued, although commenting later, "The lack of privacy and pressures on both of us have always been there."

For her, existence obviously reached a point where the future held little promise of relief. Perhaps it was too late for her to break from the old pattern and begin a new life. . . . as many ex-Washington wives have done. . . . Perhaps she had given too much of herself already. The intelligent, witty, compassionate Jane Young had been reduced to only one avenue of escape.

However it is puzzling for a number of reasons. She was a devout Catholic and chose suicide, a mortal sin. She raised her children in the church yet the police reported finding no note or message to those she left behind. Would she leave them without some explanation? From individuals who knew her, it all seems so incongruous, so unlike her. In the act itself it is rare that a woman would choose a .22 caliber pistol to end her life.

Whatever she felt, whatever her motives; her loneliness, her frustration, perhaps. . . . The bitterness against the political stage on which she found herself. . . . Perhaps the thought of further scrutiny as the pending lawsuits progressed. . . . Whatever. . . . It took from the stage the one person who lent a degree of human dignity and compassion to an otherwise sordid episode.

Congressman Otto Passman and Congressman Philip Burton—by Lew Perdue and Ken Cummins

The stories of staff abuse on Capitol Hill are not new, they have always been spoken about in hushed tones along the corridors of the Capitol and in the staff rooms of the Senate and House office buildings. The stories are timeless in their never-changing nature, appalling in their proliferation, and worst of all, they are treated so matter of factly. The dates and the names change, but the stories are the same: sexual demands, taxpayer-supported aides chauffering the member of Congress, taking care of his laundry, washing his car. The kickbacks from the staff members' pockets to help the member live a bit higher whether in direct contributions from staff salary to member, or whether the money is used to pay for things the Congressman desires; the struggle against sexual and racial discrimination in job hiring—and the problem of equal pay for equal work.

The stories are not new, but the public awareness is new, and so are attempts by both staff personnel and some members of Congress to try and correct the gross improprieties.

The public is more aware of the problems partly as the result of the Liz Ray-Wayne Hays and subsequent scandals that rocked the House of Representatives in 1976. But another contributing factor is that the double standard that Congress has set up for itself has irritated the nation.

In passing laws to prevent discrimination in job practices and hiring, the Congress was careful to exempt itself from the law. They said, "Do as I say, not as I do," and the constituents the Congress represents resent the double standard.

Each Representative and Senator has a feudal kingdom within his office. Other than administrative rules governing the issuance of pay checks and other routine areas, there are no rules governing pay or working conditions. The 17,000 employees on the Hill are not covered by any of the Civil Service regulations, and as such have no redress for their grievances.

Although both Houses of Congress have internal guidelines to protect employees from discrimination, the rules are convoluted, complex and little-known to employees.

Article 9 of the Code of Official Conduct of the U.S. House of Representatives states that "A Member, officer or employee of the House of Representatives shall not discharge, or refuse to hire any individual or otherwise discriminate against any individual with respect to compensation, terms conditions or privileges of employment because of such individual's race, color, religion, sex or national origin."

Congressman Passman and Shirley Davis.

This complacent "head in the sand" approach to solving job discrimination was shattered in July of 1974 by a 47-year-old widow with two college-age children who was fired by Louisiana Congressman Otto Passman because she was female. Shirley Davis was like a lot of women who were denied raises or promotions because they were not men. But she was luckier than most of these women because Passman was foolish enough to state his reasons for firing her in a letter.

"You are able, energetic, and a very hard worker," Passman's letter said. "Certainly you command the respect of those with whom you work; however, on account of the unusually heavy work load in my Washington office, and the diversity of the job, I concluded that it was essential that the understudy to my administrative assistant be a man. I believe you will agree with this conclusion."

Shirley Davis did not agree with the conclusion, and when she sued, she frightened the cigars out of the mouths of the crusty old men of the House.

"I realized I had been programmed to receive that letter for 20 years," Mrs. Davis told reporter Wendy Kramer. "I enjoyed my work. I was helping people I knew—my own people. I didn't know at the time that no one had ever done this [gone to court.]"

The case was originally thrown out by a judge who ruled that a Member of Congress is immune from this sort of suit. Davis appealed her suit to the Fifth Circuit Court of Appeals whose ruling threw the House into a tizzy. Representatives were outraged that they might actually have to play by the Constitution, obey the same rules they had set up for the rest of society.

The court, in its opinion, stated that "Our Constitution protects individual rights even against the mighty."

And the mighty were in an uproar. Congressional Leaders, with Speaker Thomas P. O'Neill in the vanguard, fired off an angry letter to Attorney General Griffin Bell. In the letter, co-signed by Minority Leader John Rhodes (who later withdrew his support) O'Neill said: "Having discussed this matter with a number of Members on both sides of the aisle (in both political parties) we have discovered widespread concern over the possible impact of this decision on Members of Congress . . . We therefore request and strongly urge that you exercise such authority as may be available to you under the laws of the United States to present such issues and represent such interests in an appropriate manner in this case."

O'Neill wanted to use the Justice Department to help Congressman Passman crush Mrs. Davis.

In a further letter sent to clarify his role in signing the O'Neill letter, Congressman Rhodes told Bell, "I do not believe that Members of Congress should be exempt from equal opportunity and pay provisions of Federal Law."

Bell's reply in a letter on February 11, 1977 to Rhodes stated that "I have determined that the United States has no legal basis for intervening as a party in this case." However, on February 23, 1977 the Justice Department filed a 15-page brief arguing Passman's side of the case.

The Justice Department's interference astounded people on the Hill and enraged many others. In an angry response, three members of Congress: Morris Udall of Arizona, Patricia Schroeder of Colorado and Charles Rose of North Carolina, and three Congressional staffers, filed a brief in the case on behalf of Mrs. Davis.

In addition, Congressman Don Edwards of California fired off a strongly-worded protest to Bell over his department's actions.

"The first problem with your decision, it seems to me, has to do with the separation of powers," said Edwards in a March 28, 1977 letter. Edwards is chairman of the House Subcommittee on Civil and Constitutional rights. "Congress is a separate and equal branch of the government and should act for itself when it feels that Congressional interests are at stake in private litigation. Particularly troubling with executive department intervention in the Passman case is the fact that Congress has not taken a position on the relevant questions. . . . There is rather persuasive evidence that Congress would reject the position asserted by the Justice Department in the Passman case.

"In my opinion the [court's] decision was extraordinarily comprehensive and well-reasoned, included a full discussion of those issues and there is no reason to believe that further argument will assist the court.

Edwards concluded by saying, "I do believe that the Fifth Circuit's opinion is correct and imposes no burdens upon the performance of our legislative duties. . . . For these reasons I respectfully urge you to reconsider the Department of Justice's intention to intervene in this matter."

The efforts by Shirley Davis to have justice done has turned into a full-fledged controversy on Capitol Hill with the leadership in the person of "Tip" O'Neill, split with many of those he is supposed to lead.

"I never dreamed it would become a national issue," Mrs. Davis told Kramer. "I had been by myself so long. This is a small town. When I went to court the local paper put the story on the classified page. The radio and TV wouldn't cover it. Passman was the representative here for 30 years; people try to get to me anyway they can."

"Congress has gotten too powerful, greedy and power-hungry," she told Kramer in a telephone interview. "The government is taking away our freedoms a little at a time. The members are seeing their little kingdoms being taken away, their domains crushed. They aren't servants of the people. They like the power they've gotten and don't like to give it up. He (Passman) was doing as he pleased, who was I to challenge the King?

"Well," Davis concluded, "It's time someone did it. It's not the first time it has happened, it's only the first time there has been proof."

To help all of the Shirley Davis's in Congress, nearly one-fourth of the House of Representatives has signed the House Fair Employment Practices Agreement (H.F.E.P.A.) drafted by a voluntary committee. The House Fair Employment Practices Committee was formed as a result of the agreement. It is a voluntary organization—being neither a standing nor select House Committee—composed of six members, three members of Congress and three staff members. Rose, Schreoeder and Udall are the members of Congress on the committee, Colleen O'Connor, Carla Kish and Winnie Burrell are the staff members.

They have obtained about 100 signatures from other members of Congress who have agreed not to discriminate in hiring practices, and to support attempts to set up better procedures for grievances, pay standards, job qualifications and other employment practices. The fact that three-fourths of the Congress has not signed the agreement is a national scandal.

"This standard of fair conduct parallels the things the rest of the country is held by," said Congressman Rose. "Those signing the code agree to come up to these standards."

Udall came to the heart of the controversy when he told Kramer, "There is the belief that we're a special breed, warriors on the field of battle and we can cast off anyone we like. We have exempted ourselves from a lot of laws. The belief that this is a special place makes change happen slowly.

"The fair employment practices petition is a foot in the door. People see it and think maybe it's good politics. It will take pressure from the home front for a member of Congress to sign it . . . It was a pretty good test of who really believed (in) it to sign it voluntarily . . . I'm glad she [Shirley Davis] brought the case to court."

Congressman Philip Burton and Nina Ann Coleman.

But the gains made by Shirley Davis and the House Fair Employment Practices Committee will come too late to help Mrs. Nina Ann Coleman. Mrs. Coleman, who died in January 1977, fought a long and losing battle with her former employer, Rep. Philip Burton of

California. She charged that she was forced to pay him kickbacks amounting to more than $15,000 during her tenure with him, in the form of materials, supplies and repairs necessary to be his full-time chauffeur.

In July of 1976, Perdue had written a story about Mrs. Coleman's treatment by Burton. Wanting to explore the area in more detail, Perdue called her home in January 1977. Her husband answered the phone.

"Hello, This is Lew Perdue, may I speak to Nina?"

There was silence on the other end.

"Lew, didn't you know?"

"Know what?"

"Nina died two weeks ago. I've been trying to reach you because before she died, she asked me to a gather up all her papers and give them to you in case you ever needed them."

Perdue was stunned. When he had talked to her six months before, she had known that she was dying of cancer, yet she had pressed her battle against Burton.

"She also wrote a narrative in the hospital during her last few days, until she got too weak to do it," Jim Coleman said. "She wanted you to have it."

Perdue made arrangements to pick up the material and gave his regrets to Mr. Coleman.

Phil Burton, a San Francisco Democrat, is a competitive Congressman whose love of politics had possessed him since he first came to Congress. Although a liberal, versed in the West Coast, new-left style of confrontation politics, Burton quickly allied himself with the reactionary Wayne Hays. The two of them, by mastering the arcane and little-known, turned committees and groups that others thought worthless into bases of power. Hays turned the House Administration Committee into a base to keep other members in line. Burton captured first the Democratic Study Group and then the Democratic Caucus. If Hays had not been deposed, the two might have been able to leapfrog the "stay in line" seniority system, and capture for themselves the Speaker's chair for Hays, and the Majority Leader's spot for Burton.

With Hays out of the running, Burton had to fight the battle alone, and he narrowly lost his bid for the majority leader's spot at the reorganizational meeting for the 95th Congress.

Burton's early opposition to the war in Vietnam, and his role in helping to modernize the seniority system had earned him a good reputation as a "reformer." However, his reputation as a good guy did not extend to his employees, Mrs. Coleman in particular.

Mrs. Coleman worked for Burton for two years in the early 1960's, got married and moved away from Washington. She resumed her work with his office in 1967 and worked there until January 22, 1976.

Mrs. Coleman, who said she cared for "every small whim" of Burton's for more than a decade, said in a complaint she filed with the Labor Department that her job as his appointments and personal secretary included being "a chauffeur, personal servant and hand-maiden" as well.

Her claim filed with the Labor Department alleged that she was "expected to be on call at all times and was expected to work 12-13 hours per day. . . ."

She said that in addition to driving the Congressman to his destinations, that he frequently ordered her to ferry about many of his friends including movie stars, top businessmen and union leaders.

"I had to pick him (Burton) up every morning to take him to work (he lives one mile from his office) ferry him around all day and then take him home at night," Coleman said in an interview before her death. "I remember one time when his wife made me take her downtown so she could put her fur coat in storage."

Burton's chauffeuring was underwritten by taxpayers and by Mrs. Coleman who says she was not reimbursed for her costs. When he turned over Mrs. Coleman's notes and receipts to Perdue, Jim Coleman told him that the cost of ferrying Burton around amounted to about $5,000 per year. The receipts he gave to Perdue—for gasoline, oil and repairs to her car—support that estimate.

"It was a kickback, pure and simple," Jim Coleman told Perdue. In her narrative written before her death, Mrs. Coleman repeatedly referred to the "forced kickback" she was required to make. However, to give the *other* side of the story, Burton, in two instances, has admitted that he purposely increased her salary to include pay for chauffeuring him around. Chauffeuring, he told columnist Jack Anderson "was part of her job responsibility and her pay reflected the added time." In addition, he supported this contention in an October 2, 1975 letter to the Internal Revenue Service. The letter, which was to help her justify her large deductions for chauffeuring expenses, said that she drove "at least 150 miles per week" in his service and that "one of her duties is to be available for the purpose of driving me to various functions in the Washington area as well as to and from the airports."

Anti-kickback laws prohibit the practice of deliberately inflating salaries with the expectation that the excess amounts will accrue to the benefit of the Member of Congress. In addition, Rule 3 of the Code of Official Conduct of the U.S. House reads: "A member, officer or employee of the House of Representatives shall receive no compensation, nor shall he permit any compensation to accrue to his beneficial interest, from any source, the receipt of which would occur by virtue of influence improperly exerted from his position in the Congress."

Even though Mrs. Coleman complained to the Ethics Committee, her complaint was never carried beyond the staff level. The committee took no action.

Her other taxpayer-supported duties included typing a manuscript for Burton's step-daughter. In an interview with Perdue, Coleman claimed to have spent as much as half her time some weeks doing secretarial work for Pat Tobin, who was then an assistant to Harry Bridges, President of the West Coast Longshoreman's union.

But she had other contacts with Burton's union supporters.

"A fellow named Phil Carlip of the Seafarer's Union would call up occasionally and say, 'Tell Phil I've got five big ones for him.' And every so often, he'd show up with an envelope for the Congressman."

"Now, I don't have any proof of what was in those envelopes," Coleman said, "But I was led to believe it was money."

In addition to the long hours, Coleman says she was subjected to extreme harassment and humiliation on the part of some of the Congressman's key office aides. Her contention was supported by a letter filed as an exhibit to her Labor Department case by a former intern in the office. The letter from Ms. Priscilla Ryan, dated August 9, 1976 states: "I was employed as a congressional intern in Congressman Burton's office during June and July 1975 . . . The hostility felt toward Ms. Coleman came through in an increasingly tense atmosphere over the summer . . . Several of the staff treated her particularly poorly . . . engaged in verbal banter and insults and encouraged the congressional interns not to talk to her.

"The office situation showed Ms. Coleman to be a person of tremendous strength and persistence in her job . . . in my observations (she) never initiated or provoked attacks," the letter concluded.

"It is difficult to explain the humiliation I had to endure," Mrs. Coleman says in her final narrative.

Mrs. Coleman claims that the harassment contributed to her health's decline, and several statements from physicians who treated her, back up her assertions. Yet Burton did nothing to help her, despite the fact that she was working the long hours for him.

She repeatedly asked him for help to stop the harassment.

"The first time I informed him [of the harassment]

... he laughed," she said in an attachment to her Labor Department complaint.

"The second time I informed him, he informed me that he was not a referee. The third time I informed him, January 22, 1976, he terminated my employment," her complaint concludes.

Nina Coleman and Shirley Davis are only two of the thousands of horror stories that abound on Capitol Hill. Add to them the women (and men) who have found themselves forced into a position of either losing their jobs or having sexual relations with a Congressman, and the totals are staggering. This is abuse of power at its ugliest because the people abused are not protected by the law, and they have nowhere to turn for help. They have no protection and no grievance procedures; no job standards, no pay scales and no arbiter other than the king of each office.

About the Authors of Congressional Abuse of Power Congressman John Young

NICK ROWE is a 1960 graduate of the United States Military Academy at West Point, New York. A former Green Beret, he was captured by the Viet Cong in 1963, while serving in the Mekong Delta. He escaped in December, 1968. On return to the United States he continued his military career, serving on the Army

Staff and in the Defense Intelligence Agency. He left the military in 1974, for a brief stint in politics and then returned to writing. He is the author of *Five Years to Freedom*, and *The Judas Squad*, published by Little, Brown and Company; and *The American Polo Centennial*, published by Polo Publishers. Nick's sports interests center around horses and his love of polo.

JANE ROWE was educated in New York and Paris. She was the first American woman to address the British Armed Forces Staff College and British Intelligence at Ashford, England. In 1974 she and her husband left for Texas and with Jane acting as his campaign manager, they entered their first political race. Jane's sports life centers around horses and includes playing polo and fox hunting.

3. The Energy Fiasco

Fun and games

Fast women, quick money, fancy yachts, expensive hide-a-ways, under-the-table agreements—scandalous incidents which have been commonplace for so many years in the private sector of the oil and gas industry, are following that resource into our government as Federal bureaucrats assume more and more regulatory control over U.S. energy.

Many of cases have been under investigation by the government—investigators have uncovered major scandals involving alleged bribery, sexual impropriety, and misuse of government funds and regulations. But nothing much seems to come out of these investigations and disappointed Federal investigators will tell you off-the-record that "whitewashes" occur regularly for political reasons. Thus there is at present little deterrent to misbehavior on the part of employees.

Kenneth Dupuy, former director of F.E.A.'s Atlanta Regional office was finally forced to resign his $40,000 a year Federal post. This occurred after several government investigations, and the tenaciousness of some Congressional critics and by syndicated columnists Jack Anderson, Les Whitten, Jack Cloherty and Bob Owens.

THE WASHINGTON CONNECTION

F.E.A.'s Atlanta regional office was in charge of the government's energy programs in eight southeastern States including Georgia, South and North Carolina, Florida and Alabama—all coincidentally have powerful Congressional delegations. Senators, like the powerful Strom Thurmond of South Carolina—Dupuy's power-base—were cultivated regularly.

The regional office had responsibility for the enforcement of fuel allocations and oil pricing regulations, and Dupuy established strong ties with the Congressional leaders, whom he realized could be important to his success. Because of the nature of F.E.A.'s jurisdiction, Dupuy's position carried a great deal of power and large amounts of money could be made or lost depending on decisions that he made.

For several months, Dupuy and members of his Atlanta staff were under criminal investigation for allegedly giving extra fuel allocations to gasoline distributors in return for gratuities. All have denied criminal wrongdoing, but the investigations have never been satisfactorily resolved.

Federal investigators have established, however, that Dupuy and friends often used an Atlanta apartment belonging to William Corey of U.S. Transport, Inc., of Conyers, Georgia. U.S. Transport received 21 emergency gasoline assignments out of Atlanta, the highest number granted in the area, according to a confidential F.E.A. letter to Governor George Busbee. Additionally, Federal investigation reveals that Dupuy's office raised Corey's diesel and heating oil fuel allocations substantially. Some of the emergency allocations of gasoline, diesel and heating oil were actually awarded to gas stations and truck stops that existed only on paper.

Dupuy also had more than a friendly relationship with some female members of his regional staff in Atlanta. One was Ms. X. The other young lady frequently left her infant child with babysitters so that she and Dupuy could slip away. Ms. X, who served as one of Dupuy's highly paid administrative assistants, had worked for Dupuy when he was headquartered in Washington. When Dupuy was promoted to the Atlanta job, she accompanied him. A Federal check of F.E.A. travel and per diem records revealed that she traveled regularly with Dupuy throughout the Southeastern region and even out of the region. Florida was one of their favorite states and the pair frequently had free access to accommodations in lovely resorts and tourist locations which allegedly were paid for by oil and gas interests. Trips were also made to Dupuy's Media, Texas ranch, allegedly at government expense. Charges in the Federal files include that Dupuy and his female friends charged the taxpayers for personal expenses such as cab rides, rental cars and long distance telephone calls.

F.E.A. officials became so frightened with what investigators were uncovering in their Georgia investigations that on November 18, 1976, the investigatory files were ordered to be held "without action until further notice" according to F.E.A. documents. Immediately, F.E.A.'s Atlanta Acting Director of Operations locked up the sensitive investigatory material.

However, repeated pressure by Congressman Moss of California, Dingell of Michigan, and others, continued to mount on F.E.A. National Administrator Frank Zarb, to bring the investigation to a conclusion. Finally, in late December of 1976, Zarb approved a meeting of F.E.A. investigation officials with representatives of the Justice Department's Public Integrity Section.

Justice advised F.E.A. to pursue the Atlanta investigation and let the chips fall where they may.

Although the investigation of Ken Dupuy in late 1976 was supposedly moving ahead under the direction of Robert Cook of F.E.A., a retired Army Colonel with a background in military intelligence, repeated attempts by members of Congress and the press to get an update on its progress from Energy Czar Zarb failed time and again. Finally, Dupuy, faced with a number of serious charges of federal mismanagement, left F.E.A. in the closing days of the Ford Administration and returned to Texas to work as a consultant for oil and natural gas interests.

On Wednesday, June 15, 1977, Mr. Dupuy was spotted entering Administrator Jack O'Leary's office at the Federal Energy Administration. Word quickly passed through the agency and it was generally assumed that O'Leary had summoned Dupuy for disciplinary action and final disposition of his case.

Instead, it developed that Senator James Eastland, chairman of the Senate Judiciary Committee and supposedly an uncompromising spokesman for law and order, had succeeded in urging the White House to consider Dupuy for a top energy post. Evidently, the 72 year-old curmudgeon from Mississippi had put the arm on the White House to vouch for Dupuy without thoroughly checking out the fact that the former high level energy official was under investigation for alleged bribery, sexual impropriety and misuse of federal funds.

The Carter White House also utterly failed to check out Dupuy's background before calling O'Leary and setting up the job appointment. And since the White House was evidently giving Dupuy full support, O'Leary, boss of the very agency that had been investigating Dupuy, knuckled under and scheduled the job interview.

The word about Dupuy's mid-June interview for a top staff position in the Carter energy administration quickly reached the press and in a round-about way reached the White House. Top aides in Carter's personnel office headed up by Larry King, were mortified and stunned at the slip-up and apparently Dupuy's appointment has now been stalled.

However, the very fact that Dupuy made it all the way from a position as a top level member of the Republican Administration and later an exiled federal official back to the White House for consideration for a powerful job in a Democratic Administration, shows the power of the oil and gas interests and of Senators who have the power to kill or support laws, stall or push appointments, and bog down the Government.

Consumers are doomed to lose

Price controls have never worked successfully over any long period of time. The Federal government tried to freeze prices during World War II and established the Office of Price Administration to administer its price stabilization program. A similar effort was tried during the Korean War in 1951 to 1954, and again in 1971. At the outset the general public cooperated but pressures built up for exceptions and price adjustments. Black and gray markets began to flourish in every case. Finally, the whole system of price controls became completely unmanageable and fell by its own weight into public disfavor.

Similarly, the Federal government started to control the prices of natural gas in 1954 and of crude oil and petroleum products after the OPEC countries tripled the price of crude oil in 1973. But pressures from the oil and gas industry and its representatives in Congress have caused a gradual erosion in the price ceilings. Each year the price ceilings are increased or improved for the industry. Officials in the Executive branch of government—regardless of the Administration in power—have spoken hopefully about the prospect of ending all price controls within a few years. There is an obvious financial reason why the groups that push for eliminating price controls succeed in the long run. There are heavy financial gains available to the producers when prices move upward. The windfall profits derived from sale of the same quantity of output at much high prices can be used in part to pay the lawyers, lobbyists and political leaders who worked so hard to break down the price controls. On the other hand, those consumer friends and lobbyists who struggle to maintain some reasonable restraints on oil and gas prices have no reservoir of funds or profits to support their efforts. These consumer-oriented groups and leaders must look to heaven to find their reward.

The oil and gas interests have usually been able to get their story accepted in the Senate. The House of Representatives is seemingly closer to the people and more responsive to consumer goals. Perhaps this is because Congressmen have short 2-year terms whereas the Senators enjoy a 6-year term.

The proponents of oil and natural gas deregulation start getting their decontrol bills passed in the Senate. The measures then go to the House of Representatives where, more often than not, they are amended, cut to pieces and blocked.

Another reason for the strength of the oil and gas interests in the Senate is that each oil and gas producing State has two votes, giving them a higher percentage than they have in the House where population favors the non-producing States and the consumer.

THE WASHINGTON CONNECTION

Arrogance of power

The energy industry has the most powerful and the most arrogant of all lobbies in Washington. At no time in our history has the Washington Connection been used more advantageously to further the special interests of a particular group or industry.

How can one group of businesses become such a powerful industrial empire that it out-influences all others, affecting literally every aspect of our daily lives? What are the component parts of this industry that are responsible for breeding an arrogance and wielding a power that makes it difficult if not impossible for our state and Federal governments to analyze its resources and control its objectives.

As William Greider, staff writer for the *Washington Post*, pointed out in an article in May 1977 about the U. S. oil industry staking out its role for the future, "The United States may run out of oil some day. But there will always be an Exxon. And a Mobil and a Gulf and a Texaco and so on down the list of 'majors' and 'lesser majors' who comprise the awesome corporate mass of American oil companies."

The American oil and gas industry which in 1975-1977 filled the newspapers with full-page ads of "gloom and doom" and predicted its own demise—as it does periodically—continues to work in the background to gain permanent control over all of America's energy business. The industry is doing this without hesitation, confronted by the plain fact that U. S. oil and gas reserves are being rapidly exhausted. The major oil and gas companies do not intend to give up their profitable hegemony over the world's energy industry.

If President Jimmy Carter ever cuts the government red tape holding back the expansion of nuclear power and proponents of new nuclear plant construction win the construction battles over the environmentalists and others obstructing further development, the oil companies will be in the forefront controlling the production of that nuclear power and the uranium reserves on which it depends.

If the American government ever follows through on its conversion campaign to force industrial and business shifts from oil to coal as the principal source of energy, the influence and power of the U. S. oil and gas companies will be strengthened, not weakened, because of their vast holdings of coal leases.

Scientists and lab technicians are now busily engaged in developing new technology to convert coal and shale to oil and gas in a price range that the consumer may be forced to swallow. When this happens you can be sure that the oil and gas industry will control these products from the ground to the retail marketplace.

The oil and gas industry is quietly establishing its control over the energy sources of the future—solar energy and wind and geothermal power.

While chastising Treasury Secretary Mike Blumenthal during an energy hearing on May 20, 1977, Senator Hubert Humphrey claimed that America needs to move forward post-haste on solar energy development. "The sun is free," Humphrey said, "no one can own or control it so what are we afraid of? Why don't we find ways to use it?"

Humphrey may be right that Exxon, Atlantic Richfield, Mobil and Gulf and the other handful of big oil and gas companies cannot buy the sun, but they are investing in solar technology and someday can certainly control the sale of solar home and industrial units, large-scale power-generating plants and other solar energy devices. They will then, of course, be able to set prices for solar-related materials.

Energy's interesting bed partners

The energy industry is made up of an interesting set of bed partners. These include the petroleum industry (American Petroleum Institute, Independent Petroleum Association of America, and numerous small associations); the natural gas industry (American Gas Association, Interstate Natural Gas Association of America, Natural Gas Supply Committee); the coal industry (National Coal Association); the nuclear and electric ility industry (Edison Electric Institute, National Association of Electric Companies, Atomic Industrial Forum).

The American Petroleum Institute is a lobbying organization for all of the largest oil companies in this country ranging from Exxon, the largest, to such newcomers as the Santa Fe and Union Pacific Railroads which have large oil, gas and coal interests. With an annual budget of $30 million and a staff of approximately 500 employees, A.P.I.'s responsibility is to see that laws made in Washington do not hurt their big oil clients.

In addition to these producers, transporters and marketers of energy, there are powerful allied interests that join in pressuring the Congress and the Executive Branch of the Federal Government, namely, investment bankers, insurance companies, lawyers, public relations and media consultants, suppliers of equipment, and beneficiaries of corporate largesse including universities, foundations, research institutes, and publicists. Even certain Senators, Representatives, and Governors with extensive personal financial interests in the energy areas join in the pressure game. And Federal and state regulatory commissioners and their staffs have at times become an integral part of the pressure lobby against price controls and government allocations which are in the consumers' best interests.

Government favoritism

The future of the big oil and gas companies—which has never been in doubt—is assured by the Federal government and many state governments. The big oil and gas companies have favorable leases of coal and oil and gas resources on Federal lands and beneath coastal waters. These companies also get favorable decisions from government regulatory agencies on pricing, mergers, and acquisitions. One of the biggest windfalls will be the technological benefits from the billions of dollars in taxpayers' money being spent for energy research by the Federal Government Energy Research and Development Administration.

Most of us recall various outbursts of anti-oil rhetoric and demonstrations in the Legislative, Executive and Judicial Branches of our government. Perhaps one of the most memorable occasions in recent memory was when Senator Henry Jackson, Chairman of the Senate Interior Committee, lined up the presidents of the seven largest American oil companies (nicknamed "the seven sisters") and swore them under oath "to tell the truth so help me God." The picture of the seven sisters, lined up so meekly before a powerful Congressional panel, was flashed around the world. But despite hours of intensive questioning and prodding, Jackson and his senatorial colleagues were able to gain little insight into the details and working intricacies of the powerful oil and gas industry.

In this country, after five embargoes by foreign oil exporting nations, two winters of natural gas and heating oil crises, and the worst trade deficit ever, all due to our heavy dependence on expensive foreign oil imports, our government knows little about the plans by "big oil and gas" to provide U. S. consumers with energy over the next 10, 20 or 30 years.

These corporate masters are staking out dominant positions for their companies in the energy age beyond gas and oil, an age that lies only a few years ahead.

"Trust us," the energy powers say

While the big oil and gas companies cry about huge costs for exploration and development, and small profits for their corporations at the same time they are quick to predict that energy is no problem if the "price is right." "Get rid of the government red tape and pricing regulations and within 10 to 15 years Americans can have all the energy they want" is a favorite cry of the oil and gas magnates.

Whether Americans as consumers can afford to share such optimism depends on how far we feel we can trust "big oil and big gas." If they are ideological, creative and truly dedicated to providing Americans with energy at the lowest possible cost sufficient to fuel a strong growth economy, then we can be encouraged. But if we view the oil and gas industry as a tight web of "monopolistic-minded" conspirators who have wiped out competition and hurt America's position as a leading world industrial and social power, then we need to be extremely concerned.

A look back at other monopolies

History dictates that we should always be concerned when a few big companies "own it all" and are in a position to manipulate at will supply and price and profit. We stand at that brink today with the big U. S. oil and gas interests.

Americans went through a similar experience in 1929 when a few big business leaders and Wall Street bankers controlled our economy.

Many of us are too young to have direct experience of the '29 crash. But millions of investors in the stock market at that time were average Americans who believed in the system. When the system failed and they saw their earnings lost and their economic future in jeopardy, they became disillusioned. Their confidence in the system did not return quickly and was responsible for sweeping Franklin D. Roosevelt into office in

1932. Roosevelt was a president with populist leanings, determined to create government relief and reform programs to fill the needs of people suffering from the appalling effects of the Depression.

To offset the damage created by the few shortsighted Wall Street monopolists, in his first term of office (1932-1936) Franklin D. Roosevelt rushed through Congress remedial legislation including the Public Utility Holding Company Act, the Securities and Exchange Commission Act (S.E.C.), and the Tennessee Valley Authority Act (T.V.A.). After the collapse of the Insull empire and the ignominious departure of Sam Insull to Greece to escape prosecution, faith in electric utility holding companies was non-existent. The electric utilities put on a fantastic political and public relations campaign to defeat T.V.A. and also the Public Utility Holding Company Act of 1935. But they failed in their efforts—largely due to continued widespread distrust in big business—and for a while very few lobbyists were willing to have a high profile in Washington, D. C. Associations were formed with innocent names indicating that they might be "research institutes" rather than political lobbies.

Although the oil industry was not involved per se in the 1929 market crash, due to the Teapot Dome scandal it certainly was suspect.

Teapot Dome is the name of an area near Casper, Wyoming, which was set aside by President Woodrow Wilson in 1915 as an oil reserve for the U. S. Navy. In 1921, President Warren G. Harding transferred control of the oil reserve from the Navy to the Department of the Interior. In 1922, Albert B. Fall, Secretary of the Interior, leased the Teapot Dome fields to Harry F. Sinclair *without competitive bidding*. He then leased another government-owned oil field at Elk Hills, California to Edward L. Doheny. In 1923, these transactions became the subject of a Senate investigation conducted by Senator Thomas J. Walsh. Fall resigned his Cabinet post. Great notoriety attended the investigation and subsequent criminal prosecutions. Many prominent individuals were found to be involved. Fall was convicted in 1929 of accepting bribes, and was sentenced to a year in prison and fined $100,000. Doheny was sentenced to prison for contempt of the Senate and employment of detectives to shadow members of the jury in his case. In 1927 the oil fields were restored to the government by order of the Supreme Court.

The law firm of Hogan and Hartson handled the company's defense in the Teapot Dome trial. This firm is still going strong and is one of the largest and most powerful law firms in Washington. For many years Hogan and Hartson has been retained by the giant natural gas pipeline system—El Paso Natural Gas Company. This company fought a ten-year battle in the courts in an attempt to reverse a Supreme Court decision ordering El Paso to divest itself of its Pacific Northwest system. El Paso also vainly sought relief from the Congress. The chairman and chief executive officer of El Paso, Howard Boyd, was originally a young attorney in the Hogan and Hartson law firm. We do not wish to imply there is anything improper in this, but mention it only so that the reader may understand the intricacies of the energy situation.

During World War II, the electric and oil and gas industries put their lobbying guns on the table and actually cooperated with the government in achieving an all-out effort to mobilize the country's energy resources for defense. This patriotic mobilization effort was one of the high points achieved by these and related industries. During the war emergency, executives of the electric and petroleum industries put their special interests aside and worked for the good of the country. Many—it turned out—were truly good and great Americans, some making deep personal sacrifices to promote the welfare of the U. S. A.

After the end of World War II, however, the old greed and avarice again raised its ugly head. The 1950's and 1960's were marked by unprecedented lobbying activities directed by the electric and petroleum pressure groups.

The whole subject of the energy industry and Washington politics during the 30 years from 1947 to 1977 is so amazing and intriguing that it deserves an entire book to explain and describe the actions that have been taken at the disservice of the American consumer. That book is being written now.

We want to be fair in this and all subsequent writings about "The Washington Connection and the Energy Industry."

The electric industry has been the target of intemperate attacks by a widely scattered spectrum of anti-business ideologists, environmentalists who believe in no growth of the energy industry and no growth in our nation's gross national product (G.N.P.), and poorly-informed advocates of public power. The electric industry is entitled to fight back and it is entitled to a fair hearing. Unfortunately, some electric utility leaders have—from time to time—become so infuriated by the attacks against the industry and growth, that they have stepped down to a low level in their counter attacks, thereby opening themselves up for some justified criticism.

Similarly, the oil and natural gas companies have had their natural and necessary growth to meet consumers' requirements stifled and delayed to an unconscionable degree. Environmental groups also cause problems, sometimes failing to understand the economy. We do not criticize the energy industry for fighting back against what they regard as unjust criticism. In this chapter, let us look, however, at a few real-life situations and see what happens in the real world of Washington politics.

There have been very close votes on Capitol Hill involving projects of immense and vital importance. The Senate vote on the Alaska pipeline was a tie, broken only by former Vice President Spiro T. Agnew. In 1976, Representative Krueger's natural gas deregulation bill was defeated only by the narrow margin of four votes in the House. With vast stakes running into billions of dollars, each House vote could be considered to have been of very substantial value.

The cost of the energy industry's lobbying in Washington, D. C. is terribly expensive in terms of time, materials, human and dollar costs, but it is trifling compared to the high stakes involved. These stakes are indeed so vast that it is impossible for many consumers to even understand them.

We do not have the time or space here to detail the amounts of money expended by the energy industries in gifts, campaign contributions, favors and very occasionally outright bribes that are given to Congressmen, bureaucrats, and public opinion leaders. For example, it would take an entire volume just to spell out the activities of one major oil company which distributed more than $40 million in handouts over a period of 10 years. In the heat of the effort to pass a natural gas deregulation bill in 1975/76, it was no secret in Washington that all holds were off. Everything was put into an all-out lobbying effort, everything including huge campaign contributions to cooperative senators and representatives; promises of future jobs to cooperative bureaucrats and politically appointed high-level government officials; ghost-written speeches for important public opinion formers; radio, TV and newspaper ads paid with taxpayers money; sizeable contributions to universities and foundations and similar institutions who would provide support.

Point-counterpoint ping pong

Political observers and power watchers on the banks of the Potomac delight in watching and reporting on the "muscle-flexing" between Congress and the Executive Branch. These two governmental bodies—supposedly composed of mature adults—continually test each other, probing for weak spots, each seeking to score important political and power gains over the other. Often during these battles the welfare of the country and the consumer are relegated to second place.

In 1975, the Federal Energy Administration, frustrated in its attempts to get oil and gas legislation through the Congress, reduced to writing the struggle for power between the Congress and the Executive Branch.

Titled "The Land of Us—An Energy Fable," the material was allegedly written personally by Robert E. Nipp, F.E.A.'s then director of Public Affairs as an October 1975 speech for Energy chief Frank G. Zarb. Audiences in Houston and Los Angeles wholeheartedly applauded the speech. Zarb embellished the contents of the speech somewhat and it became so popular that it was published as a booklet under his byline and thousands of copies were distributed around the country.

"The Land of Us" describes a mythical country where a gallant leader (The President) is trying to save his country (U.S.A.) from the bad influence of foreign producers (Oil Producing Exporting Countries—OPEC) of scarce resources (oil and gas) but is frustrated by a lazy, foot-dragging, bungling body of politicians (the Congress) whose only interest lies in getting themselves re-elected.

The mythical "Land of Us" fable prepared by F.E.A. relates incident after incident in which a gallant leader has proposed imaginative and creative resource development and conservation programs to make his country self-sufficient and immune from foreign embargoes, only to be frustrated by the inept and bungling political body.

Energy Czar Zarb delivered the speech some 18 to 20 times around the country in an effort by the Executive Branch to get public support for President Ford's energy proposals. The general public reacted favorably, finding the story both humorous and well timed. Several major newspapers took up the theme, editorializing at length on the "do-nothing" Congress.

Vice President Nelson A. Rockefeller, after reading the speech while on a flight with Zarb from Washington to Denver, remarked that copies should go to every taxpayer so that they can get a picture of how "bad things are in the Congress."

As can be imagined, however, members of Congress took great exception to the speech, and Nipp and Zarb came under heavy fire. Following a *Wall Street Journal* article, Nipp's Public Affairs staff was sharply reduced through cutbacks in Congressional appropriations and Zarb was called before a Congressional hearing chaired by Congressman John Dingell of Michigan to explain the intent of the speech and to be openly chastised.

"The Land of Us" incident is only a tiny drop in the Potomac political waters but it illustrates the disharmony and "devil's advocate" roles that the Congress and Executive Branch play with each other, regardless of which Administration is in power.

Since the winter of 1972-73, when shortages of gas and oil first began to 'nip' the toes of Washington politicians, top energy officials in the Executive Branch have been constantly called upon to testify before Congressional Committees and Subcommittees. Energy administrators during the Nixon-Ford era spent a very large percentage of their time on Capitol Hill—both in individual meetings with senators and congressmen and in testifying before Congressional hearings—trying to plead the cause of the energy shortage and the Administration's plans for coping with it. Much of their time was wasted in commenting on legislative proposals that various Congressmen had dreamed up for home consumption back in their districts and in answering questions about the Executive Branch's alleged failure to carry out this or that Congressional mandate. Energy policy and politics became inextricably intertwined.

In 1973-74 when William E. Simon was serving as the Nation's first strong "energy czar", he was called to testify before 68 different Congressional Committees and Subcommittees, all professing to have an interest in energy. Sometimes Simon would appear before three hearings in one day—a morning, afternoon and evening session.

Later on, while serving as Secretary of the Treasury, Simon was asked by Irving R. Levine, NBC-TV newsman, how he could put up with so much Congressional harassment which by then had placed Simon on Capitol Hill several hundred times, encompassing, in addition, several thousands of hours spent in preparing testimony. Simon good-naturedly replied that he felt it in the public interest to try to inform the Congress as best as possible on problems facing the nation but admitted that he found the spider web of Congressional Committees and Subcommittees with overlapping duties and mandates extremely confusing and wasteful to the nation.

On only a few occasions did Simon's good-nature play out in dealing with Capitol Hill politicians playing the energy game for hometown advantage. One occasion involved Congressman John Dingell of Michigan, Chairman of the Energy and Power Subcommittee of the powerful House Interstate and Foreign Commerce Committee.

Congressman Dingell issued a press statement to newsmen that he was having trouble getting Energy Chief William Simon to Capitol Hill to testify on the energy problem and that if Simon didn't appear, he (Dingell) was going to subpeona Simon and order him to show. Simon when shown a wire story about Dingell's comments, immediately phoned Dingell, angrily informing him that he (Simon) had never once turned down an invitation to testify before the

Congress regardless of how insignificant the request may have seemed or the extensive burden of his personal workload due to the energy crisis and that Dingell's comments were strictly for home consumption back in Michigan.

Simon subsequently appeared before the Subcommittee and introduced his testimony by again reviewing his long-suffering record of appearances on Capitol Hill and chastised Dingell publicly for his blatant P.R. tactics.

On another occasion, Simon had been invited by Martin Agronsky, nationally-known TV commentator, to appear in Shirlington, Virginia, a few miles outside Washington, for an early-evening 30-minute taping for distribution to educational television stations across the country. This request came at the height of the Arab oil embargo during the winter of 1973-74 and Simon accepted the invitation, believing that he could be of some value to the nation by assuring the general public that everything possible was being done to solve the heating-oil shortages and long gasoline line problems that were plaguing the general public.

Immediately prior to the taping, Simon received an urgent call from President Nixon to appear before a late evening session of the Senate Energy and Natural Resources Committee chaired by Senator Henry Jackson of Washington State. Nixon said that Simon had been requested to appear by several influential members who were deeply divided over proposed legislation involving the strip mining of coal.

A WETA-TV staff member offered to drive Simon

through the ice and snow to the Capitol, some 10 miles away and Simon took off, still not having eaten since a quick sandwich early that day. Several times on the trip, the Volkswagen spun out in the snow and ice, but finally the trip was completed and Simon appeared at the hearing room door on the fifth floor of the Capitol, just under the central dome.

At the request of Jennings Randolph, a highly-regarded senior Senator from West Virginia, Simon stayed on until midnight, answering questions about the Administration's position on various strip mining proposals, and finally sending an aide out for hamburgers and cokes at a nearby McDonald's on Pennsylvania Avenue.

After the 1973-74 Arab oil embargo, the "point-counterpoint ping pong" game on energy between the Legislative and Executive Branches began in earnest. The Treasury Department and later the Federal Energy Administration prepared a standby program for gasoline rationing. It was not put into effect. Both Congress and the Ford Administration knew that the public would be resentful and that no one could become a political hero by imposing gasoline rationing on the car-loving American public.

Only John C. Sawhill, who succeeded Simon as Administrator of the Federal Energy Administration, advocated any cutback in gasoline consumption through rationing and taxes and he was consequently "axed" on the White House meat block.

So the ping pong ball was pitched back and forth into the Congressional court and back into the

President's court. Everyone was in favor of sacrifice and putting on a "hair shirt" but no one cared for the curse that would follow the politician or government official who took the responsibility to mandate the sacrifice.

The chief reason for political timidity in coping with the energy crisis is that energy touches every facet in the daily life of all Americans. The cost and availability of energy control our use of cars, airplanes, pleasure boats, ships, domestic cooking and heating and air conditioning. Prolonged interruption of electricity or oil and gas supplies would create havoc in our cities, disrupt industrial production and damage agricultural activities ranging from fertilizers to the harvesting and storage of crops.

Opposing forces for the regulation and deregulation of oil and gas prices continue to jockey back and forth. For example, during May 1977, in testimony before the House Energy and Power Subcommittee, Presidential Assistant Schlesinger told the panel that complete deregulation of natural gas would shift an additional $20 billion from consumers to producers, thus the Carter Administration was against it. But at the same hearing, Federal Power Commission Chairman Dunham pointed out that the "roll-over" provision of HR 6831, the President's bill, which would allow expiring contracts for interstate gas to be raised from $1.45 per thousand cubic feet to $1.75, would give gas producers an additional $19 billion through the end of 1998.

At the same time, the oil and gas producers association, IPAA, was sharply criticizing the Carter Administration's energy proposals on the grounds that they expanded Federal controls over the price of intra-state natural gas, (the gas which moves from origin to use within a state) abandoned the free market concept, and put primary emphasis on reduction in demand of oil and natural gas, without corresponding incentives to increase supply of these fuels.

And so the Congressional and Executive Branch game goes on and on, the long-suffering American consumers are little closer to seeing their nation get a sound long-range energy policy.

Strange bedfellows in the conservation bed

In his address on energy to the joint session of Congress on April 20, 1977, President Jimmy Carter said that our first goal is conservation. "It is the cheapest, most practical way to meet our energy needs and to reduce our growing dependence on foreign supplies of oil." Then Carter goes on to call for higher energy prices.

Few Americans may question such an eloquent goal. We certainly do have a problem since we have the highest energy use per capita of any country in the world. We have enjoyed cheap energy because of new discoveries over the years and improvements in energy technology.

We would like to point out that the energy lobby goes all the way for conservation. Even Saudi Arabia, the U. S.'s primary source of imported oil, is telling the people and government of the U. S. that we must stop wasting energy.

Petroleum Minister Yamani, Saudi Arabia's chief voice on energy matters, is reportedly extremely disturbed over the Americans' wasteful energy ways. He was quoted recently as saying that Saudi Arabia was not going to increase the pumping and export of its finite oil reserves to the U. S. just so American teenagers could race up and down city streets in their big cars.

The oil companies have jumped on the conservation ethic with great relish in recent years, finding it still another weapon to support decontrol and deregulation of oil and gas prices. They argue forcefully that higher prices will accomplish both the objectives of increasing energy reserves by making it more profitable to explore and drill for oil and gas, and eliminating wasteful use as these commodities become more expensive.

Whenever possible the energy lobby ties in their conservation slogans and campaigns with statements of political, social and business leaders highly regarded by the consumer and publicly concerned about our fast disappearing oil and gas supplies. Meantime, of course, the lobby continues to be silent about the great increase in profits that will accrue to their benefit if oil and natural gas prices are allowed to reach the so-called "market clearing" level.

A prime example of the relationship within the energy lobby between those profiting directly or indirectly as a result of higher energy prices, and how this lobby uses every favorable opportunity to ride the "energy conservation ethic" may be illustrated by a May 18, 1977 press release issued in Washington, D. C. by the National Association of Manufacturers.

After expounding on the virtues of its Chairman, R. Heath Larry, N.A.M.'s press release gets in a good right jab to the consumer's jaw with this comment: "Mr. Larry has long championed an energy program featuring energy conservation but with heavy emphasis upon programs to stimulate development of new energy supplies through reduced regulation, well-balanced environmental programs and encouragement of market forces."

What Mr. Larry is saying, of course, is never mind that "big gas and big oil" have a complete monopoly over most of our energy supplies but throw out those bothersome governmental pricing and environmental regulations and let prices go where they may to force the consumer to cut energy use regardless of the impact on our society.

Does this posture represent a deep appreciation for human values or a fair-minded idea on how our great American system was built? Does this position by N.A.M. and the energy lobby demonstrate a "sympathetic appreciation for the American society's extensive social and economic problems? Are higher prices for energy the only answer?"

Yes, what strange bedfellows we find here—Richard Nixon, Jerry Ford, Jimmy Carter, Henry Kissinger, Energy Presidential Adviser James Schlesinger, Saudi Arabian Petroleum Minister Yamani, the National Association of Manufacturers, Mobil Oil, Atlantic Richfield. Yes, even Exxon can be found on this bandwagon—all embracing the concept of energy conservation to be achieved primarily by inflating energy prices.

Where do Federal Commissioners go?

Following the Wall Street Crash in 1929, someone wrote a book entitled "Where Are the Customers' Yachts?" Today without any particular logical relationship to the aforesaid book title, one might well ask "Where Do Federal Regulators and Commissioners Go?" The answer seems to be that they go to large law firms engaged in legal practice on behalf of corporations that are seeking certificates of convenience and necessity, or rate increases from the same commissions that were headed by the departing commissioners. This is particularly true in energy. Washington law firms are staffed by attorneys representing corporations in appearances before the Federal Power Commission, the

Federal Communications Commission, the Interstate Commerce Commission, the Securities and Exchange Commission, the Civil Aeronautics Board, and the Nuclear Regulatory Commission (formerly the Atomic Energy Commission). Many if not most of these attorneys were formerly commissioners or staff members of the Federal regulatory commissions referred to. There is, of course, nothing illegal or improper about this practice. We merely question whether it is in the *best* interests of the consumer.

Take for example the Federal Power Commission which has as one of its responsibilities the regulation of natural gas prices to protect consumers: The last three former F.P.C. Chairmen are now in Washington in the practice of law. These F.P.C. Chairmen are Joseph C. Swidler, Lee C. White, and John N. Nassikas.

In previous years, one F.P.C. Commissioner, Harrington Wimberly, became the Washington representative of Pacific Northwest Pipeline Corporation. Another former Commissioner, Nelson Lee Smith, after leaving F.P.C., was retained by Columbia Gas System. William R. Connole, after serving one term as a Commissioner, now heads up a large law firm representing numerous gas distribution and pipeline companies having business before F.P.C. Again, we suggest no impropriety and only question the desirability of such occurrences.

Various attorneys employed in the Legal Division of the F.P.C. either as General Counsel or as Deputy or Assistant General Counsel started law firms of their own or joined existing Washington law firms and maintained a prosperous practice assisting major inter-state pipelines and electric companies in obtaining cer-tificates or licenses from the F.P.C. or rate increases as the case may be.

It might be unfair to suggest that attorneys in private practice who previously worked for the Federal Power Commission, promoted regulation for regulation's sake. Nevertheless, many of them expressed concern when it appeared that Congress might simplify the regulatory process or actually eliminate Federal Power Commis-sion price controls over producers' sales of gas to inter-state pipelines. Time and again Senator Warren G. Magnuson, Chairman of the Senate Commerce Com-mittee, would interrogate nominees to the F.P.C. about their ideas as to how to simplify regulatory procedures and speed up the process of Commission regulation and decision-making. Again and again these nominees would promise to use their best efforts to accomplish the desired expeditious results. But the F.P.C. regula-tory process remained stable and unchanged. In fairness to the F.P.C., it should be said that much of the delay in the regulatory process is caused not by the Commission or its staff but by outside interveners, ap-plicants, adversaries, environmentalists and others who make it their business to oppose almost each and every proposed new power plant installation, pipeline, syn-thetic natural gas plant or liquefied natural gas terminal facility. F.P.C. commissioners have remained in office mostly for a full term of five years or more and many F.P.C. legal and technical staff members have devoted more than five years in their public service careers before resigning to accept more rewarding jobs in the private sector.

What about the revolving door at the Federal Energy Administration?

The same cannot be said for the more recent breed of "career servants" employed during the Nixon and Ford Administrations by the Federal Energy Administration. A large number of F.E.A. lawyers, executives, economists and other specialists worked for the F.E.A. for no more than one or two years before resigning to go into business as lawyers or consultants. In some cases, the same individuals who had concocted extremely complex and difficult to understand allocation and price regulations were retained by large corporations to explain what the regulations meant. This is not of course illegal, but again we do question whether it is desirable.

Among the more successful and nationally known figures who have spent relatively short terms in public service with the F.E.A., we may mention the following: Duke Ligon, former Assistant Administrator, Energy Resource Development, and David G. Wilson, former Deputy General Counsel, now together in legal practice with oil and gas clients; Frank G. Zarb, former

F.E.A. Administrator and beneficiary of secret CIA energy briefings, now engaged in energy matters with the New York financial house of Shearson-Hayden and Stone; John C. Sawhill, former F.E.A. Administrator, now President of New York University and the author of many newspaper columns and speeches on energy; John Vernon, former Deputy Assistant Administrator for Regulatory Programs, now employed by the Kuwait Government oil monopoly; Charles Owens, author of F.E.A.'s complicated price control regulations, now head of a new large economic consulting firm with offices in several major cities and whose main business is to explain the regulations to companies who are subject to them; John A. Hill, former Deputy Administrator, now with F. Eberstadt & Co., a New York investment banking outfit; Eric R. Zausner, former Deputy Administrator, now with Booz-Allen and Hamilton, Inc., a New York based management consultant firm with extensive interests in energy; Dr. Dan Rathbun, an oil and gas reserves expert now on the payroll of the American Petroleum Institute; Mel Conant, former Exxon official, later Assistant Administrator for F.E.A.'s Office of International Affairs and now a consultant; and Donald B. Craven, former energy resource and development expert, now with a prestigious Washington law firm with extensive energy interests. No, there is nothing improper or illegal about this, but again, we ask, is it desirable?

And the revolving door between other government officials and the energy industry

Bill Van Ness, a protégé of Senator Jackson, spent several years as Chief Counsel to the Senate Interior and Insular Affairs Committee, and as Counsel to the Senate Subcommittee on Energy, established pursuant to Senate Resolution 45. During the same period of time, 1974-1976, Charles Curtis was Staff Counsel to the important House Interstate and Foreign Commerce Committee, chaired by Congressman Staggers of West Virginia. In their positions, Van Ness and Curtis sat in on nearly every energy hearing conducted by Senator Jackson and Congressman Staggers, and were regarded by energy officials in the Executive Branch and the Washington energy lobby as prime conduits to these important Congressional energy officials.

In December 1976, Van Ness and Curtis resigned from their positions and formed the law firm of Van Ness, Curtis, Feldman & Sutcliffe. This firm acquired as clients Pacific Gas and Electric Company, a giant electric and gas utility in California, and Northern Tier Pipeline, a project designed to bring Alaskan crude oil to the refineries along the Northern Tier whose supply from Canada has been threatened. This Northern Tier Pipeline had been vigorously endorsed by Vice

President Mondale when he was in the Senate and also by Senator Hubert Humphrey.

Former Vice President Spiro T. Agnew snagged a good account when he picked up a retainer from the Algerian Government whose wholly-owned subsidiary is the sole producer and exporter of Algerian oil and natural gas (L.N.G.). Agnew also is employed by the wealthy Greek merchant prince John Latsis, of Athens, Greece, in an advisory capacity. Latsis has landed a super contract involving a construction program of more than $1 billion to improve and expand the Port of Jedda, the major commercial port of Saudi Arabia.

Senator J. W. Fulbright who for years headed the prestigious Senate Foreign Relations Committee has been hired by the Government of Kuwait. Kuwait depends on oil exports for much of its foreign currency.

It must be emphasized *strongly* that no wrongdoing is alleged. There is nothing illegal or mysterious involved, but we do question the desirability of intensive lobbying.

Washington Department of the Interior connections of Big Oil

The Department of the Interior has been very close to the U. S. petroleum industry for the past thirty years. There was every reason for big oil to keep close surveillance over the appointment of the Secretary of the Interior, the Under Secretary, several Assistant Secretaries and Bureau Directors. Interior controls the leasing of Federal lands, both onshore and offshore, for oil and gas drilling and development. The Bureau of Mines and the United States Geological Survey are housed within the Interior Department. During war emergencies—World War II and the Korean War—the Interior Secretary headed the mobilization of the petroleum industry. Dozens of industry advisory committees were set up within the Petroleum Administration for War (P.A.W.) in World War II and the Petroleum Administration for Defense (Korean War). While P.A.W. and P.A.D. appeared to be governmental organizations clothed with authority to allocate and ration scarce supplies of crude oil and petroleum products, the staffs and policy direction were entirely controlled by the major oil companies. Hundreds of oil company executives would serve a six-month or a one-year tour of duty with these Federal petroleum organizations. They were loaned to the government as dollar-a-year men, or as "without official compensation (W.O.C.)" men. They continued to receive their salaries from their companies. The camaraderie built up between the temporary oil executive loaned to the government and the permanent government servants permitted many off-the-record or even *ex parte* meetings and communications in subsequent years.

The major oil companies wanted a more enduring frame-work for giving their advice to government policy officials. They were not content to be called in as advisers only during periods of war emergency. So they set about convincing the Secretary of the Interior that he should have a permanent National Petroleum Council to advise him on national oil policy matters. This was done and the N.P.C. has been in existence for more than 25 years. The operation is very smooth. Members of the Council are officially named by the Secretary of the Interior. But most of the years, the industry itself, through its trade association, A.P.I., and other groups would draw up and hand to the Secretary a list of names that the oil industry recommended. Similarly, the Secretary requests the Council to make studies and report back to him on vital oil industry issues such as reserves, productivity, strategic storage program, price and tax incentives, etc. These requests coming to the Council from the Secretary usually originate within the industry itself. The big oil companies could do almost as well using their own trade associations, but the tie-in with the Secretary of the Interior has several immense advantages:

(1) It serves to immunize the participating oil companies from anti-trust suits.

(2) There is added prestige and credibility to the report when issued by N.P.C. A similar report issued by API might be suspect!

As the Federal Energy Administration emerged and became the center of government energy policy and regulation, the Department of the Interior began to lose its importance to the oil companies. They quickly focused their attention on the new energy agency. Again the oil companies and their near-relatives, the petrochemical industry, began to make personnel available for short or lengthy service in the F.E.A. Industry advisory committees proliferated. Oil company executives, experts, and attorneys served on and controlled these industry advisory committees. Task forces were appointed to develop statistical and technical data to be used for policy recommendations. Practically all of these task forces were staffed with oil industry people.

It is small wonder that so many bureaucrats who formerly helped develop energy policy for the Interior, Treasury or Defense Departments or the F.E.A. have now found lucrative positions in the oil and petrochemical industries.

Problem of recruiting competent people for top policy jobs in Federal establishments

We have reported a number of characteristic examples of apparent conflict of interest relating to Federal officials in a position to affect policy decisions with respect to energy prices, allocations, supply and conservation. The problem of conflict of interest has been studied by numerous Congressional committees and students of regulatory affairs over the last 50 years. No simple solutions have been found.

With regard to ownership of securities or property, it has been proposed that these investments be placed in a so-called "blind trust." The theory seems to be that if the Cabinet Officer or Commissioner does not know from day to day what changes have been made in his investments, he will not be improperly influenced by the fact that at one time he owned securities or property in this or that industry. However, this seems to us to be pretty much of a sham procedure done for the purpose of making the general public believe that the highly placed Federal official has suddenly forgotten about his previous investments and/or employment situation. It seems to us that anyone from an electric utility, large oil, gas, steel, automotive company, or the like would be unable to forget the loyalties and enthusiasms that he had for the particular previous employment and industrial sector in which he had invested his life savings or a substantial portion of them. To us, the blind trust is more or less a snare and delusion. (Suppose a highly positioned Federal official had at one time been in the peanut business and placed his properties in a blind trust under the control of a relative or trusted friend or attorney? Would it be possible for such a Federal official to forget all about his previous interest in such peanut business?)

We are reminded of a story that hit the newspapers a few years back about the White House energy official, Peter Flanigan, whose financial interest in an oil tanker, the *Sansinena*, had been placed in a blind trust managed by his father for the benefit of Peter's children. The tanker which had been constructed in Newport News Yards in Virginia was a "runaway" tanker operating under a Liberian flag with a foreign crew.

After being questioned about whether he had used his influence in the White House to obtain from the Under Secretary of the Treasury an exemption from the Jones Act for the *Sansinena*, Peter Flanigan indicated that he had done nothing of the sort and suggested the fact that the blind trust should be taken into account, as if to say he could care less whether the *Sansinena* did or did not get the exemption from the Jones Act which was being assiduously sought by Union Oil Company of California, which company had the *Sansinena* under long-term charter.

Recruitment of top policy officials for service in the Federal Government is complicated by these factors. If Congress or the President issues regulations barring top corporate executives and professionally trained individuals from accepting either short-term or long-term employment in the Federal Government, the Federal Government will be the loser in that it will inevitably sacrifice the opportunity of obtaining high caliber, experienced personnel. The Federal Government will then be reduced to dependence on career public servants and professionals taken from universities, foundations and various non-profit institutions. Similarly, if Congress or the President issues regulations making it impossible for government officials to obtain employment in industry, finance or the private sector except after a cooling-off period of some two to five years, such a handicap for existing government personnel would act as a deterrent, keeping many younger people from seeking to apply for government service unless they had decided to make government service a lifetime career. In either case, obstructions standing in the way of recruitment of talented individuals who have made their way successfully in business or industry or obstructions preventing present governmental officials from obtaining good jobs in the private sector will tend to reduce the quality of government personnel. The type of individual who plays it safe and refuses to move from one job to another, from industry to government, or from government to industry, is typically not a person of imagination, resourcefulness or personal courage. Some way must be found to permit the revolving door to operate without leading to corruption, nepotism, or disservice to the public interest. In wartime as, for example, in World War II, the nation was fortunate in being able to recruit as dollar-a-year men top leaders from many large industrial corporations such as Charles E. Wilson from General Electric, Donald Nelson from Sears Roebuck, General Knudsen from General Motors, Harold Boeschenstein from Owens-Corning Fiberglas, William Batt from S.K.F. Industries, and so on. These individuals served the War Production Board unselfishly and without any attempt to use their governmental positions to advance the interests of the corporations from which they had come. At the same time, all of the actions of the War Production Board and similar war agencies were under the close surveillance of the well-known Truman Committee, a Senate investigating committee of which the Chairman was Senator Harry S. Truman of Missouri. Perhaps the solution today during the energy shortage which President Carter has characterized as similar to a wartime crisis would be to have similar top-level executives drawn into government from business and industry to serve on a "without official compensation" basis and at the same time have a Congressional surveillance or policing committee ever watchful to see to it that no "hanky-panky" takes place.

The unique association of regulatory officials

The National Association of Regulatory Utility Commissioners (NARUC) provides a respectable forum for the electric and gas utilities to express their views to the regulators. Regional meetings are held throughout the year and there is one annual meeting of the entire membership. This annual meeting is always held in a popular convention city such as Las Vegas, San Francisco, Miami Beach, Chicago or New York. Utility executives and their wives attend these meetings as well as utility commissioners, regulatory staff personnel and their wives. NARUC has numerous committees whose membership and actions are controlled by the Executive Committee. The principal officers are from state regulatory commissions but the federal commissions are also members—they include F.P.C., S.E.C., D.O.T., I.C.C., F.C.C., etc. Energy policy and energy supply problems are scrutinized by NARUC ad hoc committees. The whole NARUC affords the utilities a splendid opportunity to get their *"inputs"* into the NARUC deliberations, resolutions and recommendations for state and Federal legislative programs. Many state and Federal commissioners enjoy total relaxation in the free atmosphere of the NARUC convention city.

During the long campaign to win political support for natural gas deregulation, the oil companies, working through natural gas pipeline and distribution companies, were highly successful in getting through to the important members of NARUC. The average age of NARUC commissioners is 50 years; the average term of service is 4 years. Many state commissioners are employed by the utilities after they leave public service. Others join law firms that handle regulatory matters.

Energy industry lobbyists regale the regulatory officials with arguments in favor of increased utility company profits to finance construction of new plants. They are helped in this cause by friendly bankers from Wall Street who are happy to address NARUC meetings. Their favorite subjects for discussion are (1) the need for higher utility rates of return, and (2) the desirability of removal of federal price controls over oil and gas.

Private clubs and the oil lobby

Among the private clubs most used by the oil lobby are the University Club, Metropolitan, Army and Navy, and Cosmos Club.

Some years ago, the story went the rounds in Washington that the Metropolitan Club had the wealth, the Cosmos Club had the "brains" and the Army and Navy had neither one nor the other. This, of course, was an untrue canard!

One of the special reasons for using private club facilities is protection from news reporters and groups such as Common Cause, A.F.L.-C.I.O., or Consumers Federation of America. Trysts can be held at the Metropolitan Club under high ceilings and in a dignified atmosphere. An unwritten club rule forbids disclosure to the outside world and especially the media as to who was seen dining with whom. Bureaucrats whose early years were spent in government cafeterias are flattered and sometimes overwhelmed by the grandeur of the Metropolitan Club. Some of them, especially members of minority groups, are titillated by being invited to lunch at a club which would not take them in as members, unless they were very wealthy or distinguished.

Another club favorite of the lobbyists is the Carlton Club which consists of a couple of rooms upstairs in the Sheraton-Carlton Hotel. This is a very small, discreet luncheon club. Membership includes steel, aluminum, glass, automotive and oil industry lobbyists. Exchanges of political gossip take place over card games, cocktails and lunch.

The Burning Tree Country Club became celebrated during the years when Eisenhower was President. Lobbyists who were members could brag that they had played golf with "Ike" whether or not this was literally true.

The Metropolitan Club is the elite lobbyist club in Washington, D.C. Members have included Walter Lippman, Arthur Krock, Dean Acheson, James Michener, Herman Wouk, Frank Ikard of the A.P.I. and Jim Pitkin of Texaco. The Metropolitan Club has a club rule that no business is to be discussed in the club dining room or cocktail lounge. Letters are sent to members cautioning them on this point of club etiquette. One wonders how the I.R.S. permits corporations to pay for their executives' initiation fees, annual dues and lunch expenses, if no business is conducted at this club!

The insolvency that has threatened the survival of many D.C. city clubs has been especially harmful to the National Press Club. As a result there have been repeated exhortations to members to enlist their aid in expanding the club membership. Admissions rules have been relaxed. Today there are more lobbyist associate members than there are bona fide members of the press.

The N.P.C. is a highly important forum for national

news and public opinion formation. Chiefs of state appear at luncheons, give a prepared talk and submit to questions from the Press Corps. The chiefs of state of Saudi Arabia, Iran, Jordan, Egypt and Israel have been at N.P.C. luncheons. So also have been major political candidates for the Presidency, and new and old members of the Cabinet. Top energy legislators such as Henry (Scoop) Jackson have been frequent guest speakers at N.P.C. luncheons.

Strong control of OPEC countries and American big oil and gas interests over the consumers' energy policy

During the 15 to 20 years prior to 1973, oil and gas prices increased only minimally in the U. S. And during this same time, production of oil and gas from American wells continued to grow, finally peaking in 1970. Much of the exploration and development of gas and oil during this period was carried out by independent "wildcatters" and production more or less kept up with demand.

As U. S. production peaked in 1970, however, and the independent drillers began disappearing from the American scene, demand in this country continued to grow as the Americans' appetite for more cars, air conditioners, and other oil and gas hungry devices made life here the most luxurious in the world. This peaking

271

of U. S. production coupled with continued growth in demand began placing an upward pressure on both domestically produced oil and foreign imports by 1971, a pressure kept in check only by the general price controls imposed across the board on most consumer products by President Nixon at that time.

Phase I price controls were imposed on August 15, 1971, when guidelines for the petroleum industry were essentially the same as those for the economy in general.

The quadrupling of oil prices by the Arabs in 1973-74, coupled with the quick action by American "big oil and gas" interests to take advantage of the situation, and our growing dependence on foreign oil had an immediate and important contracting effect on the U. S. economy. While it is true that we were experiencing prevailing effects of inflation at that time, the oil price increases of 1973-74 severely exacerbated the situation.

Studies by the Departments of Commerce, Labor and Treasury reveal that almost half of the nearly seven percent fall in U. S. output between 1973 and 1975 was directly attributable to oil price increases.

Once the "big lobby" moved the price of oil from $3.50 a barrel to $12-$14 a barrel, the lobby turned its attention to jacking up the price of natural gas.

THE ENERGY FIASCO

Why should OPEC countries and the "big lobby" set the price of natural gas in American homes?

All during 1976 and the early months of 1977, the oil and gas industry in the United States mounted a nationwide "educational" campaign to persuade the Federal energy officials that natural gas should be priced on the basis of parity with oil prices. Since 6,000 cubic feet of gas (6Mcf) is the heat equivalent of one barrel of oil, their argument continues to be that natural gas should be priced at one-sixth of the world price of oil as set by the OPEC monopoly.

In early 1975, the price for new gas that had been established by FPC after extensive public hearings was 52 cents per Mcf. The OPEC world price of oil was about $12 per barrel or equivalent to $2.00 per Mcf of gas. This "inequality" claimed by the "big lobby" set the stage for a block-buster price increase campaign by the gas producers. Even before the winter of 1976-1977, the Federal Power Commission which is supposed to look after consumers' interests had been persuaded into raising the price of "new" gas to $1.42 per Mcf, an increase of almost 300 percent. Now, in April 1977, President Carter declares in his message to Congress and the American people that the price of new natural gas should be $1.75 per Mcf. Note that old gas becomes "new" gas after existing contracts expire. And the "big lobby" led by such political figures as Senator J. Bennett Johnston, Jr. of Louisiana are calling for no Federal pricing regulations and a "market-clearing" price of $2.25 per Mcf. Each one-cent increase in the price of natural gas costs the American public about $200 million per year more in fuel bills. Neither historical costs nor current cost of replacement can justify a price of $1.75 per Mcf. President Carter has abandoned the traditional American idea of protecting consumers from exploitation and allowed the OPEC countries to set the price of natural gas going into American homes. The natural gas curtailments of the winter of 1976-77 have been cited as justification for the steep rise in producer prices. The disruption from gas curtailments was caused by pipeline bottlenecks, inadequate storage of gas close to the big urban markets, and failure of manufacturers to obtain in advance adequate supplies of standby fuels so that their operations might continue during periods of gas curtailment. No one has yet proved that higher natural gas prices will in fact increase gas reserves and production.

Under President Carter's proposed energy legislation, natural gas producers would increase their revenues by approximately $1 billion a year by 1980. This estimate was given by an official of the industry-oriented Federal Energy Administration, Leslie J. Goldman. Most of this increase would result from renegotiation of existing contracts between gas producers and interstate pipelines as these contracts expire, with no other purpose than to enrich the gas producers pocketbooks. The Carter Administration seeks to justify this enormous increase in the fuel bill of American consumers on the ground that the price increase is a necessary incentive to obtain new production. Even Mr. Goldman admits that the justification of further natural gas price increases is "controversial."

The Carter energy plan produces approximately the same results as would be accomplished by Congressional passage of a natural gas decontrol bill. The issue of natural gas deregulation has been around for a long time. In fact, this issue goes all the way back to the year 1949 when Senator Bob Kerr of Oklahoma, a wealthy oilman and unabashed spokesman for oil interests, introduced a bill to free natural gas producers from price control by the Federal Power Commission. At that time, some 28 years ago, Senator Kerr argued that natural gas was being used mainly by industry and not by ordinary residential and small commercial consumers. Therefore, he felt that natural gas should be treated as a non-regulated commodity, the same as steel and coal.

Congress debated the Kerr Bill for many weeks in 1949 and 1950. Finally, with the help of House Speaker Sam Rayburn of Texas, the Kerr Bill was pushed through the House by a slim margin of two votes. Observers in the press gallery witnessed a great deal of arm twisting taking place on the Floor of the House. After clearing both the House and the Senate, the Kerr Bill was finally vetoed by President Truman. The oil and gas lobby succeeded in passing another natural gas deregulation bill several years later but this second bill was vetoed by President Eisenhower. In his veto message, President Eisenhower described the petroleum industry lobbying activities as "arrogant." This bit of history is recited merely to show that the oil and gas lobby has been vigorously pushing for natural gas deregulation long before President Jimmy Carter ever addressed himself to the issue. It seems paradoxical that this new President, elected on the basis of the liberal Democratic policy platform, should now be going all-out to accomplish natural gas decontrol.

During the regime of former President Ford, natural gas decontrol legislation was again considered by the Congress. One gas decontrol bill was reported out by the Senate Commerce Committee. A substitute bill was offered on the Senate Floor during September 1975 by Senator John V. Tunney (D-Calif.). Senator Tunney's bill would have jacked up the price of new onshore gas, making it competitive with oil and would also have eliminated cost based regulation of new offshore gas supplies. In previous years, the view has been held by middle-of-the-road observers that decontrol of natural gas production will be acceptable to the Congress only if the legislation includes a windfall profits tax coupled with a plow-back condition assuring that excess profits will be used in further exploration and development. Unfortunately, the Carter energy plan does not follow this course. Carter has cast himself in the unique position where he is "out-fording" former President Ford in a move to get higher energy prices.

THE ENERGY FIASCO

Carter's energy plan and the energy lobby

Perhaps at no time in recent history has lobby activity been as intense and widespread as it has been during the last several months in connection with shaping and modifying the national energy plan which President Carter announced to the American public and to the world on April 20, 1977.

In his call for action, President Carter told the American people that "our decision about energy will test the character of the American people and the ability of the President and Congress to govern. This difficult effort will be the "moral equivalent of war"—except that we will be uniting our efforts to build and not destroy. . . We must not be selfish or timid if we hope to have a decent world for our children and grandchildren."

The April 20 date was exactly three months to the day from the time when President Carter was inaugurated as President of the United States. He had previously announced many times in advance that April 20, 1977 was the target date for this energy plan announcement. In the opinion of many serious students of energy policy, the President might well have taken a longer period of time. It appears that because of the great haste required to meet his self-imposed deadline of April 20, President Carter could not afford the time to consider inputs from such important sources within his own Administration as Secretary of Transportation Brock Adams, Secretary of the Treasury W. Michael Blumenthal, and Economic Adviser Charles Schultze. But it would appear President Carter and his top energy advisers, Dr. James Schlesinger and John O'Leary, did receive views and recommendations from the energy lobby. This lobby includes the American Petroleum Institute, headed by a former Congressman from Texas, Frank N. Ikard; the Interstate Natural Gas Association of America, headed by another former Congressman from Texas, Walter E. Rogers; the National Petroleum Council, a quasi-government/industry advisory committee headed by Kenneth E. BeLieu, a former high-level bureaucrat under both the Johnson and Nixon Administrations; the Natural Gas Supply Committee, headed by David H. Foster, Executive Vice President; National Coal Association, headed by Carl E. Bagge, former member of the Federal Power Commission; the Independent Petroleum Association of America, headed by Lloyd Unsell; the American Gas Association, headed by Bud Lawrence; and the Edison Electric Institute, headed by W. Donham Crawford. In addition to the oil, gas, coal and electric trade associations, the presidents of major oil companies were also extremely active in contacting the White House directly or in contacting governors, senators and congressmen who in turn were instructed to contact the White House energy advisers. Among the top oil company lobbyists were: Rady A. Johnson, Standard Oil

Company (Indiana); J. Carter Perkins of Shell Oil
Company; Harry D. Williams of Ashland Oil, Inc.;
Donald E. Smiley of Exxon Corporation; and N. Boyd
Ecker of Mobil Oil Corporation.

Carter out-fording Ford

President Carter's energy plan included raising substantially the ceiling price on natural gas from $1.42 to
$1.75 per Mcf and also substantially relaxing price
controls over new crude oil. The total plan was so
complex including as it did proposed new taxes on "gas
guzzler" cars and on gasoline that both the media and
the general public failed to appreciate the full scope of
the bonanza for the oil and gas producers that was
contained in the President's message.

Some spokesmen for the oil and gas industry went
out of their way to complain about the Carter energy
plan rather than to endorse it. In this manner they
helped further to "muddy" the atmosphere. Oil industry spokesmen criticized the plan because it failed to do
away entirely with all price controls over crude oil and
natural gas. Mention was made of the fact by Mr. Foster of the Natural Gas Supply Committee that the
President had backed away from a pledge that he had
made in October of 1976 that he would work with
Congress to deregulate natural gas prices. As recently

as mid-April, 1977, Governor David L. Boren of Oklahoma called on Dr. Schlesinger, urging him to see to it that President Carter honored his campaign commitment for natural gas deregulation.

For example, Mr. A. V. Jones, Jr., President of the Independent Petroleum Association of America, said:

"We think the President has very miserably failed to recognize that 75 percent of our energy now comes from oil and gas. Oil and gas are going to be the two fuels that bridge the gap, so to speak, until we can bring on coal as a primary energy source. So we must maximize domestic resources. Nothing in the President's message would lend itself to going out and finding the reserves in this country that we need to develop.

"Over a period of time, we must let oil and gas reach world market prices, or if you use Mr. Carter's own terms, their replacement cost. In his proposal he's going to have the consumer paying the replacement cost, but most of the money goes to the government in forms of a wellhead tax or a gasoline tax. This is not going to bring the consumer any more supply."

The United States Chamber of Commerce also got into the act on April 22, 1977. The Chamber said that the Carter energy plan does not go far enough in removing price controls over oil and gas. Instead of the Carter plan which provides for additional taxes to be paid on old domestic oil production and a ceiling on new gas production, the Chamber proposes removal of price controls with a provision for plowing back excess profits into further exploration and development.

Bud Lawrence of the American Gas Association said: "However, the proposed ceiling price of $1.75 per Mcf on natural gas falls short of the economic encentive required to increase gas exploration and development in the high risk, high cost, but higher yield areas. Immediate removal of Federal controls on the wellhead price of new natural gas is the realistic answer to the problem of increasing domestic production."

On Thursday, July 14, 1977, with help from some carefully planned parliamentary maneuvering and a strong push from the Carter White House, the House Commerce Committee rejected a determined gas industry effort to decontrol natural gas prices. The deregulation proposal was voted down, 23 to 20, at the end of a tense and crowded Committee session.

Fortunately the bill as finally approved by the Committee does not totally deregulate natural gas prices, it does however contain President Carter's proposal to raise the ceiling on gas prices to $1.75 per thousand cubic feet from a previous price of $1.45, a very substantial and we believe unnecessary increase.

The gas deregulation issue now lumbers its way to a Special House ad hoc energy committee and then on to the Senate. But—fortunately for consumers—it strongly appears that the forces for total gas deregulation have lost.

Congressman Tim Lee Carter, a key Republican representative from Kentucky who voted against gas deregulation and threw the gas lobbyists into an angry tailspin commented after the vote: "I became convinced that gas deregulation would be too expensive to the homeowner. The homeowner is already paying too much. Look at the extraordinary amount of lobbying that we have been under to deregulate. That should tell you something. Day after day, our large hearing room here in the Rayburn House Office Building has been packed with lobbyists who fill the seats long before the sessions began. By the time our hearings are ready to start, they line the back wall, fill the aisles and spill out into the outside corridor. I have not in all the years I've been here seen a bill harder fought. It's almost scary."

Another bonanza for oil producers resulted from the definition of new crude oil production. An earlier draft of the President's message defined "new" oil wells as wells to be drilled no closer than 5 miles from an existing oil well. After intense lobbying by the independent oil producers, this definition was revised from 5 miles to 2½ miles. What this means is that producers who already have a successful well in a field that could be characterized as developed can now drill additional wells as close as 2½ miles from the existing well and qualify for the oil price allowed for new oil production. The importance of this relaxation in the definition of new crude oil can be appreciated from the fact that the price of old crude oil is established at $5.25 a barrel whereas the price for new crude oil is presently more than $11 per barrel and may easily rise to more than $13 a barrel with adjustments for inflation. The I.P.A.A. lobbied for striking out the distance limitation altogether and granting the higher price to all new oil wells.

In discussing the matter of industry lobbying, we do not wish to imply that all lobbying efforts are necessarily in the direction of contravening the public interest in favor of some private interest or higher profits for a single company or a group of companies. In many cases, the self interest of the lobbying group may well coincide with the best interests of the general public. An example of this can be seen in what happened in the President's message to the treatment of L.N.G. carriers. In the original draft of the President's energy message, the section on liquefied natural gas (L.N.G.) suggested that the future policy of the Administration would be to withdraw all subsidies relating to L.N.G. Specifically, it was mentioned that the Maritime Administration subsidies for L.N.G. carriers constructed in U. S. yards would be withdrawn and also the Export-Import Bank would no longer grant loans for liquefaction facilities. The American Gas Association and member companies desirous of increasing L.N.G. imports to help cope with the extremely serious natural gas supply shortage lobbied intensely with Dr. Schlesinger and his aides in order to remove this anti-L.N.G. language. They were successful and the final text of the President's message included no negative language with respect to Maritime Administration subsidies or Export-Import Bank loans for L.N.G. facilities. In this instance the efforts of the gas industry coincided with the best interests of gas consumers and the general public. For example, L.N.G. projects are urgently needed in California to meet the shortage of natural gas projected for the winter of 1980-81. The industries and utilities in California cannot use coal directly. The best use of coal that is environmentally acceptable will be as a feedstock for high-BTU coal gasification plants.

Carter energy plan ommissions

The Carter energy plan, as announced in April 1977, has four significant omissions: (1) It is unfortunate that the President decided against granting Federal loan guarantees for large-scale coal gasification plants based on existing technology, (2) equally unfortunate is the omission of a program to develop use of alcohol as a supplemental motor fuel. Alcohol can be made from grains, trees, sugar crops and even from coal-gas. The high speed cars racing at Indianapolis use methanol as a fuel. Only minor adjustments would be required to permit standard cars to run on a mixture of alcohol and gasoline. A blend of 10 percent alcohol and 90 percent gasoline has been demonstrated to be practical, cost effective and compatible with air quality standards. Studies indicate that the blend can go up to as high as 15 percent methanol. A methanol-gasoline program could reduce gasoline requirements by 10 percent, with corresponding reduction in oil imports. (3)

Another Carter program omission is the electric car which offers another promising opportunity to reduce gasoline use. The electric car presently does not have the range of a gasoline-powered vehicle, although this problem can be solved by designing a hybrid system using the electric battery for low speed, in-city driving, and the gasoline motor for high speed, long-distance trips. Research and development will very likely produce better electric batteries with greater capacity and longer life. Even with the present technology, electric trucks can compete with gasoline for short-distance duties such as delivering the mail or department store packages. The electric vehicle produces no noise or air polluting exhaust fumes. Substantial quantities of gasoline could be saved if short-haul deliveries were handled by electric trucks. It is difficult to understand why the President's energy plan has placed such a low priority on electric vehicle development. Perhaps the automotive and oil industries have created an atmosphere of skepticism about the practicality of electric vehicles to the point that E.R.D.A. and other federal agencies are fearful to proceed with experiments and commercial development. Protecting existing technologies is no new thing in this country or any other.

The Congress appears to be ahead of the Administration, now as in previous years, on this issue of spending federal money to develop alternatives to the use of natural gas and gasoline. Many bills have been introduced in Congress for gasification of coal and shale-oil; alcohol-gasoline research; and electric vehicle demonstration and development.

THE WASHINGTON CONNECTION

It is natural for people employed in an industry to resist technological change. Oilmen pooh-pooh the electric car. Automotive engineers call attention to its low speed in comparison with the gasoline-fired internal combustion engine. There is a studied refusal to assess the electric car in the context of the appropriate functions it can perform. Detroit says: How long can you stretch the electric cord? The answer is longer-lived batteries and a system for recharging batteries in homes, office building garages, and at shopping centers.

The big oil companies and the big auto manufacturers already *know* about the technical feasibility of mixing alcohol with gasoline. Why does industry do nothing to promote an alcohol/gas program? How about the U. S. Department of Agriculture. Clearly, alcohol can be extracted from renewable crops. Such a program would be helpful to American farmers and at the same time reduce our dependence on oil imports from foreign countries.

Many critics have observed that the trouble with the Carter Administration approach is that it places too much emphasis on conservation and not enough on supply alternatives. We firmly believe that widespread use of alcohol fuels and electric vehicles would save far more gasoline than will be saved by the Administration's proposal to achieve conservation by imposing higher prices and taxes on gasoline and oil. (4) Another puzzling omission from Carter's *initial* energy program is *public* transportation. In view of the great importance attaching to the goal of reducing American consumption of gasoline, we feel that much greater effort should be made to persuade Americans to transfer from private cars to buses and rail transportation. If mass transit systems do not exist, obviously such a program is impossible. Therefore, it is obvious that a strong, well-financed program to construct new mass transit facilities and rehabilitate and extend existing systems should be an integral part of the national energy program.

High natural gas prices benefit consumers—a fantasy!

Natural gas is becoming too expensive for the household consumer, especially those of low and middle incomes. Yet there continues to be a determined and successful conspiracy between certain high officials in government and the natural gas industry to further raise the prices paid to natural gas producers.

A whole coterie of Washington-based lobbyists and lawyers provide the catalyst for the upward price movement. Housed in luxurious offices and commanding substantial retainers and big expense accounts, they roam Capitol Hill, the Federal Regulatory Agencies and the important Policy Making Departments, and stake out the White House to get multibillion-dollar energy decisions in favor of their gas industry clients. They are egged on by gas industry bosses and company lawyers who shuttle regularly from such energy capitals as Houston, Tulsa, and Baton Rouge, and hole up in expensive suites at Washington's expensive Watergate, Hilton, Hyatt-Regency and other hotels.

Congressional types from the gas producing states join in the cry for Federal deregulation and higher prices. This favorite hobby of theirs helps keep their campaign coffers filled with gas industry dollars and assures their continual re-election to the Congress.

Reflecting the views of oil and gas producers for higher energy prices, Senator Johnston argues succinctly that the price lid on natural gas to American consumers should not be 52 cents per thousand cubic feet as it was in 1975, nor $1.45 as in 1976, nor $1.75 as proposed by President Carter in 1977, but at "market-clearing" levels of $2.25 or higher. "When all the weeping and wailing is over with," Senator Johnston predicts that the American people "will realize we've got to have that extra price incentive for the producers to explore for more gas."

The American consumer might well argue, however, that what's good for Senator Johnston and Louisiana and its gas and oil producers isn't necessarily good for the majority of the rest of the country.

Within the executive branch, gas industry lackeys control policy-making machinery in the policy-making and regulatory agencies that result in a bonanza of preferential tax treatments and price regulation decisions of benefit to the gas barons.

As Jack Anderson and Les Whitten reported in their nationally syndicated column in April 1977, "Presidents may come and go; crises may shake the

Nation. But the gas and oil abettors keep turning up in the right places inside the government to protect their interests, remarkably unaffected by elections or politics."

The Federal Energy Administration and the Federal Power Commission are prime targets for planting gas industry stooges in policymaking positions. And as these and the myriad of other government agencies who have their fingers in the energy pie are fused together in the new Department of Energy called for by President Jimmy Carter, Washington insiders are betting that the energy interests will be more than equitably represented.

Gas and oil interests control national energy policy

A confidential memorandum on the Federal Energy Administration dated April 4, 1977, and obtained by Representative John Moss, Democrat of California, Chairman of the Congressional Oversight Committee, spells out only too clearly how the gas and oil interests control national energy policy.

Written by career Federal employees who were trying to put public interests ahead of gas and oil interests, the officials poured forth their frustrations over seven pages of typewritten single-spaced copy.

The Carter administration's energy policies, warns

the memorandum, will reflect Big Gas and Oil interests because the working data and supporting documents come from industry-oriented holdovers planted years ago within the Johnson and Nixon-Ford Administrations.

The confidential memorandum pointed out, for example, that ex-President Nixon brought Gorman Smith into the Federal Energy Office which was then operating out of the White House as a "Presidential-executive" agency in 1974. This little office became the Federal Energy Administration in 1974 and quickly mushroomed into a sprawling 5,000-person bureaucracy housed in some dozen different buildings in Washington and supplemented with sub-offices in 12 large regional cities across the country.

When Gorman Smith became head of the agency, "He called each of us in to brief him on our activities," one regulatory program manager recorded in his notes. "We were delighted with the invitation and considered this an opportunity to point out our program strengths and weaknesses and to recommend improvements. (But) General Smith then forced each of us to review our programs in terms of how to use their inherent weaknesses to achieve decontrol.

"From that point on," the F.E.A. program manager reported, "the agency's regulatory program was managed not to serve public needs as mandated by the Congress but to frustrate the small independent gas and oil man, and the consumer in general, in order to generate support for decontrol."

The General Accounting Office—which is the Congressional watchdog over Federal agencies—reported on April 6, 1977, that the F.E.A. had collected only $3.5 million on gas and oil industry overcharges totaling some $500 million.

Furthermore the G.A.O. reported that such penalties—minor as they were and usually arrived at by F.E.A. lawyers and regulatory people through out-of-court "compromises"—appeared to favor some segments of the industry over others.

For instance, the G.A.O. said that major refiners had paid penalties of $900,000 on $355 million in overcharges, or less than three-tenths of one percent, while smaller independent crude oil producers had paid $723,000 in penalties on $19 million in overcharges, or about 3.8 percent.

When questioned about the inequities by Stanley Benjamin of the Washington Bureau of the Associated Press, John F. O'Leary, Carter's F.E.A. Administrator and fifth head of that agency in its less than four-year life span, acknowledged that there were some problems. "Yes, I reviewed the G.A.O. report and I guess that everything is not shipshape in our compliance and regulatory area," O'Leary told A.P.'s Stan Benjamin. "And I have named a task force to review the program and recommend improvements."

O'Leary, a former employee of El Paso Natural Gas Company, Union Pacific Corporation, and Resource Sciences Corporation—all with intense interests in the energy area—promoted Gorman Smith to the post of Acting Deputy for the Federal Energy Administration (no. 2 spot in the agency) in the spring of 1977 as a reward for his good work.

In the depths of F.E.A.'s regulatory program, some of Smith's closest friends and former deputies continue to have direct ties to the gas and oil industry. Take for example, George Mehocic, former Exxon executive. When Smith was in control, he brought in Mehocic and put him in charge of allocating crude oil.

And take George Hall, Director of F.E.A.'s Office of General Fuels. A retired Army Colonel Hall served as a supply officer at the Department of Defense and later worked at Exxon. During the 1973-74 embargo, Hall was deeply involved in severely over-allocating fuels to foreign air carriers and to the Department of Defense. Hall has been instrumental in recruiting many industry-oriented people into F.E.A.'s regulatory programs area. Again we must mention that no illegality is involved, we question only whether such practices are desirable.

And take Colonel Don Allen. Allen is now F.E.A.'s Regional Director in Atlanta. Allen is extremely close to Gorman Smith and Mehocic—a very tight relationship. Before being assigned to Atlanta, Allen worked under Smith as Director of Specialty Fuels and Products. He was the architect of F.E.A.'s Department of Defense allocation operation, a system that in effect violated the intent and the will of Congress by providing the Department of Defense with carte blanche during and after the embargo, and which resulted in gross over-allocation to D.O.D. in time of peace while severely restraining essential civilian use, particularly civilian commercial aircraft.

And so the story goes. We have all heard the old adage by Charles Wilson: "What's good for Detroit is good for America." There's a new twist among the Federal energy regulatory agencies, "What's good for Big Gas and Big Oil is good for the American consumer."

The confidential memorandum by F.E.A. on career F.E.A. bureaucrats pointed out that the top leaders at F.E.A. under General Smith's direction "set the tone of the agency as an outright tool of Big Gas and Oil and special interests." And the career employees go on to point out plaintively: "Is it any wonder that lower-level employees here in F.E.A. have, in some instances, drifted also into the granting of special favors?" There can be little doubt that total deregulation of gas and oil prices is their ultimate goal.

When the Carter transition team came to Washington early in 1977, consumer groups immediately set about trying to oust Gorman Smith from his very influential post as acting deputy administrator and occupant of the No. 2 energy post in government. But Smith, smart to the ways of the bureaucracy, quickly ingratiated himself to F.E.A.'s new administrator, Jack O'Leary. Soon O'Leary was publicly praising Smith, pointing out that he was the one person around the agency who "had a corporate memory and could find his way to the men's room and I need that kind of help."

Surprisingly, consumers received little help from Congressman John Dingell, chairman of the House

Subcommittee on Energy and Power. But they received important staff help from Congressman John Moss of California and Senators Howard Metzenbaum of Ohio and Henry Jackson of Washington State and important moral support from such Congressmen as John Murtha of Pennsylvania, Floyd Fithian of Indiana, Patricia Schroeder of Colorado, William Brodhead of Michigan and Joe Fisher of Virginia. Despite pressure from many consumer-oriented directions, O'Leary persisted in retaining Gorman Smith as his acting deputy and openly stated his intention of moving Smith, a holdover from the Ford Administration, into a permanent job slot. To counterattack critics who claimed that Smith had been overly attentive to the wishes of giant oil companies like Exxon and Texaco, at the expense of the gasoline-buying public, O'Leary called an extraordinary meeting in April 1977 to mediate for Smith. Energy Action, a consumer research group active in energy questions, the United Auto Workers, the National Farmers Union, the American Public Power Association, the Oil, Chemical and Atomic Workers Union, and the Energy Policy Task Force, all were invited.

As reported by Robert A. Rosenblatt in the *Los Angeles Times:* "It was rather a strange meeting," recalled Alex Radin, executive director of the American Public Power Association, which represents 1,400 municipally owned electric utilities. "O'Leary mentioned at the start that this kind of meeting was a departure from previous practices, that the Administration was acting in the sunshine," Radin said. O'Leary told the group that he planned to submit Smith's nomination to the Senate for confirmation in the new job. And he wanted to explain why he felt it absolutely vital to appoint Smith. The critics were not inhibited. "Everyone seemed to be quite forthright," Radin recalled. "People felt burned by the policies of the past. They suggested it was time for the F.E.A. to make an abrupt change from the policies of the past." Familiar themes were repeated. Smith, the holdover from the bad old days, should be ousted, several of those at the meeting kept telling O'Leary. O'Leary held firm. He said he needed Smith. The session ended indecisively. No converts were made to Smith's cause. "Most of us left there with a feeling of some lack of clarity about the purpose of the meeting," Radin said. "Apparently, O'Leary had already made up his mind to appoint Smith." Rosenblatt's story in the *Los Angeles Times* received wide circulation within the Carter stronghold and prompted a discussion between the White House and O'Leary, but he persisted in sticking with Smith.

Finally, on June 14, 1977, nearly six months into the new Carter Administration, Senator Metzenbaum summoned Energy Chief O'Leary to his office and served notice that he was prepared to file suit to have Smith removed from office. Only after O'Leary reviewed the brief which Metzenbaum was prepared to file in court the following Monday, did he agree to cease and desist in his support of Smith for a permanent high post in the energy agency.

In commenting on Smith's removal, Senator Metzenbaum stated that "Smith is definitely pro-oil company oriented. In addition, it has been illegal for Smith to serve in the deputy post as a holdover for more than 30 days and O'Leary knew that this was a blatant abuse of Civil Service Commission regulations. Once we confronted O'Leary and let him know that we meant business, he folded. Today, the American consumers won a victory."

On June 15, O'Leary issued a press release, written and edited by Smith, praising Smith in words of honey. "Gorman Smith, in an action consistent with his history of dedicated service to F.E.A. and commitment to the Nation's energy problems, has asked me to request President Carter not to submit his name to the Congress for confirmation as Deputy Administrator of the F.E.A. . . . His advice and counsel have been of enormous help to me personally. I regret his decision to resign, but I admire him for his motives in doing so."

On July 15, 1977, Brigadier General Gorman Smith walked out of the federal energy business, his last day on a job which many political action groups felt that he had misused. There were several celebrations about town by the Smith critics. His dismissal was one of the fruits of victory for the consumer-environmental forces.

Consumer problems at the Federal Power Commission

Over at the Federal Power Commission, the situation is much the same. Like the F.E.A., officials there are supposed to protect the public from exorbitant natural gas prices, but frequently fail to do so.

Over the past 25 years, the oil and gas interests have lobbied intensively to secure Presidential appointments to the F.P.C. who would favor deregulation. They did not always succeed. For example, in 1972 the White House was persuaded to pick Robert H. Morse, a California lawyer, to fill a Democratic vacancy on the Federal Power Commission. At a hearing of the Senate Commerce Committee on his confirmation, it was brought out that Morse had worked for many years in a law firm that represented Standard Oil Company of California. The Morse nomination was described by Senator Frank E. Moss (D-Utah) as part of "the Nixon tradition of making a mockery of the F.P.C. Mission: to protect consumers from exploitation at the hands of the natural gas companies." Moss charged that all principal appointments to the F.P.C. were influenced by campaign contributions from the oil and gas industry.

The Senate Committee refused to confirm Morse and his name was withdrawn. Rush Moody, Jr., a lawyer from Midland, Texas, took office as an F.P.C. Commissioner on November 19, 1971. His term was to expire June 22, 1976. As expected, Moody expressed his strong bias in favor of high prices for natural gas producers in his official opinions and decisions and in public speeches. He resigned from F.P.C., effective March 15, 1975, before the end of his term, stating in his letter of resignation that he did not believe in continued price regulation of natural gas producers.

THE WASHINGTON CONNECTION

In 1973, former Congressman William L. Springer (R-Ill.) was appointed by President Nixon to be a Commissioner of F.P.C. In Congress, Springer had voted for deregulation of producer prices and also against T.V.A. and various public power projects. At the Senate Commerce Committee hearing Springer was warmly endorsed and supported by several Congressmen who had known him over the long-time period that Springer served as a member of the House Interstate and Foreign Commerce Committee.

One of the last F.P.C. appointments by a Republican President was Richard Dunham, who was appointed by President Ford in 1975 to be Chairman of the F.P.C. Dunham had worked for Nelson Rockefeller, both when he was Governor of New York and later when he served as Vice President. Chairman Dunham has championed steep increases in the national ceiling price established by F.P.C. for new natural gas sales to the interstate market.

The American public is being told that higher prices paid for natural gas will generate additional drilling and exploration, therefore additional supplies. And that these higher prices will also encourage natural gas conservation by the American working class who supposedly is wasting vast amounts heating and cooling their family homes.

Billions of dollars in natural gas profits are at stake in this great conspiracy. Three States—Texas, Oklahoma and Louisiana—produce about 90 percent of our nation's natural gas supplies. About 20 percent of the three states' production comes from Federally leased land which includes off-shore areas in the Gulf of Mexico—sources that theoretically belong to every American. Gas used within producing states (intrastate market) is not subject to Federal pricing regulations which have been in effect since 1954 and can sell for any figure.

But since 1954, natural gas sold to other States (interstate market) is subject to regulation by the Federal Power Commission.

In 1970, natural gas sold for 20 cents or less a thousand cubic feet (Mcf). The average American family uses about 112 Mcf's of natural gas per year for cooking and to heat and cool their home. And total U.S. consumption for all purposes including industrial use ran about 22 trillion cubic feet (up from 6 trillion cubic feet in 1950) annually for an industry income of some $16 billion.

But natural gas prices have risen steeply in the last seven years, in both the interstate and intrastate markets. Today, intrastate gas—which is consumed within the same state in which it is produced and is unregulated—can command a price as high as $2 or more for an Mcf. And newly-discovered natural gas flowing across state lines in the interstate market has climbed from a regulated price of 18 cents in 1954 to 32 cents in 1973, 52 cents in 1975, and $1.45 in 1976. For 1976, the gas industry boosted an income of $35 billion.

Under President Carter's energy plan proposed to the Congress on April 20, 1977, prices would skyrocket to $1.75 for an Mcf. The only relief in his proposal is that natural gas produced and sold within the same state would be brought under federal regulation for the first time and would be backed down to the $1.75 ceiling. At this price, gas is equivalent in price to a barrel of oil at about $11. When one recognizes that each 1 cent increase in an Mcf of gas means $200 million in income to the gas industry, the Carter plan will mean an additional six (6) plus billions of dollars in costs to the consumer. Even so, the natural gas industry is pleading for the Federal regulatory ceiling to be set as a minimum of $2.75 for an Mcf, with an immediate further movement toward total deregulation.

Deregulation of Federal price controls of natural gas

The drive within government to decontrol natural gas prices traces back to 1975 to discussions within the White House-based Energy Resources Council, then chaired by former Commerce Secretary Rogers Morton. It was decided early in 1975 that the F.E.A. would assume the key role in developing and furthering the Administration's objective of deregulating natural gas prices. All F.E.A. resources, supplemented by those of other agencies which could be helpful, would be pressed into service. This action was taken by the E.R.C. because it was felt that the Federal Power Commission (F.P.C.), being responsible for regulating the prices of natural gas, could not at that time assume a strong activist "deregulatory role." Furthermore, it was felt that because of a few consumer-oriented officials within the agency, the F.P.C. disagreed internally over the principle of deregulation, and probably could not wholeheartedly lead the deregulation drive.

F.E.A. resources were mobilized in virtually every area. Since Administrator Zarb was busy engineering the Administration's proposed legislation on oil policy, Deputy Administrator John Hill, a young Texan with strong industry ties, was designated in early September 1975 to chair a Natural Gas Task Force which would coordinate the agency's in-house efforts. Various departments within F.E.A. assigned some of their most knowledgeable personnel to the task force, and James Rubin of the Office of General Counsel, was placed in charge as Vice Chairman and Executive Director. Major F.E.A. segments then began developing background materials to create public awareness of the Nation's natural gas problems.

A hot P.R. campaign

The White House campaign concentrated on the threat of a natural gas shortage in the winter of 1975-76, and the need to deregulate prices in order to encourage additional exploration and the subsequent development of new gas supplies.

To give a few examples of the F.E.A. materials developed: An entire series of public advertising ideas designed by a Madison Avenue public relations firm, including radio and television tapes entitled *"A Pack of Lies"* these "hard sell" advertisements late in 1975 dismissed as false the claims that there would be no natural gas shortage. The ads also used various scare tactics and urged the public to turn down thermostats to help the United States get through the winter. A popular publication entitled *"The Natural Gas Story"*—this attractively illustrated booklet released in October 1975, with a strong pro-gas industry introduction by Zarb, traced the history of the natural gas industry, the development of a growing shortage of natural gas supplies and the potential solutions which can be undertaken by the industry and the Federal government to assure adequate future supplies of gas to meet the nation's needs. *"The Natural Gas Shortage,"* a pamphlet prepared by the Natural Gas Task Force and released in August 1975 contained a state-by-state listing of potential gas shortages. It warned of substantial unemployment in important major economic damage to the U.S. from gas shortages during the 1975-76 winter season.

Zarb and Hill also directed with the help of natural gas specialists and gas task force members in the F.E.A., the preparation of press releases, speeches, and op-ed pieces; arrangement of press interviews, press conferences and meetings with the editorial boards of major newspaper to discuss the potential 1975-76 winter gas shortage; and the preparation of statements favorable to natural gas deregulation for insertion in the Congressional Record. They and other F.E.A. officials also participated in several one-on-one interviews with reporters to discuss the natural gas shortage, the Federal price controls on interstate sales of natural gas, and to assert that "the most effective way" to increase the supply of natural gas was for Congress to deregulate prices.

All offices in F.E.A. cooperated "full blast" at taxpayers expense in preparing testimony and briefing materials for use by high F.E.A. officials to sell natural gas deregulation at Congressional Hearings and in one-on-one meetings with Congressmen and Senators. Other agencies in the Executive Branch were also utilized. Natural gas specialists at the Department of Interior and Federal Power Commission sympathetic to gas deregulation were especially helpful. F.E.A. also kept close touch with the natural gas industry and John Hill gave Max Friedersdorf and his Congressional Liaison Staff in the Ford White House, regular reports on the progress that was being made in moving the gas deregulation legislation through the Congress.

The White House "big push" for natural gas deregulation accelerated in the late summer and fall of 1975. The Senate Commerce Committee chaired by Senator Warren G. Magnuson, Democrat from the State of Washington, was busily working working away on a gas decontrol bill that did not push prices up fast enough nor remove controls soon enough for the "over-eager" Washington gas lobby and their political friends. Attention turned to ways to either get the bill properly amended within the committee or pull parliamentary shenanigans on the Senate floor and try to make changes or substitutions there.

Senator Tunney flip-flops on natural gas

A joint White House-F.E.A. review of the Senate Commerce Committee revealed that Senator John V. Tunney, Democrat from California who would be seeking re-election to his Senate seat in 1976 and was not a friend of the oil and gas industry, was perhaps most vulnerable to a change in views from anti-gas to pro-gas. For one thing, he would need campaign funds to win back the hearts and minds of the folks back home, so Tunney switched his vote on the Committee from negative to favoring natural gas deregulation. And when the marked-up gas decontrol bill from the Commerce Committee arrived on the Senate floor in September 1975, it was Senator Tunney who offered a substitute bill which strengthened the hands of the gas producers. This bill sharply jacked up the cost of new onshore natural gas supplies to Americana consumers, making it roughly equivalent in price to that dictated for oil by the Arabs. Tunney's bill also eliminated or greatly softened the price regulations governing offshore natural gas produced in the coastal waters, the property which is supposed to belong to all Americans.

F.E.A. charged with illegal lobbying

On September 17, 1976, Congressman John Dingell, as Chairman of the House Subcommittee for Energy and Power, convened a hearing into F.E.A.'s lobbying activities for natural gas deregulation. Investigators for the Subcommittee charged that the agency with lobbying in violation of law and that F.E.A. officials obstructed their investigation into the agency's improprieties.

As reported on September 23, 1976, in the Energy Users Report issued by the prestigious Bureau of National Affairs, "The Federal Energy Administration and 'certain individuals' narrowly escaped official censure by the House Commerce Energy Subcommittee for their part in agency natural gas illegal lobbying activities and for concealing and destroying information requested by the Congress."

About the Author

The authors of THE ENERGY FIASCO prefer to remain anonymous, since they are working on another highly sensitive subject. To divulge their identities at this point would hinder their investigations.

Afterword

The Lawmakers are the lawbreakers
by Lew Perdue and Ken Cummins

Afterword

One reason that the Ethics Committee—its formal name is the Committee on Standards of Official Conduct—does not take more action is due to the attitude that many of its members have toward their duty.

In interviews and conversations with many of the members a prevalent opinion emerges. The members feel that the voters of a Congressman's particular district have the ultimate responsibility for voting a congressman in or removing him for his wrongdoing.

But the fact is, the voters do *not* always get the full details of how a Congressman has violated the law or Congressional ethics. They can rarely be expected to have all of the facts on which to base a decision. Most districts are far removed from Washington D.C.

But the most important reason for rejecting the "tunnelvision" approach to Congressional ethics is the fact that even though a particular Congressman is elected by the people of one particular geographic district, once elected the Representatives are put into a truly national arena in which their actions and decisions affect the interests and welfare of the entire nation. A dishonest committee chairman, a dishonest person in the role of ranking political minority member on a committee, unethical people in the leadership can and do have an effect that reaches much further than the small geographical district from which they are elected. Their decisions affect the entire nation, and it is the interests of the entire nation that suffer. It is for this reason that it is the duty of the House to discipline and remove, if necessary, violators of the Congressional code of ethics.

But while a narrow point of view upon the part of many Congressmen and Ethics Committee members has a great effect upon inability to clean up the House, perhaps another also significant reason for the ethical lethargy is the sometimes unethical behavior of the Congressman who serves as chairman of the Ethics Committee—John Flynt, a Georgia Democrat.

The reason that more Congressmen are not investigated by the Committee may be because Flynt is one of the most blatant violators of House ethics. According to his own public admissions, Flynt has accepted free plane rides and free vacations from defense contractors, accepted money from an auto manufacturer at a time he was fighting the clean air act, engaged in a mysterious land transaction to avoid paying a tax assessment in his home county, and has leaked confidential military documents before they had been cleared for public consumption.

"A Member, officer or employee of the House of Representatives shall not accept gifts (other than personal hospitality of an individual or with a fair market value of $35 or less) in any calendar year aggregating $100 or more in value directly or indirectly from any person (other than from a relative of his) having a direct interest in legislation before Congress, or who is a foreign national (or agent of a foreign national)." That is section 4 of House Rule XLIII, The Code of Official Conduct.

In February 1976, Congressman John Flynt admitted violating that law. He admitted having received an unreported free hunting trip, courtesy of the Rockwell International Corporation. Seventeen other Congressmen, none of whom were ever questioned by the Ethics Committee, admitted similar trips. Flynt is a ranking member of the Defense Appropriations Subcommittee which is charged with approving multi-billion dollar appropriations to defense Contractors such as Rockwell. Rockwell is the prime contractor for the controversial B-1 bomber program. Rockwell has $21 billion and more, riding on the way Flynt and his subcommittee members vote.

So they paid for Flynt to have a good time at their Chesapeake Bay hunting lodge at Wye Island, Md. In February 1975 Flynt accepted. Flynt says he could see no conflict with accepting the free hospitality. He also said he saw nothing wrong with accepting free corporate jet rides from another defense contractor, Beech Aircraft.

The double standard which exists is illustrated by the punishment meted out to top Defense Department aides who also took the free hunting trips. Several were demoted and others received pay cuts. All were admonished by a letter which was made part of their permanent file. That letter reads, in part, "To maintain a public trust, our relationship must be above reproach . . . Acceptance of gratuities creates an image which is inconsistent with this standard. . ."

There is no one other than Flynt's Committee to admonish Congressmen for the same ethical transgressions and Flynt, for obvious reasons, says he does not plan to investigate the violations.

Until his death in 1975, Joe Akin, who was the manager of Flynt's Spaulding County Georgia farm, was also on Flynt's Congressional payroll at $10,550 per year. In defense, Flynt told newsmen that it wasn't of much consequence since he did "practically no farming" and said that Akin was helpful in his district congressional office.

But Flynt's farm acreage found more than just agricultural use in 1972 when the Ford Motor Company paid him $12,500 for use of some of his pasture. At the same time, Flynt received campaign contributions from two of the auto firm's top executives. Flynt was a vocal opponent of the Clean Air Act and worked hard to weaken it, much to the satisfaction of the auto companies.

Flynt and the auto company said that the $12,500 was for the storage of unsold autos made by a Ford plant outside of Atlanta, 50 miles away.

The payment, according to Newt Gingrich, a West Georgia College professor who has run against Flynt before, was *13* times the going rate for such farm land. The Ford-Flynt deal, he said, worked out to $156 per acre, when comparable farm land in the same area was leasing for $8 to $12 per acre.

According to several sources, a suitable storage area, was available at a lower cost and much closer to the plant than the 50 miles to Flynt's farm.

Real estate taxes are an outrage to many people, but most people don't think they have a right to evade them. But when John Flynt was informed that the City of Griffin, Ga. had decided to pave the road that forms one perimeter of Flynt's farm, and assess him $3,968.95 for doing so, he went to work. He sold a strip of land—5.5 feet wide and 1,210 feet long to his former administrative assistant, Clinton Brush, who lived in Alexandria, Va. at the time. The land was the strip adjacent to the road that the city had decided to pave.

In July 1972, the city mailed notices of the pavement and assessment, and Brush wrote back that he objected to the paving and would not pay unless more than 50 percent of the other adjacent property owners agreed to the paving. Since Brush owned exactly 50 percent of the adjacent land, this would have been impossible. His objection had to be overruled by the Griffin City Council.

The road was paved and Brush was sent a bill which he refused to pay until the city posted notices that they were going to seize the land and sell it at public auction.

However, the city would not have collected much at such an auction. One city official who asked that his name remain anonymous said the land was worthless.

"Nobody would have bought it and the city would have been stuck with it," the man said.

"The only thing Mr. Brush could do with that land is to build a ditch on it," said Jimmy Johnson, the city engineer. Others jokingly suggested that he was going to build a very long, one-lane bowling alley.

The land is zoned for single-family dwellings whose lots must contain at least 15,000 square feet, a fact which makes it worthless.

Initially Flynt denied that there was anything suspicious about the land deal. "He (Brush) wanted some land down here and I had some to sell him," Flynt said.

After the notices of impending sale were posted on the strip of land, a cashier's check, drawn on a Griffin, Ga. bank mysteriously appeared to pay the assessment and late penalties.

In early June of 1976, Flynt finally admitted it was a scheme to avoid paying taxes and was quoted by his hometown newspaper, the Griffin *Daily News* that "It was the most stupid thing I've done in my life."

Many people might debate that point.

While Flynt devoted most of his committee's resources in 1976 to the unsuccessful task of finding out who was CBS reporter Daniel Schorr's source for classified CIA documents, it was never revealed that Flynt had done some leaking of classified material himself. One instance, according to syndicated columnist Jack Anderson, was the premature release in 1973 of the Army's plans to close the Atlanta Army Depot, and for the stationing of a new command at Ft. McPherson. Flynt admitted leaking the plans and explained that

"There was no intention to violate any trust or confidence."

The other instance of leaks cited by Anderson involved the leaking of a General Accounting Office report on the Spewrell Bluff Dam that was a pet Flynt pork barrel project that would have created a recreation lake just a few miles from Flynt's farm. In his own defense, Flynt said he released the document prematurely since the story had already leaked and he wanted the complete story to be told. Some of the results of the study had initially been disclosed by then-Governor Jimmy Carter who vetoed the dam project and crushed Flynt's attempts to have it built.

But despite his own unethical behavior, Flynt remains as Chairman of the Ethics Committee. Perhaps many of the other unethical members of the House of Representatives feel they will be safer from investigation if they have a person like Flynt in charge.

And perhaps they have been correct. The roster of people who should have been investigated by the committee is a long one. In summarized fashion, here is a partial list taken from cases within the last two Congresses:

Robert Leggett (D-Calif.) has admitted forging his wife's name on a deed—a felony in Virginia where the crime was committed—to a home used to house his mistress and their children. No action by Ethics Committee.

William Clay (D-Mo.) May 1976 Justice Department investigation charged him with filing false claims on his travel vouchers. No action by Ethics Committee.

THE WASHINGTON CONNECTION

Ray Madden (D-Ind.) was under investigation by Justice Department for padding his travel vouchers. He was defeated in a primary. No action taken by Ethics Committee.

Otto Passman (D-La.) His padding of his travel vouchers was investigated by the Justice Department. He was defeated in a primary election. No action taken by Ethics Committee.

Henry Helstoski (D-N.J.) Indicted June 3, 1976 for accepting bribes, and for conspiracy, obstruction of justice and perjury. Defeated in general election. No action taken by Ethics Committee.

Allan Howe (D-Utah) Convicted in two trials of soliciting the services of a police decoy prostitute. Defeated in general election. No action taken by Ethics Committee.

Daniel Flood (D-Pa.) He used his political influence to get loans for several trade schools with whom he was associated. Investigators charged that as much as $1 million might have been diverted to the personal use of school administrators. A sum of $15,000 was found deposited by a school official in the account of Flood's administrative assistant. No action by the Ethics Committee.

Wayne Hays (D-Ohio) This Ohio Congressman's relationship with his tax-supported concubine has become history. However, Hays was allowed by the committee to resign with no action taken. The committee whitewashed the case by sealing the results of its investigation.

James R. Jones (D-Okla.) was convicted in 1976 of

accepting an illegal campaign contribution. No action taken by the Ethics Committee.

George Hansen (R-Idaho) was convicted on two accounts of campaign law violations. No action taken by Ethics Committee.

H. John Heinz (R-Pa.) admitted receiving illegal campaign contributions from Gulf Oil Company. He was elected to the Senate in 1976. No action was taken by the Ethics Committee.

James Hastings (R-N.Y.) convicted in 1976 of receiving kickbacks from his staff members. He resigned his seat before the trial. No action taken by the Ethics Committee.

Andrew Hinshaw (R-Calif.) convicted in 1976 of bribery. Despite requests from several members of Congress, no action was taken by the Ethics Committee.

Philip Burton (D-Calif.) was charged by his former personal secretary of padding his payroll with political cronies, and of requiring her to kick back portions of her salary to pay for chauffering him. A close associate of the deposed Wayne Hays, Burton lost his bid to become majority leader. No action was taken by the Ethics Committee despite requests from the secretary, Mrs. Nina Coleman.

Leo Ryan (D-Calif.) accused of paying $25,000 per year to a staff assistant who failed to keep regular office hours; he failed to report campaign expenditures; he was convicted of drunken driving and abused his power by threatening a judge that he would end his support for revenue sharing, when he got a parking ticket at the Sacramento airport. No action was taken by the Ethics Committee.

Joe Waggonner (D-La.) was arrested by District of Columbia vice squad police for picking up a decoy prostitute. Waggonner pulled the rule of Congressional immunity, to get police to drop charges. No action was taken by the Ethics Committee.

Charles Vanik (D-Ohio) admitted keeping a 39 year old convicted prostitute on his staff payroll even after she failed to show up for work and had moved to Los Angeles. No action was taken by the Ethics Committee.

Rep. John Young (D-Texas) accused by his secretary, Colleen Gardner, of keeping her on the payroll for sexual favors. The Ethics Committee took no action.

Thomas P. O'Neill (D-Mass.), speaker of the House conducted a campaign committee that made illegal contributions; and twisted the arms of Federal officials to do favors for at least one big campaign contributor. No action was taken by the Ethics Committee.

Harold Ford (D-Tenn.) violated anti-nepotism laws by putting his sister on his payroll. No action was taken by the Ethics Committee.

John Jenrette (D-S.C.) a company which he controls was exposed selling land that was either underwater, or which he had no right to sell to unsuspecting buyers. No action was taken by the Ethics Committee.

Charles Wilson (D-Calif) admitted converting his campaign funds to his personal use, a violation of

House ethics. No action was taken by the Ethics Committee.

Margaret Heckler (R-Mass.) admitted irregularities in travel expense vouchers. No action was taken by the Ethics Committee.

Tim Lee Carter (R-Ky.) admitted irregularities in travel expense vouchers. No action taken by Ethics Committee.

Walter Flowers (D-Ala.) admitted irregularities in travel expense vouchers. No action taken by Ethics Committee.

Bill Nichols (D-Ala.) admitted irregularities in travel expense vouchers. No action taken by Ethics Committee.

Jack Edwards (R-Ala.) admitted irregularities in travel expense vouchers. No action taken by Ethics Committee.

Carl Albert (D-Okla.), Former Speaker of the House, admitted accepting free vacation courtesy of defense contractors. He retired in 1976. No action was taken by the Ethics Committee.

The Numbers Racket on Capitol Hill

The fact that the numbers racket is flourishing on Capitol Hill, gives a sense of the easy-going attitude towards law breakers amongst our lawmakers.

THE WASHINGTON CONNECTION

The imperial world of Congress has expanded from subsidized, private dining rooms, new recreational facilities and cut-rate haircuts, cigarettes and manicures to now include its own private and apparently protected gambling operation.

Without leaving the protective confines of his office, a Congressman can place a horse bet or play a number with one of a small group of runners who provide door-to-door service to the gaming statesmen. These runners stop by the Congressional offices to pick up bets and deliver them to a former House administrative employee, who sets up shop each midday just outside the entrance to the Longworth House Office Building cafeteria, only a few yards from the door to the headquarters of the U.S. Capitol Hill Police Force.

An FBI investigation into the gambling activities was thwarted in 1977 when the man was tipped that he was under scrutiny. Law enforcement officials revealed that the leak may have come from House Speaker Thomas P. "Tip" O'Neill's office or the office of the Sergeant of Arms. Both offices have denied being the source of the leak.

The man arrived at his post around 11 a.m. each weekday and coolly and confidently dispensed numbers and collected money under the eyes of passing Capitol Hill police officers. He was often observed by Perdue and Cummins and other reporters counting large sums of money openly on a window ledge while exchanging greetings with passing police officers and House employees strolling by. Several police officers were observed and overheard placing bets.

AFTERWORD

Present and former Capitol Hill police officers said the man's operation has flourished openly for some time because officers were told privately to overlook the activity, or ignored it, they said, out of fear of "political repercussions" that might cost them their jobs.

"These officers may have sincerely had that concern," Capitol Hill Police Chief James N. Powell said. "However, I don't believe the leadership or members of Congress would interfere with us doing our jobs up here. It's never happened during the 12 years I've been chief."

"That to me is a very damn poor excuse for not doing their jobs," commented Joe Ventura, staff director for the House Subcommittee on Personnel and Police, chaired by Rep. Frank Annunzio, D-Ill.

Ventura said he "didn't even know it's going on" because the subcommittee has not received any reports of the gambling activity during the two years he has served on it.

"Most likely people just figure this is a way of life around certain people and they just leave it alone," he added.

The 73-year-old employee first denied his activities to Perdue and Cummins, but when confronted with the fact that they had continually placed bets with him during the previous three months, the Bowie, Md., resident later explained that he "might have accommodated someone" but said he had since discontinued his service.

"I'll tell you one thing, whatever it is you've got in mind is a waste of time," he said, "because it ain't anything big or small or anything."

While the man collected the bets outside, the group of well-dressed numbers runners would rendezvous at their two "reserved" tables just inside the cafeteria entrance after handing over the day's collections from Congressional offices and other office buildings. The man often came inside to confer with the group, and then returned to his post out in the hall. He continued his collections until shortly after 1 p.m., and then casually left by a normally-deserted hallway to the south of the cafeteria, past the House Publications Distributing Room, to his cab which he parked outside. Before leaving, he was observed phoning in the bets from a pay phone in the Rayburn House Office building.

When Perdue and Cummins first approached the man in early February to place a bet, he asked for a House ID. After taking money, the man told the reporters that the payoff was 600-to-1 and that winners could collect "in the Folding Room," now called the House Publications Distribution Room.

"That is a damned lie," said Frank Bechtel, deputy director of the Publications Distribution Room. "It's an absolute falsehood. I don't like that implication one damn bit. We're a business operation serving the Congress, we're not a numbers racket."

The FBI began its investigation after the reporters contacted the U.S. Attorney's office in late February to find out if an investigation was underway at that time. But just as FBI agents prepared to seek a search warrant for the man's arrest, he suddenly discontinued his activity temporarily. Sources told the reporters that he said he quit after learning the FBI was observing him.

He was back in the Longworth cafeteria a few days later but was not observed collecting any money.

O'Neill was informed of the FBI's investigation by the Sergeant of Arms shortly after it began. FBI agents confirmed that they informed the Sergeant, as required by law, before undertaking the investigation.

"This is what happens when you try to do police work and other people get into this," said House Sergeant of Arms Kenneth R. Harding. "And when they did, the guy ran."

But Harding refused to reveal whom he notified about the investigation. Gary Hymel, O'Neill's press aide, said Harding had informed him and the Speaker, but he said the leak "didn't come from this office."

"Normally, a fellow operating like this isn't the end person," Harding said. "We assume that there are other people and, in fact, we know there are other people involved."

He refused to elaborate, but said the FBI agents investigating the operation "have reason to believe that it went across state lines." U.S. Attorney Lawrence Barcella, who directed the investigation, said he could not comment. But Perdue and Cummins learned that the man reportedly had close connections with a Washington area gambler identified by FBI agents as connected with other gambling acitivites. The man denied reporting to anyone.

Chief Powell said he was also informed of the investigation after it began, but said "I didn't notify anybody."

"I understand it appeared to be a fairly open operation over there," Powell said. "It's easy to see it going on but it's hard to come up with the evidence for court. I would suspect that there are other places on the Hill where other kinds of gambling are going on, but I have no reports or evidence to that fact."

Index

325

THE WASHINGTON CONNECTION

INDEX

◤ CONDOR

BESTSELLERS

____ **THE WASHINGTON CONNECTION**
Robin Moore, Lew Perdue with
Nick Rowe $2.25 (004-8)

____ **THE CORRUPTORS**
Gerald G. Griffin $1.95 (001-3)

____ **A SURVIVAL KIT FOR A**
HAPPIER MARRIAGE
Sam Collins Jr., M.D. $1.75 (002-1)

____ **THE GREAT TOMATO COOKBOOK**
Mike Michaelson $1.75 (003-X)

At your local bookstore or forward this coupon
for ordering:

Condor Publishing Co., Inc.
Dept MO, 521 Fifth Ave., New York, N.Y. 10017
Please send me the Condor titles I have checked above. Enclosed is
$_____ (please add 50¢ to cover postage and handling).
Send check or money order—no cash or COD's. Order of 4 or more
books postage free.

Name _____

Address _____

City _____ State _____ Zip _____
Please allow at least 4 weeks for delivery.
